The Tragedy
of
Reason

The Tragedy of Reason

Toward a Platonic Conception of Logos

David Roochnik

Routledge
New York and London

Dedicated to the Memory of
Ben Kaplan (1891–1989)

First published in 1990 by

Routledge an imprint of
Routledge, Chapman and Hall, Inc.
29 West 35 Street
New York, NY 10001

Published in Great Britain by

Routledge
11 New Fetter Lane
London EC4P4EE

Library of Congress Cataloging in Publication Data

Roochnik, David.
    The tragedy of reason : toward a Platonic conception of logos /
David Roochnik.
        p.   cm.
    Includes bibliographical references.
    ISBN 0-415-90315-7.   ISBN 0-415-90316-5 (pbk.)
    1. Plato—Contributions in doctrine of logos.   2. Reason.
3. Logos.   I. Title.
    B398.L85R66   1990   90-31648
    128′.3—dc20   CIP

British Library Cataloging in Publication Data

Roochnik, David
    The tragedy of reason : toward a Platonic conception of
Logos.
    1. Logic. Theories of Plato
    I. Title
    160.92

    ISBN 0-415-90315-7
    ISBN 0-415-90316-5 pbk

CONTENTS

ACKNOWLEDGMENTS

Financial support from the Earhart Foundation allowed me to devote several summers to this project. Iowa State University granted me a semester of research leave during which I completed my penultimate draft.

I am grateful to many people here in Ames. Conversations, and disagreements, with my colleagues have been instrumental in shaping my views. Working with students has been the critical experience that led to the selection of the texts that I discuss as well as the order in which I discuss them. Steve Pett read an early version of this book and urged me to continue. The encouragement and intelligence of Gina Crandell were a constant help.

Rich White, Madeleine Henry, Barry Goldfarb, and Bill Scott read portions of the book and their comments were valuable. Charles Griswold read, and criticized, all of it. His responses were probing, insightful, and always generous. I'm certain that my work is better as a result of the many talks we've had over the years. There is no doubt, however, that all errors and confusions that remain in the pages to follow are my responsibility alone.

Prologue

This book attempts to defend a conception of reason—or to use the Greek word "logos"—that I contend can be extracted from the dialogues of Plato. The very notion of defending Plato may seem strange. Why would a philosopher enshrined for centuries as "classic" need a defense? A defense against whom and what charge? What does it mean to defend an author so long dead? Can he somehow be revived? In other words, what significance can a defense of Plato possibly attain for a contemporary audience?

The classical conception of "logos" (the full meaning of which will be discussed in the introduction below) has been under siege for a long time. At least since Descartes, logos has been attacked for being vague, unproductive, and vastly inferior to the new mathematically based sciences and technologies that were being formulated in the seventeenth century. Descartes was animated by a desire for progress and the conviction that the power and possible benefits of science had been impeded by the dominant position accorded to classical learning in European culture. He attempted to overthrow the rule of logos by redefining what counted as knowledge. In an important sense, he succeeded: there was indeed a "scientific revolution" in which Descartes' assault on logos figured prominently.

In the twentieth century, the scientific revolution has, for many, soured. This fact, however, has only led to an increase in the vehemence of the hostility voiced against logos. Critics such as Nietzsche and Heidegger, and most recently Derrida, have accused logos of fathering the Cartesian project. Logos is, for them, ultimately the origin of, and hence culpable for, the life-denying woes of the technological world. And Plato is typically taken to be the undisputed Father of the logos tradition. For such critics, there is an unbroken line leading from Plato to Descartes to biotechnology and word processing.

Nietzsche's early book, *The Birth of Tragedy*, written in 1871, makes this clear. Here Nietzsche, who was a trained classicist, argues that with the arrival of Socrates (or Plato),[1] a terrible transformation occurred in ancient Greece, one that gave rise to a profound sickness that has subsequently plagued Western culture. A spirit of "theoretical optimism," of hyper-rationalism, took hold and displaced what until then had been the basic and very healthy impulse among the Greeks: the spirit of tragedy. (A full discussion of "tragedy" will be found in the introduction below.)

> Socrates is the prototype of the theoretical optimist who, with his faith that the nature of things can be fathomed, ascribes to knowledge and insight the power of a panacea, while understanding error as the evil *par excellence*. To fathom the depths and to separate true knowledge from appearance and error, seemed to Socratic man the noblest, even the only truly human vocation. And since Socrates, this mechanism of concepts, judgments, and inferences has been esteemed as the highest occupation and the most admirable gift of nature, above all other capacities.[2]

For Nietzsche, the theoretical optimism transmitted by Plato is a virulent disease. By equating knowledge with goodness, Plato ostensibly vilified and repressed other human capacities such as willing, feeling, creating, and playing. By elevating the importance of the mind, he downplayed the wonders of the body, and by searching for a timeless Truth he degraded the indisputable fact of human temporality. Plato set into motion a series of ideas and events that has culminated in a Western culture denuded of life and left only with its dehumanizing science and technology.

> And again: that of which tragedy died, the Socratism of morality, the dialectics, frugality and cheerfulness of the theoretical man—how now? might not this very Socratism be a sign of decline, of weariness, of infection, of the anarchical dissolution of the instincts?[3]

From a variety of quarters Plato has been damned repeatedly as the architect of a hyper-rational and oppressive world. The very word "Platonic" no longer refers only to the historical figure or his work. Instead, it is often used to label traditional Western rationalism itself, with its antiquated and offensive commitment to the Truth. Consider, for example, a remark made in the preface to a volume of essays published in 1987 and significantly titled *After Philosophy*. Its contributors include Rorty, Foucault, Derrida, Habermas, Davidson, Dummett, and Putnam. It is clear that they were chosen for their diversity. Nevertheless, says the editor, "all are agreed in their opposition to the 'Platonic conception of Truth.'"[4] (The last four words of this sentence, as well as the procedure of capitalizing the first letter of "Truth" in order to highlight it with scorn, are taken from Richard Rorty.)[5]

What is the relationship between the (supposed) "theoretical optimism" inherent in the "Platonic conception of Truth" and Greek tragedy? A good explanation is found in Martha Nussbaum's recent work, *The Fragility of Goodness*. She argues that in the *Protagoras*, for example, Plato attempts to develop a "science of practical reasoning." Armed with such knowledge, philosophers could eliminate the suffering caused by moral conflict and escape from the dangers and contingencies that ordinarily seem to plague human life. By contrast, Greek tragedy not only depicts, but also wisely affirms, the vulnerability of human goodness and the very emotions that Plato despises. As a result, Nussbaum agrees with Nietzsche and characterizes the dialogues as "Plato's anti-tragic theater," as "theater purged and purified of theater's characteristic appeal to powerful emotions, a pure crystalline theater of the intellect."[6] For Nussbaum, the dialogues, unlike the classical Greek tragedies, are hyper-rational denials of the fragility and uniquely beautiful pathos of being human.

To a large extent what follows is a response to Nietzsche and scholars like Nussbaum. In other words, the principal charge against which I shall defend Plato is this: that he is "anti-tragic." I shall do so because I believe that it is an extremely serious accusation. In other words, I *agree* with Nietzsche and Nussbaum that tragedy is both illuminating and affirming of the value of human life; to deny it, therefore, *is* a sign of decline, of infection, of a hyper-rationalism gone awry. I further agree, with Nietzsche and his epigones, that the world of twentieth-century science and technology is genuinely dehumanizing and in need of revitalization. I do not believe, however, that Plato is the evil genius lurking behind these developments. Indeed, I think that precisely the Platonic dialogues can supply a revitalizing alternative to the scientific or technical conception of rationality today so predominant.

Nietzsche's disciples, many of whom have become quite fashionable and whom I shall call "the subversives," are engaged in a wholesale rejection, or deconstruction, of the Western tradition of reason.[7] While it is not difficult to sympathize with their dissatisfaction, even their rage, at the technocratic worldview, their own response is no more fulfilling. The Western tradition is not homogeneous. While it may be true that the specifically technical conception of reason developed in the last 400 years is dehumanizing, classical logos is not the culprit. For it is possible, I shall argue, to extract from the Platonic dialogues a conception of logos that is compatible with the life-affirming insights of tragedy.

This book thus reflects three related concerns. The first is with Plato. Through a discussion of a small selection of his works I shall attempt to show that embedded within the dialogues is a "tragic conception of logos." By the end of the book, I hope that the meaning of this phrase will be clear. The second is with Descartes and the founding of the technical conception of reason. I shall show how Descartes attacks and fundamentally alters classical logos. The result is an impoverished conception of reason, one that is unable to do justice to the significance and value of human experience. The third is with the subversives. I shall argue that through a great irony they, the grand deconstructors of Western rationalism, and Descartes, the founding father of the technical conception of reason, hold complementary positions. They can be conceived as two extreme positions that are like "flip sides" of a single coin. The Platonic conception of logos, as I move toward articulating it, will offer a third, a middle way, one that is richer and more humane than the two extreme views flanking it.

A caveat about the strategy that informs this book: What follows is itself an imitation of a dialogue. By setting a series of texts by a wide variety of authors—Sophocles, Aristotle, Plato, Descartes, Spinoza, Heraclitus, Derrida, Rorty, Hesiod, Homer—into opposition with one another, I shall attempt to generate a conceptual drama whose goal is to exhibit the nature or structure, which I have already described as tragic, of logos, the main character of the story.

I shall follow this approach for the following reasons. I am convinced that the Platonic conception of logos can be of real value, and not just academic interest, for the contemporary debate about the fate of reason. I want to exhibit that conception and thereby make it accessible. This, I have decided, requires giving voice to a competing set of views and forcing them to confront one another; for such competiton is, I shall argue, of the essence in Plato's thought.

The most obvious, and perhaps the most telling, fact about Plato's writings is that he never presents a "theory," a monological argument, about a single specified subject. He only writes dialogues.[8] It is of course true that the character Socrates is usually the "hero" of his work, but as has been argued many times, it is illegitimate, and perhaps even impossible, simply to equate Plato with any of his characters.[9] All of Socrates' statements—his arguments, assertions, myths, similes, and jokes—are placed in a specific dramatic context composed of a particular time and place and a series of characters. Socrates' remarks, therefore, are always addressed *to* someone for a specific reason and so are conditioned by the contingency of their dramatic context. As a result, it is illegitimate to isolate any given Socratic statement and christen it "Platonic." The full meaning of the statement emerges only as part of a dramatic whole.

Beginning with the assumption that the dialogue form is an essential component of Plato's thought, I make two further claims. First, several of Socrates' most critical interlocutors hold views that are significantly similar to those of our own subversives. I refer to sophists such as Protagoras, rhetoricians like Gorgias and Thrasymachus, and a poet (more accurately, a "rhapsode") like Ion. I shall argue that these characters represent positions that prefigure the work of thinkers such as Derrida and Rorty. They were, in other words, ancient versions of the subversives. As a result, the Platonic dialogues are well equipped to comment on contemporary issues.

Second, the Platonic conception of logos can only be made intelligible insofar as it emerges from the *conflict* between Socrates and his subversive interlocutors.[10] A sizable portion of what follows is devoted to clarifying and substantiating this assertion. This book is an attempt to extract and to defend the Platonic conception of logos by reproducing such conflict in the form of a series of textual oppositions. If I am correct in my comparison between Socrates' sophistic and poetic interlocutors and the subversives, then it becomes entirely possible that the dialogues can help us, even today, participate in the battles currently being waged over the future of reason.

A final note on my strategy: The first "scene" of this drama contains a discussion of Aristotle, not Plato. It would be a serious mistake to conflate the two and attribute to them joint authorship of "the classical conception of logos." Their disagreements are profound. Nevertheless, I have used Aristotle to help illuminate what I take to be a critical feature of Plato's thought. Aristotle's vision of the value, range, and security of logos is more comprehensive, and in an important sense more optimistic, than Plato's.[11] Beginning with Aristotle allows me to show by contrast the great awareness Plato has of the limits . . . the tragic limits . . . as well as the goodness of logos.

In what follows I shall not presuppose any knowledge of Greek philosophy or literature and when a Greek word is used, its meaning will be given. The scholarly references I have chosen to include will be confined to the notes (and largely to works in English). When needed I shall supply the primary text that is under discussion. (Unless noted, translations will be my own and have been formulated with an eye toward readability.) Finally, I shall try to explain what prompted the many transitions from section to section, from text to text, that occur throughout the book. My hope is that anyone willing to think seriously about the issues under discussion can benefit from this work. More particularly, I would like to address those readers who are troubled by the omnipresence of the technical version of rationality and, as a result, are tempted to join a noted philosopher of science in saying "farewell to reason."[12] I urge such readers to reexamine the tradition they are tempted to abandon and in particular to ask whether, in damning Plato, they have not misidentified their enemy. Is it possible that the Platonic conception of logos, far from representing the theoretical optimism deplored by Nietzsche, includes a tragic awareness of its limits as well as a life-affirming understanding of its goodness?

But what if you were hurled into a time warp and came face to face with the Ancient Greeks. The Greeks invented trigonometry. They did autopsies and dissections. What could you tell an Ancient Greek that he couldn't say "Big Deal."

—Don DeLillo, *White Noise*

INTRODUCTION

A TRAGEDY

> Is there a pessimism of strength? An intellectual predilection for the hard, gruesome, evil, problematic aspect of existence, generated by well-being, by overflowing health, by the fullness of existence?
>
> —Nietzsche, *The Birth of Tragedy*

Before proceeding into the main current of this work, three terms require explanation. Two appear in the title of this book and the third, more precisely a descendant of the third, already was featured in the prologue. These are "tragedy," "logos," and "techne."[1]

Tragedy was a form of drama that reached its peak in Athens during the fifth century b.c.e. The name itself seems to come from words meaning "goat" and "song." This could indicate that the earliest tragedies, which took place sometime before the fifth century, were performed in contests whose prize was a goat. However, as is true of so much about classical Greek drama, the question of its origins remains obscure. Scholars do not know exactly how or why or when tragedy originated. All that can be said with confidence is that it reached its pinnacle in Athens during the fifth century.

Even this assertion, however, needs qualification. From the three great tragedians, Aeschylus (510–450), Sophocles (496–406), and Euripides (476–406), only some thirty-three plays remain. Seven each belong to Aeschylus and Sophocles, nineteen to Euripides. The manner in which these particular plays managed to survive the centuries of transmission is itself noteworthy. The seven each of the two older playwrights were the result of editions compiled by later scholars for use in various schools. Since both authors wrote scores of plays, we cannot be at all certain that the particular plays chosen for the editions were truly representative of their entire corpus. We do not know precisely who chose them or what criteria they employed. It is obvious, therefore, that we do not have enough text with which to construct a historically complete or defensible characterization of either Aeschylus or Sophocles.[2]

The situation is slightly better with Euripides. In addition to an anthology, we have several more of his plays. These were preserved when a small portion of a complete alphabetized edition was discovered. (Notice how many of Euripides' plays begin with the English *H: Hecuba, Helen, Heraclidae, Hippolytus).*[3] Euripides has frequently been described by commentators as the most perplexing of the three tragedians. His work has been most resistant to classification because his tragedies are extraordinarily diverse and often seem quite strange. It is possible, however, that this wide variety is a consequence not of some unique characteristic of Euripides, but of the simple fact that we have so many of his plays. In other words, if more work by Aeschylus had also survived, perhaps we would respond to it with a perplexity similar to that often felt after a study of Euripides.[4]

In short, Greek tragedy was a highly complex and multiplicitous genre, and we simply do not have enough textual data to be confident in making generalizations about it. Even with the thirty-three plays that remain it is dangerous to generalize. What, for example, does Euripides' *Hecuba* have in common with Aeschylus' *Oresteia* such that both should be called tragedies? It is clear that the safest and historically most prudent course is to speak of Greek "tragedie*s*" and not "tragedy."

But this is not typically done. At least since Aristotle (380–320), critics have yearned for a general definition of tragedy. For some reason, this word exerts a strong appeal. "Tragedy," in the hands of Aristotle or even thinkers far less than he, somehow becomes a provocative and luring notion. Why? Because critics can use it to speak about human life as a whole. Tragedy, they say, can tell us something fundamental about ourselves. Aristotle puts it this way when he compares tragic poetry to history:

> [Tragic] poetry is more philosophical and serious than history. For poetry speaks more about what is universal, while history speaks about what is particular. That which is universal is, for example, what sorts of things a specific type of person will say or do according to what is most probable or even necessary. It is this at which poetry aims (1451b5–10).[5]

Tragedy teaches us about types of human beings and general patterns of behavior. It can thus be used as an occasion to comment, not on this or that particular person, but on what it means to be a human being. This is why Aristotle believes that drama should be included as part of a well-crafted educational system. Critics since Aristotle have followed his lead and books abound with titles such as *The Spirit of Tragedy* or *The Tragic Sense of Life*.[6]

As stated above, the relationship between such philosophical or critical versions of tragedy and the hundreds of actual plays that were once performed in Athens is not obvious. Even Aristotle probably did not consider all of them since he wrote over one hundred years after their performance. Despite its enormous influence in shaping the critical reception of tragedy, Aristotle's account in his *Poetics* is not a historically verifiable characterization of tragedy. When speaking of "tragedy," therefore, I make no pretense to refer accurately to the hundreds of plays performed some 2,500 years ago. Instead, I have been inspired by a few of those plays, particularly Sophocles' story of Oedipus, to forge a conception of tragedy that I believe can be put to good use in articulating a conception of human life and knowledge.

"Tragic" is an adjective widely, and poorly, used today. If a child is struck down by an incurable disease, the reporters call it "tragic." This event is sorrowful, terrible, and catastrophic. But it is not tragic. Tragedy does bespeak sorrow and catastrophe. Its essential movement finds the hero changing from what seems to be a reasonably good state of affairs into a bad one. As Aristotle puts it, tragic drama requires a *peripeteia*, a reversal or "a complete swing in the direction of the action" (1452a22–23).[7] The child's death surely does involve a reversal for both the parents and the child. Still, it is not tragic. Aristotle explains that a tragedy must be sparked by an action performed by its hero. This he calls a *hamartia*, an error or mistake in judgment. This is a very difficult word and notion for scholars to pin down with certainty (1453a10 and a16).[8] The important point here is that the hero must be at least partially responsible for his catastrophe. He must be causally implicated in the course of his reversal. The child did nothing to bring about her illness, and so her death is not tragic.

The hero's *hamartia*, however, is not the sole or sufficient cause of the reversal. The hero is implicated in a world, in a network of causes and effects, that is not exclusively of his making. There is a dimension of "necessity" or "fate" in the hero's life. His catastrophe is thus as much a consequence of his necessary involvement in a world beyond his control as it is of his own action. It is precisely this duality, this delicate blending, of causes that characterizes tragic catastrophe.

This is vague. To clarify, let us consider Oedipus as an example. (This tends to be Aristotle's procedure as well.)[9] He is doomed, fated to kill his father and marry his mother. He was not consulted or made aware about this course of events before it occurred. Nevertheless, it is the inescapable fact of his life. But Oedipus is surely no puppet or purely passive victim.

He is quite capable of instigating actions on his own. He becomes furious at an old man who hits him. He kills the man in retaliation, not knowing that it is his father. This is surely a *hamartia* (a mistake, not a sin and, given the mores of the time, perhaps not even an egregious character flaw) and it sets into motion the sequence of events that constitute the tragedy. Oedipus is both the active instigator of his tragedy, and its unwitting victim. He was cursed. Suffering was mandated for him. But the consequences of his patricide were brought about by *his* killing of his father.

This is still vague. How can such a contradictory blend of notions, determinism and freedom, fate and human agency, be made compatible? The key notion here is that the tragedy of Oedipus is the story of a man implicated in a context of events only for some of which he is responsible. This context, or structure, includes past events, his *hamartia*, his character, and his destiny. Oedipus was partially responsible for his downfall; a tragic hero has a history of which he is in only part author.

This description of the dual causal network in which the hero is implicated remains vague and perhaps contradictory. Furthermore, it is not particularly informative about tragic drama, for even if it is true, then presumably it should apply to all human beings. In order for a tragic drama to become truly dramatic, the hero has to be more than an ordinary human being. As Aristotle puts it, he must be renowned and successful, as well as a decent human being. These characteristics are necessary in order for his reversal to have an emotional impact on the audience. More precisely, the hero must be sufficiently good so that his reversal will cause the audience to feel pity. On the other hand, the hero should not be so good that his reversal seems to the audience to be arbitrary and a perverse trick of a cruel world. He must be sufficiently good so that his downfall is not caused by his evil or vice (but by his *hamartia* and fate), but not exceptionally good. (See 1453a7–12.) He must be a man whom the audience can admire but still can identify as being one of their own.

Precisely this combination of characteristics is found in Oedipus. He is a good king and highly regarded by his citizens. But as one character says to him, "Neither I nor these children sitting here at your throne in supplication equate you with a god. Instead, we judge you to be first among men in the fortunes of life and in the dealings with the world above (31–34)."[10]

The tragic hero, while identifiably human, has a certain drive or impetus to act on a grand scale that sets him apart from other men. He is impelled by an urge for some form of greatness. The hero pushes to the fullest extent of his power his ability to act. He then collides with the limits of his efficaciousness. In other words, the hero misjudges the boundary that separates his role as the author of his destiny from his role as a victim of that which is beyond is control. Above all else, through its portrayal of the hero's catastrophe a tragedy discloses *limits*. In the course of the collision between the hero's ability to act and the context that limits it, the spectator of the tragedy feels pity. The hero's suffering at the hands of a world beyond his limited control is undeserved. Oedipus, for example, did nothing to merit his curse. The spectator also feels fear. Since Oedipus is readily identifiable as a fellow human being, it is conceivable that a catastrophe like his can befall any who witness it.

With the hero's reversal comes a "recognition," which Aristotle defines, quite simply, as "the transformation from ignorance to knowledge" (1452a30). Upon his reversal the hero realizes, among other things, where his ability to act is limited by a world beyond his control. Tragedy in this sense is an educational experience. Since the audience can identify and thus suffer with the hero, the drama teaches them where they, as human beings, stand. It properly orients them in the larger world in which they reside. As a result, the audience goes through a "katharsis," a purging or (as one commentator recently has put it) a "clearing up" of one's vision so that human limits can be accurately seen and fairly evaluated.[11]

The recognition of one's limits involves what is virtually a paradox. Consider, for example, a woman whose ability to walk has been limited (from the time of her birth) by the four walls of a cell. How would this woman come to an understanding that these walls are in fact limits? The four walls of the cell dictate the area beyond which she is not able to walk. To understand this, the woman would have to realize that there is something beyond her cell. To understand a limit requires somehow going beyond that limit. The woman would either have to gain a peek of what is outside the walls or would have to crash against them in order to learn what they are. Both options would bring pain. The first would force the woman sharply to revise her vision of the world. Her cell, which had previously been regarded as the world entire, would become transformed into what it actually is: a highly limited enclosure. The second would bring with it the pain of colliding with an inflexible boundary. Thus, to orient herself and her cell properly in the larger context of the world beyond, the woman would have to suffer.

Something like this goes on in tragedy. Because of the hero's urge to act on a grand scale, he crashes into the limits of human efficaciousness, limits which most human beings rarely approach. It is in this sense that tragedy teaches its audience. It tells us that we are actors whose greatest strivings bring us into unwanted collision with our inescapable limitations.

We are those who at our best must suffer the realization that we cannot achieve the greatest of our goals.

This all sounds terribly negative. Tragic recognition, however, does not bring with it despair or paralysis. Instead, it brings katharsis and affirmation. It infuses our lives with awareness. It purges us of that false confidence that can lead to exaggerated claims for ourselves. It instills within us the deepest understanding of our real capacities. Such, at least, is the conception of tragedy I will employ for the purposes of this book.

Let us consider more closely the tragedy of Oedipus. When the play opens he is the good king of Thebes, a responsible father and husband. He is not extraordinarily good: his virtue is that of a man and not a god. As such he is fully recognizable by his citizens and the audience as one of their own. He is, or so he thinks, ruler, *tyrannus*, of Thebes.[12] He gained this rule by successfully saving the city, whose king had just been killed, from the oppression of a terrible monster, the sphinx. This he accomplished by answering the famous riddle: What stands on four legs in the morning, two in the afternoon, and three at night? Oedipus rightly declared that this describes a human being. The city was saved and he was awarded the throne and the former king's wife.

This ability to solve the sphinx's riddle tells much about Oedipus. He is a man convinced that by the rigorous application of his intelligence problems can be solved. As a result, when Thebes is struck by a second crisis, a plague that has made barren the fruitful plants of the earth, the cattle in the field, and the women of the city, Oedipus firmly believes that he can repeat his inaugural performance. When he is approached by an elderly priest begging him to aid the citizens, Oedipus' first response is this: "My pitiable children. Known and not unknown are the longings you bring to me. For I know well that all of you are sick" (58–60). These few words, three of which refer to knowledge, reveal what confidence this man has in his ability as a problem solver. He is convinced, for example, that he has already taken the right first step toward eliminating the plague. He has sent his brother-in-law, Creon, to the Delphic Oracle for advice.

When Creon returns from Delphi he brings the disturbing news that the plague is caused by the fact that the murderer of the former king, Laius, is yet alive in Thebes. Once again, Oedipus acts decisively and boasts that "I will bring to light, from its beginning, this event" (132). Oedipus, the believer in the therapeutic effect of light, orders all citizens who might have relevant information to step forward. He threatens with punishment any who might withhold what they know or might actually be harboring the criminal. Finally, he curses the murderer: "Whether he worked alone or with others, may he live out a miserable life miserably! And I pray that if with my knowledge he should be living in my home, that I myself may suffer this curse" (246–251).

Oedipus' strategy is that of a detective who calls in his witnesses. First is Teiresias, the blind prophet of the god Apollo. In many ways, Teiresias' first lines express the keynote of the entire play: "Oh woe upon woe, how terrible is intelligence when it does not profit him with intelligence" (316–317). The prophet has here called into question a belief that is, to Oedipus at least, obviously true: that intelligence and the capacity to solve problems, that light, is good. Teiresias, despite his blindness, predicts the result of Oedipus' interrogation; he sees that Oedipus himself is the murderer of Laius. At the beginning of this scene, however, he refuses to say this, for he understands that this disclosure would wreak havoc on the king and his family. Teiresias understands that if Oedipus succeeds in his investigation, which is motivated by his good intention to save (what he thinks is) his adopted city, he will at the same time fail.

Oedipus is outraged by Teiresias' silence. In his frustration, he accuses the old man of killing Laius. In fact, he draws up an entire scenario: Creon wanted to usurp Laius' throne and joined forces with Teiresias, who was motivated by a desire to secure a high position in the new regime. Together they plotted the ambush. This accusation, which the audience knows is false, is finally enough to provoke Teiresias to speak. He declares that Oedipus is the murderer.

The audience knows that Oedipus' scenario is ill conceived and dreadfully wrong. In fact, Creon is loyal and Teiresias innocent. Sophocles, however, makes it clear that even though he is wrong, Oedipus, given the facts available to him, behaves rationally. First of all, Oedipus has no reason whatsoever for suspecting himself. For years he has been the good king of Thebes. As the play later makes apparent, he is a man honest about himself and at this point he simply is unaware that he has killed Laius. By contrast, he does have reason to suspect Teiresias. When the city was plagued by the sphinx and her riddle, the prophet did nothing. There is even reason, however slim, to suspect Creon, for it was Creon who suggested that Oedipus send for Teiresias (see line 288). Creon also had a motive; since Laius was childless, as the queen's brother he was next in line to the throne.

The decisive problem with Oedipus' scenario is not that it is wrong. Given the lack of further information, as an initial hypothesis it would actually have been quite plausible. Oedipus' error is that he is far too confident and assertive about his scenario. He treats the results of speculation as if they were facts.

The next three major scenes are interrogations that lead to recognitions. In each, Oedipus successfully questions a witness and so comes closer to the terrible realization that Teiresias was right: he himself is the criminal he so actively seeks; he is guilty of the very crimes of which he accuses others.

The first witness is his wife, Jocasta. In what will turn out to be a stroke of brilliant irony, she tells him not to believe Teiresias, for prophets are unreliable (709). Her skepticism is based on a single experience. Many years earlier it was prophesied that the son she bore to Laius would murder his own father. But (as far as she knows) this did not happen. First, Laius was killed by robbers "at a place where three roads meet." Second, Laius had taken the prophecy seriously and had pierced his infant son's ankles and left him to die in the mountains. The earlier oracle now appears obviously false; Teiresias, therefore, should be ignored (708–725).

Jocasta's story triggers Oedipus' memory: he himself had killed a man at a place where three roads meet. In a manner that is typical, and admirable, Oedipus does not shy away from the truth. He interrogates Jocasta further and discovers exactly where these three roads were, what Laius looked like, and with what sort of party he was traveling. Unlike his earlier speculation, Oedipus' conclusion here, that he murdered Laius, is based on compelling evidence.[13]

This scene (726–755) discloses the fundamental pattern of *Oedipus the King*. Through his own power of rational investigation, Oedipus has recognized a portion of the truth. (Which he announces by saying, "Oh god, these things are now all clear" [754].) He has gone through a reversal. His earlier confidence in both his innocence and his ability to understand the world around him has eroded. From Aristotle's point of view, this type of reversal is the best and most tragic: "The finest form of a recognition occurs simultaneously with a reversal, such as the one in the *Oedipus*" (1452a32–33). Indeed, the most elemental tragic pattern is precisely the coupling of recognition and reversal. As the hero comes to realize that his former judgments about himself were mistaken, as he comes to understand his limits, his fortunes are reversed. Insight brings suffering and a revision of his conception of himself. Oedipus' revision is in terms of his ability to know. He thought he was a master detective whose success would bring happiness. But it is his very success that causes him to recognize that he was mistaken.

Oedipus describes in detail how he came to murder an old man at the place where three roads meet. He had been the crown prince of Corinth, a neighboring city. One day he had heard a rumor that he was not the legitimate child of the king and queen of Corinth, but a bastard. Determined as always to find out the truth he confronted his parents.

Despite their assurances he went to the Delphic Oracle to learn definitively about himself. The oracle, however, told a terrible tale. It announced that he would lie with his own mother and murder his father. In response, Oedipus acted decisively. He did not return to Corinth and so, as he thought, he eliminated the possibility of his committing the crimes of incest and parricide. As he traveled he came to a crossroads where he met a party surrounding a high-ranking dignitary. The old man sitting in the distinguished carriage hit him as he was passing. Oedipus retaliated and killed all in the party but one. During his interrogation of Jocasta, it seems unmistakable that this victim was Laius.

There is, however, one possible way of escaping this awful conclusion. Jocasta had said that several robbers, and not just one, had committed the murder. In addition, there was one survivor of Laius' party, a old man who is now a shepherd, who was an eyewitness to the event. Oedipus demands that the shepherd be brought to him for interrogation.

Despite this apparent "escape clause," it is clear that Oedipus realizes that he did kill Laius. (This is evidenced by the fact that even when the shepherd is brought to him, Oedipus does not ask whether he was the murderer of Laius.) What is not known is only that Laius was his father. Oedipus has every reason in the world to believe that the king and queen of Corinth, the only two people he has ever identified as parents, are truly his parents. His abrupt leaving of Corinth was well motivated: he wished to keep his parents from harm. The audience has to sympathize with Oedipus here. How many of us would ever doubt that the most secure and enduring of all relationships, that to our parents, is in fact suspect? Oedipus operates, as would any of us, on the assumption that the way the world seems, and has seemed for his entire life, is the way it is. What differentiates him is only his great confidence that he sees his world accurately.

The Jocasta scene provides Oedipus with a single fact or premise: He killed Laius. He is as yet unaware of the final conclusion: that Laius was his father. For this Oedipus must interrogate a second and third witness. The second is a messenger from Corinth. He comes bringing the news that Polybus, King of Corinth and supposed father of Oedipus, is dead. This appears not to be altogether bad news for two reasons. Oedipus will now inherit the throne and, at the same time, is free from the oracle's prophecy: since his father is dead, he can no longer be the murderer of his father. However, since Polybus' wife Merope is still alive, Oedipus fears that he might still commit incest. He expresses this fear to the messenger who in turn attempts to assuage Oedipus. There is no reason to fear returning to Corinth, the messenger says, because Merope is not Oedipus' real mother. Oedipus was a foundling, brought to the childless royal family of Corinth by this messenger himself. The messenger had been a shepherd at the time and had received an abandoned infant from another shepherd. And who was this other shepherd? "He was called Laius' man" (1042).

This is Oedipus' second recognition. He now realizes that Polybus was not a blood relation and that, therefore, it is in principle possible that he killed his father. He now understands that he does not know who he is. When the Corinthian messenger remarks that the infant Oedipus was found on the slopes of Mount Citharon, had pierced ankles, and was given to him by Laius' man, Jocasta, whose own son was given identical treatment, knows full well the truth. Her husband and the father of her children is also her son. Oedipus himself is not certain that this is the case. After all, he has no memories of being exposed on the slopes of Citharon to die. He wishes to continue his investigation and demands that the third witness be brought to him. Jocasta rushes off the stage, soon to commit suicide. Before doing so she urges Oedipus to end his search: "By the gods, if you value your own life, don't seek this out!" (1060–1061). "Oh you wretched man, may you never know who you are" (1068).

Oedipus does not heed Jocasta's warning. As always, he plunges forward, determined to find out the truth, confident that the truth will heal. The third witness, the Theban herdsman who was a member of Laius' original party and who had handed the infant Oedipus to the Corinthian, appears. He confirms these facts, these worst suspicions. He thus identifies Oedipus as husband of his mother. The scene closes with Oedipus speaking these lines: "Oh my god, that all things should now come clear! Oh light, let me see you now for the last time! Since I am one who has been revealed as born in the wrong, as having lived with those I should not have lived with, as having killed those I should not have killed" (1182–1185). Oedipus, the believer in light, leaves the stage and destroys his own eyes.

The final scene of *Oedipus the King* directly confronts the audience with the challenge of tragedy. The blind and bloodied Oedipus, having discovered who he is, having learned that his confidence in himself as a rational problem solver is now empty, returns to the stage. And, almost miraculously, he is as yet unbowed. He has not been destroyed by his catastrophic revision of his understanding of himself. He is strong enough still to make certain demands upon Creon, the new ruler. He asks, for example, that he be exiled and that his daughter, Antigone, be allowed to stay with him (1436–1469). Where does Oedipus get this strength to remain standing on stage in full view of the audience? Why wasn't he destroyed? Why doesn't he destroy himself? Such questions typify, I suggest, the great challenge of this tragedy.[14]

Tragedy somehow affirms. The chorus ends *Oedipus the King* by saying,

> You who dwell in ancestral Thebes, look upon this Oedipus, he who knew the famous riddle and was the most successful of men. Who among the citizens did not look upon him with envy. Into what a great wave of disasters he has crashed. So that, looking at that final day, count no mortal happy until he has passed the limit of his life suffering no pain (1524–1530).

Look upon and learn from Oedipus.[15] Even though his story is about the catastrophe suffered by a man who thought he could see the world clearly (and in fact could not), the chorus has not abandoned the hope of seeing. They still want us, the audience, to look and learn. But to learn what? The tragedy of Oedipus is a paradigm. He thought that with knowledge alone he could heal his city and himself. Furthermore, and even worse, he thought that knowledge was best expressed as answers and straightforward solutions of problems: he thought that his answer to the sphinx's riddle, "man," was evidence that he actually knew something about being a human being. He thought that the question "who am I?" could be answered as simply as a riddle. By the end of his drama, he has learned that his life, so carefully and honorably maintained, had been nurtured on ignorance. The tragedy thus ends, not with the abandonment of knowledge, but with a new kind of knowledge: knowledge of ignorance, of limits; knowledge that life is not simply a riddle to be solved; knowledge of what it means to be a human being.

Oedipus succeeds as a detective: he learns the answer to the questions "who killed Laius?" and "who are my parents?" But his very success brings catastrophe and causes him and the audience to revise their understanding of his success. More important than Oedipus' prowess as a detective is the knowledge he and the audience gain at the end of the play: We learn that life is fundamentally insecure and that, as a result, it cannot be reduced to a riddle. Oedipus the detective learns that life cannot be simply solved.

Oedipus is not destroyed. He stands with the strength generated from having recognized his true place in the world. Such recognition came at a high price. His fortunes were reversed and it was Oedipus himself, through his intensive interrogation of three witnesses, who caused this. Recognition and reversal are simultaneous in this play. Together they culminate in a new, well-chastened knowledge. *Oedipus the King*, which finally can be described as a tragedy of knowledge, teaches us that we must acknowledge the precariousness of our understanding of even that which is most familiar. The world given to us by our parents, the world on whose paths we have stepped for all of our lives, cannot be counted certain. This realization is painful. But it is true.

This play, particularly its structure, functions as the model for what follows. The first moment of this tragedy is assertion: Oedipus claims to know. His assertion is directly challenged by Teiresias. But to Oedipus, Teiresias is only what he seems to be: a blind man speaking to one of good sight. After his interrogation of the three witnesses, Oedipus realizes Teiresias was right and that he himself was blind to the truth that the unseeing Teiresias saw. The testimony of each witness contributes an essential piece of information or premise that helps to undermine the initial claim. Finally, when the syllogism is complete (I killed Laius; Laius was my father; therefore, I killed my father), the initial claim has to be fully revised. But the claim to knowledge is not totally abandoned, for the play ends with a new form of knowledge, the tragic knowledge of limits.

B LOGOS

> For, as we say, nature does nothing in vain; and human beings, alone of the animals, have logos.
>
> —Aristotle, *Politics*

What follows is the tragedy of logos. But what does "logos" mean? The easiest answer comes from the dictionary. Liddell and Scott divide it into two basic components: (1) the word, or the outward form by which the inward thought is expressed; (2) the inward thought itself.[16] This dual nature of its meaning gives "logos" extraordinary range. Primarily it refers to those outward sounds that express thought. Logos differs from "voice" or the production of mere sound. It is the ability to give voice to some reasoned thought. Word, sentence, talk, speech, explanation, language, discourse, story, argument, rational account—all these function at different times as the proper translation of "logos." It can also be rendered as "thought, reason, rationality, calculation," when it refers to the "internal talk" that goes on within. "Logos" thus comprehends virtually all that is verbal and rational within us. The one phrase that begins to capture both of these meanings is "rational account," a speech that attempts to render rational or intelligible any given phenomenon.

A third meaning should be added. "Logos" can refer to something like "rational structure." It can refer to that which exists outside of the human mind or the voice. For example, Heraclitus begins one of his aphorisms by saying, "having listened not to me, but to the logos, it is wise to agree that all things are one."[17] This logos is not a human speech or thought, but the structure of the world "out there" that can be apprehended by human beings (who use their logos) and then expressed in language (in logos).

Logos is what is found on this page. It is what I use in trying to communicate as best as I can what I think is important. It is what the reader employs in trying to decipher and then evaluate the meaning of my words. Logos is what Oedipus believes in. Early in the play, during one of his most assertive and confident moments, he states, "I examine every logos" (291), every possible explanation of the city's problems, in order to discover and effect a cure. It is logos in which he invests his hopes and his conception of which he must eventually revise.

Even after having clarified somewhat the meaning of its two principal words, the phrase that best titles the content of this book, "the tragedy of logos," remains obscure. By contrast, "the tragedy of Oedipus" is not difficult to understand. Oedipus is a character who, in a complicated way, is responsible for his reversal and catastrophe. Because of his own drive toward greatness, he collides with the limits of his efficaciousness—and this very collision discloses to the audience something about the nature of human existence. But how can there be an analogous story about logos?

The "tragedy of logos" implies that logos itself has a history in which it figures as a character whose reversal is inevitable. Logos has limits that it cannot surpass and against which it must collide. Such an assertion is quite similar to what many philosophers have said. Kant, for example, devoted much of his career to articulating "the limits of reason." But to attribute a tragic "fate" to logos is to do more than document its limits. It is to suggest that not only does logos have limits, but that it *must* collide with them. This implies that in its initial "scene" logos does not know its limits. Like the tragic hero, logos has some sort of internal drive toward greatness; it is driven to go beyond the bounds of its legitimate efficaciousness and suffer a catastrophe. Logos, through the intensity of its initial self-assertion, will instigate the developments that are to follow on these pages. Through a series of examinations it will progressively come to realize that it is incapable of sustaining or justifying its initial claims. As a result, it will finally be forced to revise those claims in light of its discoveries. It will suffer reversal as it comes to realize its limits.

What differentiates the treatment afforded to logos on these pages from, let us say, a Kantian critical analysis of reason, can be understood as largely a matter of the *form* of what follows. Kant makes purely theoretical arguments. In other words, he gives his reader reasons to believe that the conclusions he advocates are true while those of his opponents are false. But if logos has a tragic "history," then this type of argumentation is not an appropriate means of expressing it. The only form that can do justice to, can appropriately express, the tragic history is a *drama*. The reader must apprehend not only the argument leading to the conclusion that logos has limits, but must witness the entire surge of developments that logos undergoes. The goal is not to articulate theoretically the limits of logos, it is to witness a character who undergoes a reversal. We (the audience, the readers, those who care for logos) need to suffer as it makes its journey from confident self-assertion to the revision of its claim. Only by undergoing this entire sequence of events, from the first moment of assertion to the later stages of revision, can we truly appreciate the tragedy of logos.

Perhaps a comparison with Sophocles will help clarify. Consider the following statement: "in *Oedipus the King* Oedipus gains self-knowledge and learns that his previous confidence in his rational prowess was ill advised." This statement is probably true. However, neither it nor a highly refined version of it can convey the full force of the actual developments of the play. The drama includes all the movement from Oedipus' initial self-confidence to his catastrophe. When, at the beginning of the play, Oedipus says (as I reformulate), "I am the son of Polybus of Corinth," he is wrong. At the end of the play when he says, "I am Oedipus son of Laius," he is right. But the latter statement does not simply replace the former. Being initially wrong is as integral a part of Oedipus' story as is being right; his drama is precisely that of moving from ignorance to knowledge. He must be initially wrong in order for him eventually to become right and for his story to unfold.

Theoretical arguments do not work this way.[18] For the theorist, being wrong is to be avoided at every turn. His goal is to establish through good reasoning what is true and right. Drama differs. It tells a story and so asks the reader to participate in each of the different chapters of the hero's tragedy. The teaching of the drama is not simply its conclusion: it is the work in its entirety. What follows has three chapters that together comprise the history of logos. There is no simple statement of the thesis of this book. What occurs at the beginning is not a premise in an argument. It is a moment in a drama. Even though it will later be revised, it cannot be eliminated, for it is as much a part of logos as the third chapter.

To return to the issue at hand: logos is a word whose meaning is extremely broad. Part of the intention of what follows is to clarify it. Logos is tragic; that is, like Oedipus it undergoes a series of changes, a movement, from self-confident assertion to a revised conception of who it is. This movement requires that logos collide with its limits and thus have revealed to itself and to its audience the inadequacy of its initial claims.

There is a problem, however. Who is to say what logos is? There are many versions of logos and people do not agree on what it means. Even if what follows succeeds in clarifying a specific sense of its meaning, what reason would there be to believe that the conception of logos depicted on these pages is an accurate representation of logos itself? Why, in fact, should anyone agree that "logos itself" is a meaningful phrase? Even if we concur that the word is to be translated as "rational account" or "reason," there would still be sharp disagreement about what these words mean. A physicist, for example, when asked to give a logos of the human body, would do so given his own version of what constitutes a rational account. His logos would be composed largely in the language of mathematics and would explicate the body as a moving object in space. The biologist, when asked the same question, would present quite a different story and might use a language not nearly so mathematical. More different still would be the logos given by a sculptor concerned only with the body's lines of beauty and grace. It seems clear that "logos" is necessarily a controversial term.

An example of this controversy was already alluded to in the prologue. There it was stated that Descartes radically altered the classical conception of logos. To prefigure the lengthy discussion of this issue that is to follow, in the seventeenth century only a certain type of logos was deemed legitimate, namely that identified with technical knowledge (or "techne," the term to be discussed next.) Before that period of European history, particularly during the age of classical Greece, logos was not restricted in this fashion. It was much broader and embraced technical knowledge as only one of its several parts. The philosophers of both the seventeenth century and ancient Greece affirmed logos. But they fundamentally disagreed on what it meant. What would happen if contemporary representatives of these two competing positions were to debate one another on just this issue, what is logos? How would it be possible to settle the dispute between them? To ask an analogous question, how is it possible to establish that the conception of logos to follow below is "right," is in fact reflective of the human capacity for reasoned discourse?

To settle such a dispute or establish such a claim requires explaining what the best meaning of "rational account" really is. In other words, one of the competitors would have to justify the contention that his version of logos is right and his opponent's wrong. But this attempt at justification is very peculiar. To determine that a certain version of rational account is correct would require giving a series of explanations. The attempt to give explanations, however, requires *already* having a conception of logos to guide that attempt: giving explanations is precisely the task of logos. How, then, is it possible to defend a contention, and not just assume, that a certain conception of logos is correct?

In order to give a complete defense of a specific conception of logos it might be necessary, for example, to explain what the human power of rationality really is and what types of objects it is able to handle successfully. On the basis of these two explanations, an argument might then be needed to certify that a specific type of language, of reasoned discourse, is the appropriate vehicle for expressing the conclusions garnered by the use of rationality as it comes to understand those objects that it studies. Consider the physicist. In order for him to explain why mathematics should figure so prominently in the logos of an object, he first must explain how it is that the mind (or the brain) gains information about those objects in the world treated by physics. On the basis of this, he would then be able to explain why it is that mathematical physics is the paradigmatic form and offers the best means of speaking knowledgeably about the world.

(Physicists, of course, don't usually engage in this sort of enterprise; they do physics. Philosophers of science are usually assigned the sort of task just described.)[19]

Again, there is a problem. If the physicist is required *first* to explain the brain, the world, and the connection between the two, in order to justify his conception of logos, then has he presupposed what he needs to prove, namely a conception of what it is that constitutes a good rational account or explanation? Has he "begged the question"? The physicist had to have a working conception of logos in order to explain how the brain receives information. But where did he get this from? Framing such a conception was supposed to be the goal or the end, and not the beginning, of this endeavor. The physicist had to begin by using the very conception of logos he was supposed to justify.

This seems like cheating. "Begging the question" is a serious offense. A basic goal and an animating impulse of logos, no matter what particular version one has of it, is to explain, justify, or defend its conclusions. To beg the question is to presuppose, rather than establish, a conclusion. In itself, the phrase "begging the question," is difficult to decipher. The Latin phrase of which it is a translation is *petitio principi*, which literally means "begging the beginning." The Latin is more faithful to the original phrase coined by Aristotle who also spoke of "begging the beginning." But what "beginning" is referred to here? One scholar suggests that the best way to understand this is to imagine a game.[20] Person A begins the game by asserting a thesis. Person B is required to ask A a series of questions in order to force A to make a series of admissions. His final goal is to use these admissions against A's thesis. B "cheats" if he asks A, right at the beginning, to admit that A's original thesis was wrong: the goal for B is to force A to admit to independent reasons that will show that A's thesis is wrong, not just begin by saying it was wrong.

Some sort of game like this may well have been played by the students in Plato's or Aristotle's school. The key idea is that when someone "begs the beginning" he fails to provide reasons for the conclusions he wants to establish. And this is cheating. For example, you may wish to prove Homer was the greatest poet. In order to prove this you offer as a supporting statement, "all people with good taste believe that Homer was the best poet." When pressed again to defend this statement, and to explain how you identify someone with good taste, you say, "I can always tell if somebody has good taste because they always prefer Homer to other poets." Such arguing is circular. You have used one reason (people with good taste prefer Homer) to support a conclusion (Homer is the best poet), and then backed up the supporting reason with a disguised version of the conclusion (a person with good taste is one who believes Homer is the best poet). The conclusion is being used to support itself and, as a result, what seems to be an argument is no argument at all: it is simply an assertion of an opinion.

All human beings carry with them a host of opinions. What is supposed to differentiate the person of logos from the one without is the commitment to giving reasons explaining why one opinion is superior to another. The physicist has an opinion as to what logos is. But why this opinion is worth holding is not really explained by his attempt to justify his conception of logos; it is assumed.

The physicist is not being singled out for blame. This dilemma would plague any representative of a competing version of logos that attempts to justify itself. There is something inherently peculiar in this task. In order to carry on an investigation into the nature of logos one must *begin* with a conception of logos. After all, it is logos that is responsible for investigating things. But how, then, will it ever be possible to certify with confidence what logos is? If in fact this turns out to be impossible, then does every representative of logos begin in an irrational manner, with an unsupported opinion of what it means to be rational? This question will be discussed repeatedly below. Indeed, it is the critical problem that will propel logos into its catastrophe. Logos, as we soon will see, is driven to examine itself, to attempt to know itself. The result of this examination will force logos to conclude that it is unable to be rationally confident about who it is. It will suffer at the moment of this recognition for it will be forced to revise radically its understanding of itself.

Rather than attempt to explain here what particular conception of logos will be used in this book, let me only indicate that I will attempt to clarify what I mean by "logos" in the first chapter following this introduction.

C TECHNE

This word did not appear in the prologue, but it was present in the form of its cognates "technical" and "technology." Since "techne," as well as its descendants, will play a critical role in the tragedy of logos, it is important now to consider its meaning at some length.

Again, let us begin with the dictionary. "Techne" (plural: "technai") derives from an Indo-European root that refers to "wood." For example, the "*tekton*" (a very old Greek word) was the woodworker. In the earliest times, building houses from logs and branches was probably an activity performed by an entire family or group. But as human society became more settled and more elaborate homes were needed, greater strength and cleverness were required by the house builder. The activity of the *tekton*, or "techne," came to label that particular skill uniquely possessed by one member of the community and needed by all.

In subsequent centuries the meaning of the word progressively widened. From its very narrow origin, where it named only woodworking, it came to refer to many different skills. By the time of Homer (around 750 b.c.e.), the meaning of "techne" had been freed from the *tekton*. It meant skill or cunning or craft in general. One might well ask why woodworking, rather than metallurgy or something else, became paradigmatic for technical skill in general. "The activity of the carpenter differs from that of the smith through its more rational character. It demands a capacity for intellectual solution to particular tasks . . . a capacity to combine and improvise which, if explained to the layman, is comprehensible, but whose individual tasks, to be coordinated purposefully, remain the priority of the specialist."[21]

The above is the view of one scholar only and is speculative. Nevertheless, even if it is not completely accurate, it tells much about how the word was probably heard in ancient Greece. By 750 b.c.e. "techne" meant intelligent skill in a very broad and general sense. A good example of just how broad this sense was can be gleaned from a passage in Aeschylus' play *Prometheus Bound* (which dates some three hundred years after Homer). Prometheus, a god, stole fire and techne from other gods and gave them to humanity in order that they might survive. In his elaborate description of his gift, Prometheus says:

> For indeed you know of the sufferings of mortal men, how before I placed intelligence in them and made them possessors of their own minds, they

were foolish. I will tell you, not because I blame humanity, but because I gave men the things I did with a good intention.

At first these men, though looking, looked in vain; they listened but did not hear. Like the shapes of dreams they muddled through their long lives in random confusion. They did not know how to build houses that face the sun, how to work in wood. As a result, they lived underground like small ants, in holes. They had no reliable means of telling the onset of winter or flowering spring or fruitful summer; but without knowledge they did everything until I showed them the rising and the setting of the stars, all so hard to discern.

And lo and behold, number, pre-eminent of all clever devices, I discovered for them, and the combining of letters, memory of all things, the mother of the Muse, a good worker (442–461).[22]

Prometheus goes on to list more of the specific skills he distributed to humanity: animal husbandry, sailing, medicine, prophecy, metallurgy. He closes by saying, "all technai to mortals from Prometheus come" (506).

There are at least two kinds of techne on Prometheus' list. The first might be described as "productive," that type of knowledge, like woodworking, that brings into being a useful artifact that aids in the direction of human affairs. This is perhaps the most obvious sense of the word. "Techne is a deliberate application of human intelligence to some part of the world, yielding some control over chance; it is concerned with the management of need and with prediction and control concerning future contingencies."[23]

"Techne," however, is broader than the quote might suggest, for it is also typified by arithmetic, simply called "number" in the passage and described as preeminent among all "clever devices." Why does arithmetic, which in itself produces nothing, receive this accolade? One reason at least is that many of the technai Prometheus mentions probably made use of some form of arithmetic: the house builder, the "meteorologist" who charts the risings and settings of the stars, and the sailor each performed a variety of calculations in their work. Each of their technai required some application of arithmetic. The woodworker had to measure carefully the dimensions of his house before cutting his timber.

There is, however, a consideration more basic than the fact that the various technicians actually employed arithmetic in their work. Arithmetic is paradigmatic, even constitutive, of techne in general. For example, all technai have a *determinate*, that is limited, subject matter. Woodworking is about one subject only: the production of useful artifacts from wood. The woodworker, insofar as he is a woodworker, knows nothing about the rising and setting of the stars, for that is a separate subject. Since arithmetic is about number, and number is the very basis of determinateness itself, the simple fact about technai, that subject X is a self-contained unit of study separate from subject Y, is itself a "quasi-arithmetical" notion. To say that woodworking studies wood, while meteorology studies the heavens, is to select wood and the heavens as units distinct from each other. Arithmetic and mathematics in general reflect, in purest form, the activity of making distinctions. The number three is not the number four; a three-sided polygon is not a four-sided polygon. A line can be drawn between two corners of the four-sided polygon in order to distinguish two separate three-sided polygons. It is the very essence of mathematics to make such unambiguous distinctions.[24]

If the above is too abstract, consider this: All technai are relatively *precise*. When their practitioners are asked a question about their work, they are usually able to answer clearly. Without some measure of precision a techne loses its credibility. Mathematics is prototypical of techne insofar as it is the most precise of all subjects. In a similar vein, technai ordinarily result in some kind of expertise or authority that is widely acknowledged. There is, for example, usually little controversy that the doctor, and not the engineer, knows how to help us when we are sick. Criteria can be established to determine clearly who the expert, the master, in a given field really is. Furthermore, the expert can then transmit, either to peers or students, her mastery of her subject. In these senses, too, mathematics is paradigmatic. More than any other subject, the answer to a mathematical problem is certain, clear, and definitive. In the broadest sense, we can count on mathematics.

Because it is teachable, precise, not controversial, and authoritative, a technical subject, like medicine, is typically thought of as the best and most obvious example of knowledge. It is to the master of such a subject that most people would point when asked to identify one who knows. In this regard techne might further be described as "ordinary" knowledge; that knowledge people ordinarily recognize. Again, in times of sickness most people are willing to defer to the judgments of the doctor.

This last comment suggests another characteristic of techne, the one most clearly implied by the passage from *Prometheus*: A techne produces results that often are beneficial and as a consequence quite desirable.

All of these attributes of techne, that it can be mastered and taught, that it is precise and not controversial, are derived from its first characteristic: that it has a determinate subject matter. Only because medicine, like computer science, electrical engineering, or carpentry, is a very limited and well-defined subject can it be mastered and then taught. Only because medicine has clear boundaries that separate it from other subjects can the person who has become an expert doctor be identified. People do not become experts in everything; they are experts about something very specific.

There is another, still related and critical, feature of a techne. It is *value-neutral*. As mentioned, the results of such knowledge can be quite beneficial. Medicine, for example, can produce health. There is no guarantee, however, that the doctor will use her knowledge properly. Instead, the techne of medicine can be used for good or evil. With her knowledge, the doctor can heal a sick child or implant a deadly virus in an otherwise healthy patient. The doctor's technical knowledge permits her to take either of these actions. But when the situation arises, which will she choose? Obviously, the overwhelming majority of doctors will cure the child and refuse to implant the virus. But why? They are decent and reasonable and have taken an oath never to harm a patient. But why be decent? What makes the oath binding? Why shouldn't the doctor implant the virus and refuse to heal the child? There is nothing within the techne of medicine itself to answer this question. It is only in its use or in the larger human context in which it makes its appearance, and not in the subject itself, that medicine takes on a value. Medicine itself does not study how it should be used or applied.[25]

Here again, mathematics is paradigmatic. With its formal beauty and marvelous precision mathematics is silent on the questions that emerge from the uniquely human realm of value and meaning.

The fact that mathematics is constitutive of techne is hardly made explicit in Aeschylus. It is, however, made quite clear some years later by Plato in his *Republic:* "This lowly subject which comprehends the one and the two and the three—I mean in general arithmetic and calculation—isn't it the case that every techne and science must have a share in them?" (522c5–8).

There is obviously some sort of overlap between "techne" and "logos." As already indicated—and this point is crucial—for the Greeks, and unlike Descartes, the two words are not identical. For both Plato and Aristotle there is a type of logos that is broader than, and so can embrace within it, techne. This "larger" type of logos can, for example, take up the issue of how the products of techne should be used.

The three words "tragedy," "logos," and "techne" will function like guiding paths in what is to follow. Logos has a tragic structure and techne must always be kept in view in order to illuminate it. These three roads will eventually meet during the course of this book. They surely have not yet been fully clarified. What follows is devoted to doing just that.

Chapter 1

Logos Is
Unconditionally Good

A The Classic Assertion

(1) Aristotle's Vision

Aristotle was right: human beings are, by their very nature, "the animals who have logos." What this means is that logos is what essentially characterizes us. Without it we simply would not be who we are. To put this in different but related terms, logos is what is best about us. In order to become fully and best human it is necessary to exercise our capacity for logos to the highest degree possible. Because logos plays this crucial role in human life it is fair to say that not only is it good, but that it is unconditionally good; there is no occasion, no condition or set of circumstances, that negates the goodness of logos.

Aristotle's famous assertion is found in the first chapter of his book the *Politics,* in a passage that analyzes how a city (a polis or "city-state") comes into being.[1] Briefly the process is this: A polis, which is a type of community (*koinonia*), is a natural entity that emerges from equally natural, but more primitive, communities. The first of these primitive communities is the household, a gathering composed of at least two pairs: a male and a female, and a ruler and ruled. The first pair is hardly surprising, for it is an obvious biological requirement. The second is puzzling. Aristotle claims that the joining of a ruler and ruled is as natural and as necessary for survival as the relationship between male and female: "Those that are by nature fit to rule and those fit to be ruled must be joined together for survival" (1252a31).

One reason that Aristotle makes this comment is because he believes that such hierarchies are found in all of nature. The relationship between ruler and ruled is not, in other words, an artificial imposition foisted by one group of people on another in order simply to benefit themselves. It is natural. The best example of what Aristotle means by the natural ruler and ruled is found in the relationship that obtains between the psyche (the soul, spirit or mind) and the body.[2] "An animal is first of all composed of psyche and body. Of these the former is by nature the ruler, the latter is the ruled" (1254a34–36). (Aristotle's teaching on animals in general would take us rather far afield. Let us then concentrate only on human beings.) The psyche is able to use foresight, intelligence, and calculation to direct the workings of the body toward preestablished goals. Because it has such a natural ability, the psyche *should* rule the body. It fails to do so only in those people who are truly wretched and in whom "the body rules the psyche on account of this person being totally out of shape and contrary to nature . . . it is clear that it is according to nature and beneficial for the body to be ruled by psyche" (1254b1–8).

In an analogous fashion, some human beings are more adept at giving orders because they are better at using their intelligence to foresee what is needed in the future. These are the "natural rulers." Those who are "naturally ruled" are better suited to use their bodies to fulfill these orders. No doubt this sounds shockingly elitist to our modern, egalitarian, ears. But it must be remembered that Aristotle is here talking about natural, and not legal or conventional, distinctions. In other words, if person A rules person B only because A's country has conquered B's, or because the laws stipulate that B cannot himself rule, then this is not a natural, but a conventional, ruler/ruled relationship. Aristotle would deny that it is good. Only if A rules B because A is truly more intelligent than B, only if the relationship between A and B benefits *both* parties, would Aristotle call it natural and good.

When the male/female and ruler/ruled are themselves combined, they form the household, a small communal unit required for human survival. The second stage of development is the village which comes into being through the combination of households. This more advanced community facilitates day-to-day living and enhances the security of its members. Eventually, households join together to form a polis, the most complex and self-sufficient of human gatherings. Once they are joined together in the polis the range of human concerns can be greatly expanded. No longer is survival or the secure continuation of life the sole goal of the community. Once they become political, human beings can strive to live a good life (1252b16–34).

It is not necessary here to evaluate the anthropological or historical accuracy of Aristotle's assertions. Instead, our goal is to understand how he looks at the world and why he is right in making his famous claim that human beings are the animals who have logos. The most striking feature of the *Politics'* analysis of the polis is its reliance on nature. All the developments charted by Aristotle are seen by him to be fully natural. They occur in accord with and in fulfillment of human nature. Natural entities are purposive. They have a "telos," a goal or end, toward which all their parts and their entire activity are directed. Human being has as a dimension of its essential makeup a purpose: to be political. The biological coupling of females and males is for the sake of the continuation of the species; the joining together of households is for the sake of achieving a higher degree of security. Finally, the coming into being of a polis is for a purpose that encompasses the previous two: the living of a good life. Only in a polis can human beings become what they are capable of being. None of the prior stages (nor their purposes) were complete in themselves. They were like children who have not yet matured. Only with the advent of the polis do they successfully emerge into what they truly are.

This type of reasoning is a prime example of Aristotelian teleology, his logos of the telos of natural entities. Aristotle declares that "as we say, nature does nothing in vain" (1253a9–10), that natural entities have some final state toward which their development is directed. As a result, a full account of such an entity must include an analysis of its telos. This type of account is sometimes referred to as the "final cause," which is an answer to the question "for the sake of what?" To understand properly any natural entity, this question must be answered.[3]

The telos functions as a standard by which to measure individual instances of a natural entity. If, for example, it is part of a tree's nature to have leaves, and a particular tree is diseased and does not have its full share of leaves, then that tree is rightfully declared deficient. Similarly with human beings: since the polis is the telos of communal development, a human being without a polis is not fully human and so cannot live a good life.[4] Human beings are political animals.

Aristotle's teleology has been out of fashion for centuries and no doubt sounds strange (offensively arrogant even) to a reader unfamiliar with it. Our scientific age, ever on the search for those particles that cannot be seen or that theory which can embrace all of the universe, dismisses the notion of natural purposes. As one scholar puts it, "the beginning of modern thought can be defined by the decay in the belief in that universal teleological order."[5] Later in this book we will examine a pardigmatic example of such a dismissal and consider whether it is justified. For the moment, let us try to suppress our familiar preconceptions and look at the world through Aristotle's eyes in order to see whether his vision can illuminate our experience at all. The polis, he says, is natural and is the culmination of a process of development.

This chapter began with Aristotle's declaration that human beings are by nature the animals with logos. It then stated that they are political animals. These two descriptions are related.

> And why human being is a political animal more so than any bee or other gregarious animal is clear. For nature, as we assert, does nothing in vain;

and human beings alone of the animals have logos. Any usage of voice can indicate pleasure and pain, and so voice belongs to the rest of the animals (for their nature has come to this point, namely to have perception of pain and pleasure and to indicate this to one another.) But logos is for the purpose of clarifying the beneficial and the harmful and as a result the right and the wrong. For this is unique to human beings, that they alone have a perception of good and bad and right and wrong . . . And the sharing of these things makes a household and a polis (1253a7–16).

Having logos is the precondition of being political. Human beings join together in communities because they can speak to one another. We do more than make sounds indicating pleasure and pain; we can articulate reasoned thoughts about what is right or wrong, bad or good. It is a sharing, a bringing to voice, of a set of values that constitutes a polis.

But what is logos for Aristotle? The passage above seems to indicate that it is just this capacity to discuss and clarify right and wrong. It is the ability to speak rationally about, with the hope of attaining knowledge, questions of value. This sounds strange; one might rather expect logos to be described as the capacity to discern what is true or false. Why does Aristotle here give priority to what is good or bad, right or wrong? For one thing, he is talking about politics, whose very essence is the human ability to speak about values. In other contexts, such as his *Metaphysics,* he examines logos more from the point of view of truth and falsity. But what, then, is Aristotle's real view of logos?

For this let us return to the passage about the coming into being of the polis. Aristotle's *Politics* itself gives a logos, a rational account, of the polis as a natural entity. As such, in this text Aristotle functions as a "physicist," one who gives a logos of some natural entity that has a *physis,* a nature. He articulates something essential about the nature of human beings. He would do much the same in a biological work examining the nature and structure of a fish. Aristotle observes, looks at the world, and then articulates what he sees. In a biological text, Aristotle might study human being as a mammal with a certain type of heart, lungs, etc. In the *Politics* he looks at human being in its political or communal aspect. And what he sees is that the capacity to speak rationally about values is essential to, or even coextensive with, the polis.

We should notice that in the passages from the *Politics* that have been discussed there are no arguments; Aristotle has not proven that his views are correct. Instead, he seems to tell what he sees as the truth about human beings. This is his standard procedure. Aristotle is above all else a "theoretician," a word that comes from the Greek *theorein* meaning "to look at" or "to see."[6] He looks at the world and then tells us what he sees. As Heidegger puts it, "the logos lets something be seen . . . namely what it is about; and it does so either for the one who is doing the talking (the medium) or for persons who are talking with one another . . . Discourse . . . lets us see something from the very thing which the discourse is about."[7]

The following passage also should indicate how closely Aristotle's conception of logos is related to vision.

> All human beings by nature reach out for knowledge. An indication of this is the affection we have for our senses. For even disregarding their usefulness, we are fond of them for their own sake; and more than the rest, we are especially fond of the sense which is through the eyes. For not only when we are going to do something, but even when we're not about to do anything, we prefer seeing, generally speaking, to all the rest. The reason for this is that sight, most of all the senses, enables us to know things and it makes clear many distinctions . . . (*Metaphysics* 980a20–28).[8]

Sight is frequently used, both in English and Greek, as a metaphor for knowing. (We speak of insight, having a bright idea or an illuminating discussion.) It is not, however, only a metaphor since for Aristotle it (along with the other senses) makes an actual contribution in the process of acquiring knowledge. Aristotle is extremely confident about the reliability of our senses. They can be trusted for they can report accurately to us information about the world (about nature) "out there." Through a complex process that he describes in his book *De Anima*, Aristotle shows how the senses constitute the first stage in the attainment of knowledge. It is not necessary here to examine the details of that process. Instead, let two further citations give some indication of how greatly Aristotle trusts our ability to see, and then say, the world as it is.

> For it is on account of wonder (*thaumazein*) that human beings, both now and at first, began to philosophize. At first, human beings wondered about the odd things that were right in front of them. Gradually they progressed and were perplexed about much greater matters, like the changes of the moon and sun and stars, and about the generation of the universe (*Metaphysics*, 982b12–17).

> Seeing (*theoria*) the truth is in one sense difficult, in another easy. An indication of this is the fact that even though no one can adequately grasp it, all of us cannot miss it entirely. Instead, each of us is able to give a logos (*legein*) about some part of nature and even though as individuals little or nothing is added to the truth, from all of us contributing together something grand comes about (*Metaphysics*, 993a30–b4).[9]

These two short passages tell much about how Aristotle understands the human relationship to the world out there. In the first, he talks about wonder. The Greek word here, *thaumazein*, is etymologically related to *theorein*, which means to see or to look at. Wonder, seeing objects in the world and being both amazed and perplexed by them, is the origin of philosophy. It is because we see things that puzzle us that we begin the search for knowledge. The search is progressive. Starting from that which is right in front of us, we are able to advance in our inquiries until we attempt to understand the nature of the universe itself. There is thus a continuity in our searching. The wonder-ful things in our immediate vicinity trigger a process of inquiry that eventually leads us to questions about the much larger whole that embraces these things. As such, we can and should trust our relationship to the world around us. When we are perplexed by what is in front of us, we can be confident that our puzzles, as well as our solutions, will lead us toward greater and more comprehensive questions. We are beings directed outwardly toward the world, approaching it with wonder and the desire for knowledge, worthy urges that should be affirmed and carefully nurtured.

The second passage reformulates this theme. Seeing the truth is in one sense easy. Nobody can get it all wrong. Why? We are at home in, part of, the world. Simply to be alive requires being able to see some of the world accurately; we typically walk around, and not into, ditches.[10] What we see is actually out there to be seen. Our senses rarely lie. No one can see everything, and some surely see more sharply than others, but by pooling together the visions of many we can see something grand.

In this passage Aristotle evinces a great trust not only in the human ability to see without distorting the world out there, but to articulate faithfully that vision. "Each of us," he says, "is able to give a logos (*legein*, related to logos) about some part of nature." Language, according to Aristotle, is able to communicate, without distorting, the truth about nature, the world out there to be seen. To elaborate, consider the following passage from *De Interpretatione*:

> Spoken sounds are symbols of affections of the psyche, and written words are symbols of spoken sounds. And just as written words are not the same for all men, so spoken sounds are not the same for all. However, those first things of which these [spoken sounds] are signs, namely the affections of the psyche, are the same for all, and the actual things of which these [the affections of the psyche] are likenesses are also the same (16a3–8).[11]

Aristotle asserts that language can faithfully reflect actual things in the world. The psyche, in the process of sensation, is affected by these objects. These psychic affections, these sensations, are what Aristotle calls "first things." They are the primitive constituents of knowledge. Spoken sounds, especially words, are signs or representations of these affections.

Human languages obviously differ and in this sense are a matter of convention. But those first things for which language provides signs are "the same for all"—they are a consequence of the psychic ability shared by all human beings to sense accurately the world. Furthermore, that world, that set of actual objects out there, exists independently of the human ability to sense it; nature too is "the same for all." All of this implies that language can in principle provide us with a window to nature. By speaking carefully, knowledgeably, we can see clearly objects in the world.

This is precisely the function of Aristotelian prose: it aims to let be seen those objects of which it speaks. This is also why Aristotle so often seems assertive rather than argumentative. Often he is not trying to prove anything, he is attempting to tell his readers what is before their eyes. The task of the reader is to do more than study Aristotle's text or dissect his arguments; it is to evaluate his assertions by examining the world in which we live.

As with his teleology, Aristotle's "method" (his *methodos*, his way of going about the job of gaining knowledge) is today poorly regarded. As will be discussed below, the modern scientific project begins with a fundamental distrust of what is before our eyes. It begins by rejecting the testimony of common sense and ordinary language. By contrast, Aristotle has confidence that ordinary language can make a valuable contribution to the project of articulating the natural world as it is. For Aristotle, the ordinary, the usual, is also "ordinal"; it presents an order, sets a standard. Modern science begins with a rejection of ordinary language and an attempt to replace it with one much more reliable and precise.[12] For Aristotle the way things ordinarily seem, and the way most people talk about most things, tell much about the way they are. The way things ordinarily seem is of no interest to the modern scientist. He has dispensed with purposes, has little interest in the teachings of common sense, the testimony of the naked eye, or the speakings of ordinary language.

It is not only the scientists who have dispensed with Aristotle. To the contemporary subversives like Derrida and Rorty, for example, the notion that language can achieve transparency and thus allow an object spoken about to be "seen" is preposterous. Indeed, for Derrida there is probably no notion more offensive than that offered by Aristotle in *De Interpretatione*. The hierarchy presented in that passage—objects in the world, sense perceptions of those objects, spoken signs of those perceptions, written signs of that which is spoken—represents to him "logocentrism," the illegitimate confidence that the human voice can become a transparent medium through which the world can be made present, at its worst. For Rorty it would represent the antiquated notion that the mind can be "a glassy essence," a mirror to the world. Both thinkers (and many readers) would reject utterly Aristotle's great hope.[13]

From a variety of perspectives, then, Aristotle is a "dead dog," a naive philosopher whose time has fortunately passed.[14]

It is thus hardly to be expected that at this point the reader should be "converted" to Aristotelianism. The most to be hoped for is that Aristotle's vision will at least be considered as a way of looking at the world and the human capacity for logos. His is a logos of common sense. It attempts to explicate the ordinary "look" of things and not the "laws" that lie behind such appearances. It seems, for example, that the parts of living beings do have purposes. It is tempting to say, for example, that eyes are for seeing. It seems that language does refer to objects in the world. In one's daily life there are very few occasions to doubt one's sense perceptions. Aristotle's logos, as opposed to most contemporary versions, seeks to affirm this dimension of human experience. This is, I suggest, its greatness and beauty. As one commentator puts it, Aristotle "is a professional human being."[15] His logos is the effort to tell us what our earthbound, purposive, ordinary, experience is like. In any case, the "logos" which functions as the title of this book is Aristotle's. It is the distinctly human ability to see and say the world as it is.

Before clarifying further what "logos" means, a final point about Aristotle's "method." Consider the following comment he makes about his book *The Nicomachean Ethics*, the study of what is a good human life:

> Our subject would be sufficiently articulated if it should achieve the level of clarity that is appropriate to its subject matter. For the same degree of precision should not be sought for in every logos, just as it should not be sought for in all the things produced by craft. That which is fine and right, the very subjects of ethics and politics, contain much difference and instability. As a result they often seem to be a matter of mere convention and not nature. Good things too are characterized by such instability because harm often accrues to many people as a result of them. Some men are, for example, destroyed by wealth, others by courage.
>
> Therefore, it will be satisfactory in this particular kind of study to show the truth roughly and in outline and, since we are speaking from and about something that only usually holds good, to make our conclusions in a similar manner. It is necessary for the reader to accept what is said in the following in the same spirit. For it is a sign of an educated man to seek that degree of precision that is appropriate to each area of study. And what this appropriate degree is, is determined by the nature of the object being studied. For it

seems to be nearly the same thing to accept a probable conclusion from a mathematician as it is to demand a rigorous demonstration from a rhetorician (1094b11–27).[16]

What is crucial in this passage is the *heterogeneity* it allows for in the various branches of knowledge. Different subjects, or logoi, take up different objects. Arithmetic, for example, studies numbers; physics studies change. As a consequence of their having different objects, these subjects achieve varying degrees of precision. What degree of precision is to be expected in any given study results from "the nature of the object being studied." And these objects differ. The subject of the rhetorician, one of Aristotle's examples, is (broadly speaking) the means of persuading human beings. As a result, the rhetorician must know what techniques are best used under what circumstances. When, for example, is it most effective to make an appeal to pity? When should invective be employed? Being able to answer these questions requires some knowledge of human psychology. It is a mistake, says Aristotle, to expect the rhetorician to be able to achieve the degree of precision that is achieved by a mathematician. The latter studies only formal, purely abstract and invariable objects. From the mathematician we should expect the highest degree of precision. But only one who is ignorant would apply this same standard to the rhetorician; his subject matter is too variable, too complex, too muddy, ever to be made as clear as mathematics.

The world itself is heterogeneous, filled with objects that differ in kind. Logos is the articulation of the world. Therefore, to do justice to that of which it speaks, logos must accurately reflect such heterogeneity. The logos constituting the *Nicomachean Ethics* or the *Politics* takes up human being in its social or political dimension. In this sense, their subject matter is the same as that of the rhetorician. It would therefore be a mistake to demand from them mathematical precision.

As we shall see below, the contrast between the Aristotelian teaching on precision and that belonging to those who created modern science could not be more different. Aristotle's distinction between mathematics and those subjects that study human beings is fundamental: ethics and politics simply cannot attain mathematical precision. Contrary to the founding spirit of modern science, this fact does not disqualify these logoi from attaining the status of knowledge. Although it is true that in one sense all types of knowledge are the same (for they are all a result of *theorein*, of seeing), in another sense, types of knowledge differ: their objects are heterogeneous. Some, particularly those that concern the human community, are by nature imprecise.

Finally, let us return to the passage from the *Politics* (1253a7–16) in order to decide what "logos" means for Aristotle. In it can be found two aspects of logos. First, there is that which is at work in the text of the *Politics* itself, namely Aristotle's capacity to articulate his vision of a particular natural entity, human being in its political dimension. Second, there is the logos exhibited by the particular entity being studied in the text: the discussion of right and wrong which human beings undertake in the polis.

For Aristotle, then, logos is a capacity to see and then bring to voice what really exists in nature; to make clear the truth of an entity. It is also the ability to clarify what is right and wrong, to speak rationally about values. In an important sense, however, these two sides of logos are connected. Since that which is right and wrong is measured by a natural telos, logos can achieve the truth about what is right and wrong. When a woman says of a particular tree that has only a partial filling of leaves, "that is a bad tree," she speaks truthfully. Similarly, when she says of a deed, "that action is a crime; it is destructive of the polis and so it is bad," or of a person, "he's worse than the guy next to him," her statements might well be true. There is no great disparity between articulating the truth and the value of an entity. Both are rooted in the ability to see that entity clearly.

To summarize: Logos is the ability to give voice to what is in the world; and values themselves are located in the world in the form of the various purposes latent in natural entities.

Logos is definitive of who we are: rational beings, living together in a common world to which we have good access (if only we see and talk straight). We converse with one another, seek knowledge about what is right and wrong, true and false. This description becomes the standard by which we should evaluate ourselves. Logos is our telos, it is good, and the extent to which we fulfill this capacity is the measure of our worth. We are "meant" to seek the truth in conversation and to attempt to articulate what is right and wrong.

Aristotle makes this same point in different terms in the *Nicomachean Ethics*. Here he claims that logos is the "proper function" (*ergon*) of humanity. He says this in the context of asking, what is the highest good a human being can attain? The answer, in broadest terms, is "happiness" or "flourishing" (*eudaimonia*). His "argument" goes something like this: Every techne and action, every goal-directed activity and choice, aims for some good. Medicine aims for health, shipbuilding to build a ship, military strategy for victory. All human activities are, it seems, purposive: we do things for a reason, namely to achieve some goal, some good we think desirable. Furthermore, these goals are hierarchically ordered. A student goes to class in order to pass a course; he desires to pass the course in order to graduate; he desires to graduate in order to get a job so that he may gain financial security . . . and so on. Aristotle claims that this ascending series of goals must terminate at some highest goal.

> If among the things we do there is some telos which we desire on account of itself, and we desire other things on account of it, and if we do not choose everything on account of something else, it is clear that this [highest] telos is the good and the excellent. [That there is some highest telos is evinced by the following: if there were no highest telos, our goal-directed activities] would proceed indefinitely. As a result our desire would be empty and vain. [Our desire is not empty and vain; therefore, there is a highest telos.] (1094a181–22)[17]

The highest goal is what Aristotle calls *eudaimonia*. It is that which is desirable in and of itself; it leads to nothing more desirable and so we do everything for the sake of it. If there were no such highest good toward which human desire led, then desire would be empty. In other words, we would continually be striving for objects that in principle could not satisfy since their attainment would bring only the desire for new objects. Without a stable terminus toward which desire can aim, all desires would be essentially the same—that is, they could not be ordered and significantly distinquished—and life would be empty and without direction, meaningless in just the terms used by the depraved Macbeth: "a walking shadow, a poor player that struts and frets his hour upon the stage and then is heard no more."

It does not seem to occur to Aristotle to entertain the possibility that life is meaningless and desire vain. He does not, however, explain why. Perhaps he is so impressed by the fact that those around him act as if life were meaningful that he does not feel the need to call this into question. Human beings generally do go after goals: we get out of bed in the morning and ordinarily act as if our goals were worth pursuing and our lives were meaningful. We take steps toward achieving what we deem good and attaining what we desire. We rarely collapse in despair or behave like Macbeth. No great argument is needed to establish the fact that desire is not empty and vain; only an honest look at those who live around us. It is only those whose conception of logos has lost all connection to the ordinary, to the commonsensical, who could entertain the proposition that life is meaningless.

One might agree with Aristotle that life is not experienced as meaningless, but still object to him by saying that there is no reason why, in fact, there actually is a terminus or highest goal of human desire. Again, Aristotle might respond by saying that without a final standard there would no ultimate way of measuring any given desire. There would simply be an indefinitely shifting series of desires, none of which would in principle lead anywhere. No desire would be higher than any other and therefore it would finally be impossible to distinquish desires that are positive from those that are not. The student planning to move up in the world and the low-life wanting to sell drugs on the street would, if they were to be evaluated on the basis of what they want, become indistinquishable. In this sense, if there were no terminal goal, all desire would be vain, a condition Aristotle finds inconceivable.

Even if we grant the above, however, Aristotle's statement really tells us little, for without a better understanding of what *eudaimonia* is we do not learn much. Therefore, in order to flesh out his claim Aristotle asks, is there a function, a basic type of activity or work, that uniquely characterizes human being? If so, then actualizaton of that function would constitute our telos and would become the highest, most desirable, form of activity available to us. *Eudaimonia* would be that activity.

Our function is not procreation or nourishment: these activities we share with plants. It is not self-motion or sense perception: these we share with other animals. The only activity that is uniquely ours, that makes us what we are, is logos. More specifically, Aristotle here calls it "the practical aspect that belongs to the human being who has logos" (1098a3–4). By "practical" Aristotle means "that which has to do with right and wrong." Our capacity, therefore, to discuss rationally (with the hope of attaining knowledge) questions of value is our unique function. By actualizing it we flourish, for it constitutes our *eudaimonia* and what is best about us.[18]

Logos is good; we are "meant" to discuss, to try to understand. Even further, logos is unconditionally good. Because it figures so prominently in the very composition of our lives, there is no condition, no external fact or situation, that can qualify or conditionalize its goodness. It just is good. We reason, talk together, and so become who we best can be.

But unless we are misty-eyed worshipers of a dusty past, isn't the above all so much empty boast? Who is to speak so confidently of the human telos? Who is to say that Aristotle's vision bears any relationship to real life? One could object even more strongly and argue that such bold talk of a human function is not just misguided, but actually oppressive. Does Aristotle hide behind the facade of "nature" in order to impose his conception of rationality, of human life, upon unsuspecting readers? Has he suppressed a plurality of voices by insisting that his alone speaks what is true and good? As suggested above, Derrida and Rorty would certainly say yes. The Aristotelian, the classical, assertion infringes upon human freedom, robs us of our polymorphous ways. Aristotle is a "logocentrist," an "ethnocentrist." He grants his own way imperial sway and calls it good. But, say the subversives, there is no human Good . . . only goods. There is no natural purpose whose goodness is unconditional . . . life is but a series of conditions. ("Never yet has the truth hung on the arm of the unconditional": *Thus Spoke Zarathustra*.)[19] To speak of natural rulers is to perpetuate oppression and perform an act of violence.

Any number of objections could be brought against Aristotle. On what grounds, a critic could ask, does the ordinary become ordinal and receive the privilege it has in Aristotle's thought? One could accuse Aristotle of the "naturalist fallacy," of moving from the "is," from the analysis of what a human being is, to the "ought," to what a human being ought to be or do. One might well object that his confidence in language to express the natural structure of the world neglects the powerful forces of subjectivity that always infect our speaking. Aristotle's critic might well say that we make the world do what we say; we don't say the world as it is. The critic could object that Aristotle's "natural" world is so highly structured that it denies the reality of flexibility and change. She could even go so far as to complain that it is precisely Aristotle's insistence on the goodness of logos that has brought a plague upon us, one caused by the unregulated spread of technology, by reason run rampant. To his critic, Aristotle's arrogance is stifling, his teleology a weapon for enslavement.

There is, however, a form of argument that can offer support to Aristotle's vision and help fend off his opponents. We noted above that Aristotle himself simply asserts what he sees as the truth. In what follows, logos actually presents an argument for itself. Not surprisingly, its conclusion will be that logos is unconditionally good.

(2) The Protreptic Logos

Assume the following: All human beings wish to do well.[20] The last four words are ambiguous, but intentionally so. They are broad enough to make the initial assumption worth accepting. Put it this way: All human beings wish to attach the adverb "well" to their doings. From the worst criminal to the best of men, all human beings move forward with an eye toward doing well. We move from where we are toward where we hope and plan to be with the aim of some sort of enhancement. Human action is intentional: we act for reasons. Even when to normal eyes an action seems perverse or harmful, the agent does it because he thinks doing so will enhance himself. Take the man who inflicts bodily harm upon himself. Even one so deranged must believe that self-harm is better, in some sense of the word, than his previous condition. The heroin addict who imbibes a large quantity of a drug known to be harmful does so because he believes, however incorrectly, that it is "worth it." The brief and intense pleasure of the drug is counted, however inarticulately, by the addict to be better than the life free from drugs. The use of heroin eventually leads to degradation and this indicates that the addict's judgment is ill conceived. Nevertheless, simply because the addict acted freely and consciously, the use of the drugs is in some sense a consequence of wishing to do well.

"Wish to do well" is a useful phrase precisely because it is broad enough to include within it all human intentions. We can reintroduce the word "*eudaimonia*" here. Human beings vary greatly in their conception of what *eudaimonia* is; but we are linked by our desire to achieve it.

The above of course has to be specified further. What follows from the initial statement, "all wish to do well"? How do we go about trying to do well? First, by acquiring the good things that we desire. This is obvious because we believe that in the attainment of these good things lies the condition for *eudaimonia*. Actually, the statement that human beings desire good things is not accurate. Since we so often err in determining what is good, what we desire is more safely described as what we think is good. The drug addict desires heroin, which is not in fact good. Nevertheless, he is still motivated by a desire for what he (incorrectly) thinks is good.

And what, generally, do human beings think is good? The list need not be surprising. Wealth, health, physical beauty, a good family, talent, fame, good luck . . . all are typical examples of good things most of us want. Less typical and more elevated would be virtues such as good sense, justice, and bravery. The specifics on the list are not crucial; what matters is that there is such a list filled with items deemed good and so desired by those who desire to do well.

But there is a problem. The items on this hypothetical list are not actually good; they are neutral. Wealth, for example, can be used for, can bring, benefit or harm, good or evil. A woman may use her wealth either to buy heroin or to buy books. Her money, while sitting in the bank, is neutral and brings no benefit to her. Only upon being *used* does it bring benefit and so become charged with value. The argument being proposed here now has four stages: (1) human beings wish to do well; (2) to accomplish (1) we wish to possess what seems to be good; (3) what seems to be good is actually neutral; (4) neutral items must be used properly if they are to bring benefit and become genuinely good. Use becomes the critical notion.

How then does one use neutral items properly? With knowledge. With the successful application of reason or logos neutral items become good. An analogy can be offered with carpentry. How does someone use well the raw material that is wood? Only with the knowledge supplied by the carpenter. It is only knowledge that shapes the unformed neutrality of a material into that which is good. If the items on our hypothetical list are truly analogous to wood, then it is only knowledge that can consummate our wishing to do well. It is, therefore, a lack of knowledge that characterizes the heroin addict's failure; he thought, incorrectly, that the drug was good. He did not know what he was doing.

The conclusion of the argument is now obvious: Logos, the striving for knowledge of how to use neutral things properly, is the highest activity available to those who wish to do well. It is unconditionally good because it, and only it, supplies us with the necessary means to transform the neutral into the good. Even money, that most powerful of motivations, that most apparent of goods, is really only neutral until it is used; and only logos can guide properly its use. Logos alone is the true source of *eudaimonia* and thus nothing, no external fact or circumstance, can conditionalize or call into question its goodness.

This type of argument is traditionally described as or simply called "protreptic," a term that derives from the Greek verb "*protrepein*," which means to turn (*trepein*) someone forward (*pro*), to urge them onward, upward. More specifically, it refers to a type of persuasive speech used to exhort or encourage the listener to pursue some course of action. In this particular case, it means to exhort someone to engage in logos, *in philosophy*, in the quest for understanding of the good use of neutral items.

Aristotle was right: logos is good. This is not to imply that anyone using her reason is simply by that fact doing what is proper. It is of course possible that logos may err. The doctor, for example, after having deliberated thoroughly, may conclude that it is good to heal a vicious criminal of a curable disease. In fact, this decision may prove to be wrong; it may well be the case that the doctor should have let the criminal die. Even so, such an error would not invalidate the claim that the doctor's use of her logos was good. Admittedly it strayed. But it can be corrected. This is another way of putting the protreptic point about logos: it is potentially self-correcting. If it errs, it is open to criticism, to rational self-inspection and improvement. Such openness is testimony to its unique goodness: only logos can correct itself.

There is another sense in which logos is self-correcting. Imagine that someone objects to the protreptic argument. As an alternative, this person might propose that "logos is not good and thus we ought not to philosophize or pursue knowledge." There is, however, a problem with this objection: precisely insofar as the opponent here has arued (has given reasons for, has attempted to defend his position) that one ought not to engage in logos, he has engaged in logos. In other words, in the very act of trying to refute the goodness of logos, this person has used logos and so has given testimony to, has implicitly affirmed, the belief that logos is good. In this sense logos is able to embrace (to correct) even those who seem opposed to it. Even those who deny it is good, insofar as they try to make sense to another person, must use logos and so to it they give the nod.[21]

To summarize: The protreptic logos demonstrates that in order to do well one must use one's possessions properly and that this can only be done with knowledge. It concludes that seeking such knowledge is the highest, the most important, of all activities. Against possible objectors, it argues that even if someone using her logos makes a mistake, logos is able to correct itself. Similarly, all who deny the goodness of logos in fact affirm it (precisely in the attempt to deny it). All of this is evidence that Aristotle was right, that logos is unconditionally good.

(3) The Indirect Argument

Another way of supporting the claim of logos is through what is known as an indirect argument. This type of argument begins with a proposition that is the opposite of that whose proof is desired. Consequences are drawn from this initial proposition that are found to be unacceptable or contradictory (or absurd). As a result, the initial proposition itself must be rejected and its opposite accepted. In this particular case the assumption will be that logos is *not* unconditionally good. Consequences will be drawn that will force us to reject the assumption and accept its opposite.

If logos is not unconditionally good, it is either unconditionally bad or conditionally good. The second of these two options is weaker than the first. (The first is a more negative and harsh judgment than the second.) As a result, if the second generates unacceptable consequences, then the first would generate consequences that are even more unacceptable. Therefore, only the second formulation—logos is conditionally good— needs to be examined.

If logos is not unconditionally good there must be some condition or set of conditions that can negate its goodness. And what would this be? In a sense, it does not matter, for whatever this condition is (call it X), by definition it stands over and against logos and is not itself susceptible to treatment by logos. For reasons soon to be presented, if X negates the goodness of logos, then X negates the power of logos to identify it. As a result, if logos is not unconditionally good, then we are prohibited from saying what it is that negates its goodness. After all, saying what something is, is precisely the task of logos. For the moment let us translate logos as "reasonable speech." If X negates the goodness of logos, then X is incapable of being articulated in reasonable speech; X looms in silence. It could be anything.

Let me try to clarify. There are times when it seems good not to be reasonable. For example, it might be the case that musical improvisation and sexual intercourse are activities that reason impedes. When trying to improvise on the saxophone it is good to suspend the processes of analysis, justification, articulation, etc., since successful improvisation requires giving free rein to the musical imagination. Not only can this imagination not be analyzed, but the attempt to do so actually impedes the creative process. If we ask the musician "how did you come up with that tune?" or "will you tell me how to do it myself?" no answer is or should be forthcoming. If we attempt to force the musician to answer such questions while he is trying to play, we might destroy the music.

It might well be true that improvisation and good sex require suspension of rational activity. These examples, however, do not damage the claim that logos is unconditionally good. Because they can be identified, reasons can be given as to why these nonreasoning activities are good and how they function as conditions apparently capable of suspending the goodness of logos; these activities can be "embraced" or "surrounded" by logos. Among human activities most are best accomplished when accompanied by logos. Some, however, are best when left untouched—and there are good reasons for this. Sexual intercourse, for example, is good. It is good because it leads to procreation, because it furthers intimacy, and because it is fun. In order to be good, sexual intercourse is best left untouched by reason. Here the instinctive moves of the body best guide themselves.

While the assertion "it is sometimes good not to be reasonable" is true, it does not conditionalize the goodness of logos. That logos is unconditionally good does not mean that logos is needed at every single moment. It means that it can identify and then explain why any given activity is good. If logos can do this, if it can locate all such activities within a broad rational context, then its goodness will not be negated by some X that can be rationally identified. By surrounding, by explaining, that X, it will render the X subordinate to itself. It will embrace the X and not let it stand outside as an independent critic.

The above does not imply that there can be no X. The key point the argument makes is that if there is an X, it cannot be identified. It must remain hidden in silence.

The advocate of the X is, in the eyes of logos, an enemy, a criminal who threatens its authority. If the X exists (and cannot be identified), logos would be dethroned, subordinated to an inarticulate "something" that is "out there" in dark silence. Such a view produces unacceptable consequences. A world ungoverned by logos is one without rational standards. For example, if the X exists, then logos would no longer have ultimate authority in the adjudication of disputes over values. Should a doctor heal a vicious criminal or not? If logos is not unconditionally good, then in principle logos has no right to claim that it, and not something else, not some X, ought to be finally responsible for determining what should be done. What, in the absence of logos, would determine what should be done? The X can take an indefinite number of forms. The doctor may simply follow customary practice and obey the standing conventions of the day. She may consult a religious or political authority. She may act on a subjective impulse or intuition; she may simply do what she wants or take a vote.

If X exists, then all exertions of logos—all efforts to determine rationally what, for example, is right or wrong—are conditionalized. If one judges that the criminal ought to be treated because the proper duty of the doctor is to heal, then that judgment will have to be made conditionally. The X looms, capable of negating the validity of that judgment.

To put this point in other terms: If X exists and cannot be identified, then the situation that results is *relativism*. The goodness, appropriateness, the value of all exertions of logos will be relative to the condition that is capable of negating them. And this condition, as has been stated, is in principle hidden from the view of logos.

Relativism is an often stated and familiar doctrine, although it is not usually formulated as it has been above.[22] (The formulation just presented is not, however, what is most crucial. The key is the conclusion: Relativism is the consequence of denying that logos is unconditionally good.) When it is specifically addressed to questions of value (when it is ethical relativism) it implies that no action has any value in and of itself. An action is good or bad only relative to the person or group performing or advocating that action. One doctor may heal the criminal; another may refuse treatment. One society may force its doctors to heal all patients by means of its legal code; another may allow the doctor more discretion. Neither action, neither system, is in itself good or bad. Both are good, but only from the perspectives that each holds. Relativism implies that the question should the criminal be healed? cannot be answered except in terms that make reference to the individual doctor or to the doctor's society. Neither the doctor nor the society can be made to answer the demand that their values be defended in terms other than those that make reference to themselves, to their own perspectives. In this sense, relativism implies that the question should the criminal be healed? cannot finally be answered at all. Such questions are ultimately not in the purview of logos. They are a matter of convention, custom, law; perhaps they are a matter only of subjective desire. Whatever they are a matter of cannot finally be rationally defended.

Relativism is disease, is pollution, for it negates the efficacy of logos. It destroys the possibility of a complete rational debate of fundamental questions. If relativism holds, there is no reason to be reasonable about— to examine thoroughly—questions of value; for ultimately these are questions about which logos can have no authoritative say. If relativism holds, value judgments become groundless: there would be no firm ground, no discoverable reason, upon which any value judgment could be securely based. Relativism is thus the enemy, the usurper, who would dethrone logos the king.

But relativism is untenable; it is a position that cannot be coherently held. It is a position whose consequences few, if any, can actually live. For the relativist, all value judgments are ultimately equal in the sense that none can muster a final defense of itself. This implies that if person A makes judgment P, and person B makes judgment R, and P is directly opposed to R, A (according to the relativist credo) must accord to B full equality with himself. Relativism forces A to suppress his urge to compete with, to defeat, B in rational argument. Again, I do not refer to a debate that could occur between A and B as to whose position is most in conformity with prevailing custom. The debate I consider occurs when someone asks, "but is R *really* better than P, and if so why?" This is the debate prohibited by the relativist.

Such a view is at odds with the way people live. It surely is not likely, for example, that a doctor who adamantly believes that all life, even that of a criminal, must be honored, will accept with equanimity the fact that a colleague who disagrees with her has a view of equal rational worth to her own. We desire to give voice to our opinions, to try to elevate them to the status of knowledge. Relativism denies that desire. What it does instead is homogenize all desires. All desires and values are equal precisely insofar as none is ultimately defensible. Such equality is unacceptable, unlivable, a denial of what is patently true about human beings. It is simply not the case that, when questioned hard, persons A or B are willing to declare that their values are no more defensible than their opponents'. To declare that it is the case, is to defy the phenomena of ordinary life.[23]

Relativism is unhealthy for it forces its advocate into a kind of silence.[24] It denudes him of his urge to bring forth his own set of values into the light of rational defense.

Relativism is unacceptable. Therefore, the initial proposition that generated it as a consequence—that logos is conditionally good—must be rejected. We are thus constrained to affirm the opposite assertion: Logos is unconditionally good. Logos is our telos, our essence. To deny this is to plunge into the darkness of silence and to rob human beings of what is best.

And yet . . . this defense of logos, this classical assertion, is problematic. For doesn't the protreptic argument have holes? With it did logos manipulate its audience (or its opponent)? Even if the opponent accepts the first three premises, that we all wish to do well, that as a result we desire good things, and the things we desire are actually neutral, he is not forced to agree to the final conclusion, that knowledge of the proper use of a neutral item is the condition of *eudaimonia*. This conclusion assumes without proving that something like a "proper use," one that can be grasped by knowledge, really exists. If it is true that things do have a proper use, then it may well be the case that knowledge is necessarily the most desirable of goods. But it must be shown that proper use does in fact exist. Perhaps it does not; perhaps use is a matter, not of being proper, but of being pleasurable or of fulfilling a desire. Perhaps there is nothing to be known. If that is the case, then surely logos is not the highest good. There may not be a highest good.

To put the same objection into different terms, in its protreptic argument logos imposes the analogy between carpentry and the use of neutral items upon its audience. (It argues that just as the carpenter forms the neutral material of wood into useful artifacts, so does logos transform the neutral items on the list of apparent goods into genuine goods, those that are used properly.) The critic of logos can object that this analogy is misleading. The carpenter uses wood as a passive material and has a techne to form that material according to design. But what analogous design is there in using apparent goods such as wealth, health, and physical beauty? If logos presupposes that there is such a design, then it begs the question and assumes what it purports to prove: that knowledge (the discovery of design) is the highest good.

According to the critic, the protreptic logos is not an argument at all: it is *nothing but exhortation*, urging, pleading for its cause. It is groundless and nothing but a proclamation of its own desire. The critic turns the very charges logos brandishes against its enemy against logos itself.

A similar objection can be aimed at the indirect argument. It argues that the consequence of stating that logos is only conditionally good is relativism and that the relativist would make value judgments groundless, reason-less. This it declares unacceptable. But in fact all the indirect argument actually does is outline the consequences of relativism and then express its distaste for them. That's not enough. The charge of groundlessness would only be effective if it could be shown that there is actually a ground. This the indirect argument did not do.

The indirect argument assumes that if logos can identify a given activity, even one that is apparently nonrational, and if it can explain why that activity is good, then it has rendered that activity subordinate to itself. But even if this is true, why does this type of subordination make logos better than that which it is explaining? Perhaps this type of subordination is exactly what should be avoided.

In sum, in the indirect argument logos simply voices its disapproval at those who disagree. As a result, the indirect argument is just a disguised version of protreptic. It is nothing but an urging "forward"; but, the critic will ask, forward to what? It is nothing but a plea that a specific desire, for the classical version of logos, be privileged. Such a plea, which accuses those who disagree with unreason and shameful groundlessness, is cloaked in the authoritarian mantle of Reason, but in fact is no more substantial than the pleas of its opponents.

Logos now stands accused. It began with untarnished confidence that it was the ruling principle of human life. It saw itself as happily at home, king of a natural world that welcomed it, a world whose purposes could be understood and articulated. But now logos is accused of being a tyrant, of leading a regime based on nothing but empty assertion and an ungrounded declaration that it can discover the purposive structures of nature. Logos cannot ignore this charge, for its most basic commitment is to providing an account, a defense, of its claims. Indeed, such a commitment is what best animates it—and so logos welcomes the opportunity to respond to its critics. Its initial response came in the form of the protreptic and indirect arguments. But these failed for they each presupposed what they pretended to prove: that logos is good, that neutral items can be used properly, that values are a matter of reason. Logos will have to respond again.

Before proceeding to that response, we will pause for a digression. The view of logos being developed on these pages is inspired by certain texts of Greek philosophy and literature. In order to show how such a view can retain any vitality in facing the contemporary world it is necessary to engage in the following historical sketch. Its purpose is to show where logos fits in a larger context—to show, in other words, how the ideas being presented in this book can both challenge and illuminate (by contrast) the ruling ideas of today.

As we will see next, an essential component of modern thought takes its bearings from logos. It does so negatively: it accuses logos. The accusation against logos is a vital impulse behind the technological world. Logos, in the full and rich sense championed by Aristotle, has been under attack for hundreds of years by the proponents of modern science.

In what follows, we will examine select writings of Descartes and Spinoza, two of the great architects of the modern worldview. We will see that both are fundamentally directed by the desire to dethrone Aristotle, to strip logos bare of all its mighty pretensions. What they offer instead will be a conception of reason with a greatly restricted purview, one that resists the Aristotelian temptation to speak about the purpose and goodness of natural entities. It should become clear that this is a conception under whose sway we today live.

The attack against logos comes not only from today's rulers (those progeny of Descartes who were utterly successful in breaking logos's hold on the throne). Recently, especially with the warm welcome accorded to French thought here in America, the attack has come from another perspective: that belonging to the contemporary subversive. And this attack has become ever more shrill and widely felt. Thinkers such as Derrida and Rorty have made their considerable reputations based upon their assault on logos. Both follow the lead of Nietzsche, who prophesied so well the furies of the century.[25] Nietzsche explicitly calls into question the goodness of logos, particularly its belief that it can adjudicate the question of value. For him, such a belief is the most pernicious form of the "theoretical optimism" he saw plaguing the modern world. For him, to elevate logos to the throne is to suppress the free play of human life. The belief that good and evil can and should be a matter of authoritative reason is blasphemy against the urgings of creativity. For Nietzsche there is no world out there, safely structured, amenable to the probing eye of reason. Instead, the world is like a river, ever flowing, whose banks ever change, a river never to be stepped in twice. Elevating logos to the throne is a means or device to deny this temporal flow and is thus evidence of a hatred for life. Nietzsche's best work aspires to remedy this hate, to repudiate those "rational/natural" standards whose real purpose is to deny time's incessant flow. His goal is to infuse thought with "the meaning of the earth" and to affirm the very incompleteness that is being human.

The next section, then, has three parts and purposes: (1) to show briefly how the modern scientific project, as typified by Descartes and Spinoza, includes a fundamental assault on logos; (2) to show how the contemporary subversive, despite appearances to the contrary, actually shares a great deal with Descartes and Spinoza. Despite the fact that Rorty and Derrida complain of the tyranny of reason and of the "hyper-rationalism" of the modern world, their views as to what rationalism is are surprisingly similar to the early-modern proponents of the scientific revolution.

The third goal is this: (3) to show that the complaint against logos, in both its early-modern and contemporary (subversive) genres, was prefigured in antiquity. There were Greeks themselves who complained of the tyranny of logos and sought its overthrow. One of them, a man named Protagoras, offered a critique as profound as any delivered by today's fashionable critics. To restate a line from the epigraph of this book, "What could you tell an Ancient Greek that he couldn't say 'Big Deal'?"

It is important to realize this: So many recent voices simply recast, often with a great deal of ornamentation, ancient messages. In Athens itself a dispute raged between the proponents and the opponents of logos. Each side was eloquently and powerfully represented. This was not an abstract dispute carried on in the pages of professional journals. Instead, each side championed a living option, a basic human possibility. As a result, the ancient dispute had an intensity and immediacy rarely found today. Revivifying it can thus be of value in helping us situate ourselves within, and clarifying the terms of, the often numbingly abstract, technical, and highly professorial debates of today.

B THE CRITIQUE OF LOGOS

(1) Protagoras

Protagoras offers a profound alternative to the classical conception of logos (which, as I hope is clear, is now simply being called "logos"). In important ways, his challenge is similar to those attacks on logos presented by Derrida, Rorty, and today's "great" subversives. Before we begin Protagoras' story, some background is needed.

Protagoras was the greatest of a group of highly influential teachers who appeared in Athens around the middle of the fifth century b.c.e.: the Sophists. "Sophist" is derived from "*sophos*," meaning wise or clever or skillful. Men like Protagoras traveled from town to town offering their *sophia*, their wisdom, for sale. They were the first professors, or paid teachers, in Western culture. And what did they profess? As usual, the historical question is not easily answered; the data on the actual man Protagoras is scanty since virtually none of his writings remain. For the purposes of this chapter I will largely rely on what Plato, in his work the *Protagoras*, had to say about the Sophist.[26]

There is a saying attributed to Protagoras from which I also will take my bearings: "Human being is the measure of all things; of that which is, that it is; of that which is not, that it is not." This statement is the clarion call of relativism. It asserts that what seems to be the case to a given person, is the case. As such, it implies that there are no absolute, no natural, structures or standards that exist independently of the human beings who hold them. Since the human activity of measuring and holding standards varies from place to place and from time to time, Protagoras' famous dictum really asserts that all structures and standards are in a state of change. What, for example, seems to be the case to a person living in Athens may differ quite sharply from one living in Sparta. What seems to be the case to a twentieth-century woman may not be the same as what seemed so to her great-grandmother. No one has a privileged view of things; all views share an essential status: they are perspectives on, and measures of, things.

This is, of course, oversimplified. Relativism has many varieties: one can be relativist concerning values, knowledge, reality, or any mixture of these. What sort of relativist Protagoras is has been a matter of scholarly debate. Furthermore, when Protagoras says "human being," what does he mean? Does he refer to each and every one of us as individuals? Does he refer to human society? Or does he have the species itself in mind? Finally, what exactly does he mean by "things"?[27] What follows will, in part, present Plato's effort to answer these questions.

Before proceeding to that, a bit more background. Assume that Protagoras' relativism applies to values. As suggested above, this is the easiest and I believe most illuminating way to begin a discussion of relativism. Assume further that when he says "human being," he refers to individuals and not the species. (This tends to be Plato's assumption.)[28] This would imply that Protagoras believes that it is possible for a variety of human beings to function as a variety of measures of values. This would be true even if these human beings lived in the same society, were about the same age, and had similar social standing. If these assumptions are plausible, then it is clear that the sophistic teaching is deeply threatening to the traditional authorities of Greek life. If human being is the measure of what it means to be a good citizen, for example, then it is possible for one to be a good citizen in any number of ways. An obedient soldier, a disobedient soldier, an earnest participant in political affairs, and a recluse, are each, by their own lights, good. The relativist does not permit us to rank these people; they are equal in that they each have a particular perspective on what is good. And since no perspective is intrinsically better than any other, there is nothing by which their differences can be reasonably measured (except another perspective . . . and so on.)

Two comments: A typical Greek polis, indeed any community based on a traditional and stable sense of right and wrong, would find such a view repugnant. A traditional society is, very simply, one in which the norms of the children are consistently formed by those belonging to their parents; where, in other words, the old is implicitly taken to be the best. The Sophist, if he holds the position sketched above, attacks the very soul of this type of polis. He challenges its right to command the loyalty, and even the lives, of its citizens. Why, for example, should I be willing to die for my country (as was my father) if I acknowledge the principle that there is no substantial difference between my country and its enemy? If the ideologies of both are merely perspectival measures of the good, then I would be a fool to consider one genuinely superior to the other. The native and the old have no priority over the foreign and the new; both are but measures shifting like the sands on a beach.[29]

A second comment: There is one type of community in which the sophistic teaching (the relativism sketched above), even if it cannot be officially endorsed, can at least flourish—a democracy. In a polis ruled by the people, authority is granted only to that proposal, person, or group that wins the approval of the people. No individual has a right to impose his opinion on the polis, for no opinion can be declared authoritative or absolute. The opinions of the people, of course, vary over time. Furthermore, the people are highly susceptible to being influenced by someone adept at winning their approval. *Rhetoric*, the art of persuasion, thus commands the highest premium in a democracy. Whoever is most persuasive will win the day.

In our contemporary democracy the persuasion of the people takes place largely through television and the manipulation of visual images. In Athens, the first democracy of the west, it took place through spoken words alone. Therefore, it was to Athens that the Sophists flocked. They offered to teach the most ambitious of the young men how to be successful in political persuasion: they taught rhetoric. The relationship between relativism and rhetoric is intimate. If human values truly do not have any intrinsic worth and are but relative to those who hold them, then there is no hope that rational debate, that logos, will be able to provide an authoritative defense of such values. What remains to be said about these values, therefore, is not an account of their goodness, but a speech designed only to win their approval. The author of that speech, the rhetorician, need not be committed to the goodness of the values he champions in public. Since no value is intrinsically better than any other, the rhetorician is free to champion any value whatsoever. In other words, *if relativism offers an accurate description of human values, then rhetoric replaces logos as the most fundamental human activity.*

The Sophists, the ancient relativists, understood well the human and political consequences of their beliefs. Relativism is an attractive position. Today it is widely propounded by a great number of people (including the subversives). At first glance relativism seems commonsensical and benign: it seems to acknowledge the obvious fact that people differ greatly in their value systems and beliefs and that such differences are worthy of respect. But relativism has a harsh underside to it that is rarely brought forward. If values are relative, then what determines which value will, or should, be held at any given time? The relativist believes that all values are, from the point of view of reason, equal: they are all perspectives. But all communities make decisions about values; they do not, indeed cannot, allow all values to flourish. Instead, each community decides which values will regulate it. But how are such decisions made? What is the relativist's answer to the question, how are, and how should, the values that inform any given community be determined? Obviously the answer would not be "by a reasoned defense," for the relativist denies that any such defense is possible.

The Sophists realized that their views committed them to a rather disturbing thought: The values that are operative in any given community have no basis other than the fact that they are in command. Values are the result of a competition, a struggle, for supremacy. In other words, the sophistic view implies that the fundamental issue concerning human life is not what is good or bad, right or wrong; it is power. Whoever emerges victorious from the arena in which the struggle for power takes place determines which value will hold sway.[30]

One of Sophists' followers, a man named Callicles who appears in Plato's *Gorgias*, makes this point quite clear. He says:

> But nature herself, I think, declares that it is right for the better to take advantage of the worse and the more powerful to take advantage of the powerless. It's clear that the right has been determined as follows both among the rest of the animals, and in all the cities and races of human beings: the strong should rule the weak and take advantage of them (483c9–d6).

This is an unusually straightforward description of the core belief of sophistry from one of its more perceptive students. Life is a power struggle. The strong should rule, not because they have a better set of values, but because they are able to rule. Who rules "deserves," simply by virtue of ruling, to rule.

Another Sophist, Thrasymachus, puts the same point into quite similar terms when he defines justice as "the advantage of the stronger."[31] The "stronger" refers to those who hold political power. Thrasymachus assumes that those who rule do so for their own advantage. If the ruler, the one with power, decrees that X is just, then X is just simply because the ruler has decreed it so and can enforce his decree.

Both Callicles and Thrasymachus state their views in the midst of arguing against the philosopher Socrates. In Plato's dialogues Socrates functions as the representative of logos (although, as we will see, Plato's view of logos—while sharing much with Aristotle's—differs significantly from it as well). This means that Socrates believes that the questions, what is just? what is good? can and should be answered, not by a power struggle, but by rational inquiry. X is not just only because some ruler has decreed it so; X is just if and only if it can be rationally shown that X is just. Even the fact that the ruler and all who hold powerful positions believe that X is just does not legitimate X. Reason, logos, is the only tribunal for legitimation. The best activity for a human being, then, is not rhetoric, the quest for power, but philosophy, the public search for knowledge of what is good and just.

Callicles believes that he himself is a powerful man capable of dominating others through his rhetorical prowess. As a result, Socrates' views are offensive, even preposterous, to him. Callicles believes that life itself is a power struggle and that he is thus acting according to nature in attempting to gain political power. Socrates' views would turn life "upside down." They would repress the creative impulses men have and seek to replace the urge to dominate with intellectual inquiry. Socrates wants to find out what justice is, and this becomes the question animating so many of his conversations. For Callicles such a philosophical question is absurd: what is just is what is to the advantage of the stronger. The goal of human activity should therefore be to become as strong as possible in order to gain advantage and exert control over others. Some men have the "right" to impose their will on others. In a world with no enduring standards to function as intrinsically worthy restraints upon the desires of men, there is no principle to prevent those who are powerful from having more than their neighbors. If they can succeed in taking advantage, there is no reason for them not to do so.

Callicles enlists the aid of the Sophists in order to win the power struggle he takes as his world. To him, Socrates represents a pernicious diminution of human energy. By denying relativism, by claiming that logos can discover a set of values that is in principle binding upon all who are rational, Socrates denies the human urge to dominate. The "real man," according to Callicles, wastes no time asking "what is The Good." The real man imposes his particular version of the good upon his audience. By contrast, the philosopher, the lover of logos, is weak, cowardly, afraid to assert himself in the world. As a result he spends his time, not in the corridors of power, but in corners whispering to a few young people he can manage to convince to listen to him. Because of his life-denying and escapist set of commitments, Socrates is doomed never to say anything "free and great and vigorous" (484d). He is doomed to be a passive player in the game of political struggle.

Nietzsche, in whose shadow stand Derrida and Rorty, was inspired by men like Callicles. "The Sophists are no more than realists: They formulate the values and practices on the level of values—They possess the courage of all strong spirits to [know] their own immorality."[32] Morality (in its Socratic version) implies that since values can be rationally discovered they should function as principles applicable to all human beings. Morality thus demands that no one should exert force or behave in any other irrational manner in order to place himself above another. For Nietzsche and Callicles such Socratic morality is a ploy to suppress the strong, to repress their creativity and will to power. As Nietzsche's character Zarathustra says;

> Truly, men gave themselves all their good and evil. Truly, they did not take it, they did not find, nor did it come to them as a voice from heaven.
>
> Only man placed values in things to preserve himself—he alone created a meaning for things, a human meaning! Therefore, he calls himself "man," that is: he who evaluates.
>
> Valuing is creating: hear this, you creators! Valuing itself is of all valued things the most valuable treasure.
>
> Through valuing alone is there worth: and without valuing the nut of existence would be hollow. Hear this you creators!
>
> Change of values—that is a change of creators. Whoever must be a creator always annihilates.[33]

Nietzsche's career was devoted to exposing the stultifying morality of his nineteenth-century Europe. To do so required him to attack logos, for it is logos that declares that values can be a matter for reason, that there are reasons to do and not to do various things. But such reasoning, such morality, inhibits life, makes it old and stale. And Nietzsche, inspired by the brilliant Callicles, wanted life to be unleashed. All of his followers, in one way or the other, agree.

The students of the Sophists, then, were men who had broken with the traditional sensibility of their world, who did not believe that their fathers' opinions were necessarily the best. They wished, instead, to further their own political ambitions and were eager to employ the expertise of the Sophists to aid them. Their commitment was not to "The Good," understood as a rational object that exists "out there" in a world we all share. Instead, they were committed only to their own self-interest. One such young man appears in the prologue of the *Protagoras*. To him, then, let us turn.

(The following will include a somewhat detailed discussion of Plato's dialogue. In particular, the question, "What view of techne does Protagoras hold?" will be carefully considered. As mentioned in the introduction, "techne" plays a pivotal role in explicating the tragedy of logos. Why this is so will now begin to emerge. The full import of this section, however, will not become fully clear until later in the book.)

The story begins just before dawn. Socrates is awakened by his young friend Hippocrates who is terribly excited. He has heard that Protagoras, the famous wise man, is in town, and he wants to meet him. Since he is too young to visit Protagoras alone he asks Socrates to accompany him. Hippocrates is eager to be made wise and willing to pay Protagoras a large sum of money for his tutelage. Socrates, who is clearly devoted to the young man, is concerned that Hippocrates has lost his wits and so asks a series of questions that are designed, first, to calm the boy down, and then to force him to reflect more carefully on what it means to be a Sophist.

Socrates' first question is broad: "Tell me, Hippocrates, now that you are going to visit Protagoras and are willing to pay him a fee for what he will teach you, whom do you think you are visiting and who do you expect to become?" (311b) To illustrate what he means by this, Socrates offers the following analogies: If the young man were to approach his namesake, Hippocrates the famous doctor, with the same intentions that presently motivate him to approach Protagoras, he would do so in order to become a doctor. If he were to approach Polykleitos or Pheidias, he would do so in order to become a sculptor. What, asks Socrates, is the analogous profession in which Protagoras would offer instruction? Hippocrates is forced to answer "sophistry" and to imply that he is himself eager to become a Sophist (311e4). I say "forced" because, as mentioned above, in the traditional eyes of the polis, sophistry is shameful. It is an admission that there is no secure ground on which to base the citizens' loyalty to the set of values that the polis represents. Accordingly, Hippocrates, who still retains some of that loyalty, blushes when he answers Socrates' question (312a2).

Socrates' method of questioning here is one he uses often. He employs what I will call the "techne-analogy."[34] He places Protagoras' claimed field of knowledge (or, Hippocrates' perception of that field) into an analogy with very typical technai such as medicine or sculpture. As noted in the introduction, a techne has a determinate subject matter. Medicine is about something very specific: the workings of the human body. Sculpture is about the formation of images in stone. Both are relatively precise in their methods, capable of being mastered and then taught, and easy to identify as noncontroversial examples of knowledge. By using the techne-analogy, Socrates forces Hippocrates to locate Protagoras' sophistry into the following analogical pattern: As the doctor is to medicine, and the sculptor is to sculpture, so Protagoras is to X. What is the X, the presumed field of expertise, Protagoras is able to communicate? Who is the Sophist?

Hippocrates' first attempt at answering is "Just as the name suggests, he is the man who is knowledgeable about wise things" (312c5–6). Such an answer, however, fails to meet the criterion that Socrates, through the analogy, has imposed on this discussion: it is not sufficiently determinate. Both the painter and the carpenter, two noncontroversial possessors of a techne, would claim that they, too, are "knowledgeable about wise things." (This doesn't sound quite right in English; the word "*sophos*" is, however, broad enough to make it sound right in Greek.) The former would rightly claim that he is knowledgeable about the production of images. What analogous product can the sophist claim?

Hippocrates answers again: "He is knowledgeable about making someone clever at speaking" (312d6). This is exactly the answer we would expect. The sophists were famous for teaching rhetoric, the art of clever, effective, speaking. As Socrates later says, Hippocrates is a young man who "desires to become big in the city" (316b10); that is, he is politically ambitious. Clever speaking seems to him to be the key to gaining his goals. But Hippocrates' second answer, at least as formulated here, still does not satisfy Socrates. Again he uses the techne-analogy to explain why: The master player of the lyre can make his student clever in speaking about playing the lyre. With respect to what similar object does Protagoras make his claim? The problem with Hippocrates' second answer is the same suffered by the first: It is not sufficiently determinate.

Hippocrates is at a loss. He admits that he does not know how to identify what Protagoras teaches. Such an admission, however, is really a step forward for him. He now is aware that he does not understand what the Sophist actually teaches. Only when he is armed with such awareness, will Socrates take him to meet the Sophist.

When Socrates and Hippocrates actually confront Protagoras, Socrates asks the Sophist a similar set of questions. He begins broadly: "What will accrue to [Hippocrates] if he associates with you?" (318a3) Protagoras answers, "Young fellow, if you associate with me, on the very day you join me you will go home a better man; and on the successive days, there will be similar progress. On each day you will become progressively better" (318a6–9).

This answer is not satisfying. If Socrates' question had been directed at Zeuxippos, the famous painter, the answer would have been: Hippocrates will get better *with respect to painting*. So, too, if the question were asked of Orthagoras. His answer would have been *in fluting*. With respect to what, in what, about what, will Hippocrates improve if he studies with Protagoras? Two points should already be clear: Socrates is not receptive at all to Protagoras' boast and he is preparing to do battle against it. Second, the techne-analogy is an effective weapon with which he can challenge his opponent's claim. It forces his opponent to specify exactly what he claims to be knowledgeable about.

Protagoras responds: "My subject (*mathema*) is good counsel about domestic affairs, how one might best manage his own household; and about political affairs, how one might be most capable (*dunatotatos*) in both acting and speaking in the affairs of the city" (318e5–319a2).[35]

Socrates, in typical fashion, immediately reformulates this "advertisement."[36] He replaces Protagoras' word "*mathema*," a broad term indicating anything that can be learned, with the more specific "techne," and ignores the matter of domestic affairs. Protagoras' claim, as now interpreted by Socrates, is to teach the "political techne and to promise to make men good citizens." The Sophist enthusiastically agrees with this description.

Protagoras, at least according to Socrates, possesses a unique techne. Unlike all the others, its very subject is value. To use the word that later becomes prominent, Protagoras claims to teach political *arete* (319e2), or excellence. He teaches men how to excel in political affairs. This claim is both peculiar and instructive. A prominent feature of techne discussed above was its neutrality in matters of value: the doctor can use her knowledge for good or evil. Protagoras, by contrast, claims to have a techne by which he can make men good citizens. Furthermore, this claim should appear quite problematic given our description of Protagorean relativism. If that was accurate, what does the Sophist mean when he says he makes men "good" citizens? We shall see that these questions haunt the rest of this dialogue.

Socrates is not at all happy with Protagoras' claim, and he again uses the techne-analogy to attack it. In the Assembly, the basic forum of political debate for the Athenians, if a question is explicitly a technical one, an expert is consulted. If, for example, a ship is to be built for the polis, and a decision has to be made about the design of that ship, the master shipbuilder is called. To him the other members of the polis defer. If an ordinary citizen, a layman, were to challenge the shipbuilder, he would be laughed down. On technical questions it is altogether reasonable to defer to the expert. By contrast, if the issue is one laden with the question of value, if it is a matter of policy, then all citizens are equally capable of contributing to the debate. All citizens, for example, should debate whether a ship *should* be built with city funds. The two cases, Socrates concludes, are *disanalogous:* there do not seem to be technical experts whose subject is value. If this is true, then the subject Protagoras claims to have mastered and be able teach, the political techne, doesn't exist. In less polite terms, Socrates has just accused the Sophist of being a fraud.

Socrates' analogy clearly does not prove that there is no political techne; it only shows that the Athenians, who might be wrong, think there isn't. Socrates does not tell us why he believes the Athenians are right, but he does give a clue. He offers a second argument that political *arete* is not a suitable subject for a real techne. He observes that it is often the case that excellent fathers are unable, despite their best efforts, to make their sons equally excellent. Kids go bad (319e–320b). By contrast, a shipbuilder can, with a good deal of reliability, train his apprentice. As parents know, it is not even clear what sort of teaching is required for an education in that most peculiar of subjects, *arete*. It is just this lack of clarity, this peculiar matter of communicating successfully a knowledge of value, that leads Socrates to assert here that political life, whose essence is *arete*, is disanalogous with techne. (It should be noted, however, that this is not equivalent to saying that political life is irrational.)

Socrates has challenged the teachability of the Sophist's subject matter and thus his livelihood. In response, Protagoras tells a long story. In it, I suggest, we will get a good picture of what he teaches and of what he thinks a good life is. We will see further in what sense he offers an alternative to Aristotle's beautiful vision of logos and why someone like Nietzsche would find him so attractive.[37]

Protagoras' Story (320c8–323a4)

320c8   There was once a time when there were gods, but mortal creatures did not exist. And when the allotted time arrived for their generation, the gods formed them within the earth by mixing earth and fire and various blends of fire and earth.

When the gods were about to lead [mortal creatures] towards the light, they ordered Prometheus and Epimetheus to outfit them and to distribute to each of them powers as was fitting. Epimetheus asked Prometheus if he could do the distributing himself. "After I have distributed," he said, "you check it out." And because he persuaded him in this way, he did the distributing.

320d8   In his distributions, Epimetheus attached strength to those creatures without speed and he outfitted those who were rather weak with speed. He armed some, while to others who were without arms he gave another nature and devised another power for them which they could use to survive. To those he made small he distributed winged flight or an underground dwelling. And those he augmented with size, he saved by means of this size. He distributed and compensated the rest of the mortal creatures in this fashion. He devised these measures with caution so that no species would be annihilated.

321a3   After he provided for them ways of avoiding mutual destruction, he devised protection from the divine seasons. He clothed some with both thick hair and solid skin which was sufficient to ward off both the cold and the heat . . . Then he provided different types of nourishments for each; to some, vegetation from the earth, to others the fruit of trees, to others roots. Finally, he did allow some to serve as the food for others . . .

321b6   Because Epimetheus was not at all wise he was unaware that he had squandered the powers on the animals that don't have logos. The human race still needed to be outfitted by him and he was at a loss what to do. Prometheus came to him while he was at a loss and inspected his distribution. He saw that the other animals were suitably outfitted with all things, while the human race was naked and unshod and without beds or weapons. Furthermore, the destined day on which the human race had to go out from the earth into the light had arrived. So Prometheus, who was at a loss as to what form of survival he could provide for the human race, stole from Hephaestus and Athena technical wisdom together with fire; without fire technical wisdom could not possibly belong to anyone or be at all useful. Thus they were given to the human race.

321d4   In this fashion, humanity obtained the wisdom needed for survival. It did not, however, have political [wisdom], for that was in the hands of Zeus. And it was still not possible for Prometheus to enter Zeus' home on high; in addition, Zeus' guards were fearsome. But Prometheus secretly entered the common dwelling of Athena and Hephaestus, where they enjoyed doing their technical work, and stealing the fiery techne of Hephaistos and the other which belonged to Athena gave them to humanity. Because of this humanity gained resourcefulness in matters of survival. Later, it is said, Prometheus was punished for his theft because of Epimetheus.

322a3   When humanity had a share in the divine portion, alone among the animals it first of all, on account of its kinship with the divine, acknowledged the gods and undertook to construct altars and statues of the gods. Then, by means of techne, it quickly articulated voice and names and discovered dwellings and clothes and shoes and beds and nourishment from the earth.

322a8   At the outset, human beings, having been furnished in this manner, dwelt scattered all around: there were no cities. They were being wiped out by the wild animals since they were weaker than the animals in every way. Even though the productive techne was quite enough for them in terms of supplying food, it was still deficient in the fight against the animals. This is because human beings did not yet possess the political techne, which includes military skill. So they sought to gather together and save themselves by founding cities. However, when they did gather together, they did wrong to one another, because they didn't have the political techne; as a result they were scattered once again and faced destruction.

322c1   Zeus feared that our race would be entirely detroyed and so he sent Hermes to human beings to bring respect (*aidos*) and a sense of right (*dike*); the purpose of this was to engender orderliness and the bonds of friendship which would tie the cities together. Hermes asked Zeus in what manner he should give a sense of right and respect to human beings. "Should I distribute them in the same manner in which the technai were distributed? These were distributed as follows: One man who has the medical techne is quite sufficient for many laymen. And this is true for the rest of the technicians (*demiourgikoi*). Should I place a sense of right and respect among human beings in this fashion, or should I distribute them to everybody?"

322d1   "To everybody," said Zeus, "and let everybody have a share in them. For cities would not exist if only a few people should have a share in them, as is the case with the other technai. And make this a law which comes from me: he who is unable to have share in respect and a sense of right will die as a disease of the city."

322d5   So it is, Socrates, that both the Athenians and other people believe that when the logos is about the *arete* of carpentry or of some other craft, only a few should be allowed to deliberate. And, as you say, they don't allow someone who is not one of these few to enter the deliberations. This is quite reasonable, I might add. By contrast, whenever they meet for a consultation on political *arete*, which is to be resolved entirely through justice and moderation, it is reasonable to allow every man to enter. This is because it is appropriate for every man to a have share in this *arete* or there would be no city at all.

This story presents the fundamental elements of Protagoras' "worldview." (The fact that it does so in the form of a "myth" is significant and will be discussed below.)[38] With his story, Protagoras attempts to overcome Socrates' objection to his claim to teach the political techne. First of all, the story tries to explain the fact that only a few are able and allowed to give advice as to how, for example, to build a ship, while all citizens are invited to debate questions of political *arete* or value: *aidos* and *dike*, the constituents of political *arete*, were, unlike the technai, distributed to all by Hermes. By saying this, Protagoras seems to acknowledge Socrates' objection that political life and techne are, at least in this one sense, disanalogous.

Once Protagoras makes this admission, however, problems arise. If techne is that which is paradigmatically teachable, and political life is disanalogous with techne, how can the Sophist's claim to teach the political techne be sustained? It is clear that in order to survive as a professional teacher Protagoras must show that the disanalogy is not total. Later in the dialogue he presents a series of arguments that are designed to do just this. He cites, for example, the widespread use of punishment as evidence that *arete* is teachable. Men punish others in matters that they believe are a consequence of "practice and exercise and instruction" (326d6–7). By contrast, they do not punish someone for that which is beyond their control, say for being small. Since men do punish others for political wrongdoing, political *arete* is teachable.

Of course, such an argument doesn't prove that *arete* actually is teachable; it only shows that Athenian men (Protagoras' example) think it is. But the intention of his argument is clear: Protagoras wants to draw the analogy between political *arete* and techne. Carpentry and geometry are uncontroversially teachable. The "punishment argument" is meant to show that *arete* is similar.

In response to the Socratic objection that fathers do not always succeed in transmitting their excellence to their sons, Protagoras offers a similar argument. Fathers send their sons to school and seek to provide them with numerous instructors in virtue. In school the sons learn, from the poets for example, of good men. The city itself tries to teach the sons by means of the laws (325c–326d). Therefore, he concludes, *arete* must be teachable. Again, however, his argument only shows that fathers think *arete* is teachable. Again, his intention is clear: Protagoras wants to suggest that *arete* is analogous to techne.

But Protagoras must yet confront Socrates' objection: Why do fathers so often fail to instruct their sons in *arete*? Carpenters do not often fail to transmit their knowledge of carpentry? Or do they? At this point Protagoras again attempts to draw the analogy between what he teaches and techne. There is, he says, variety in natural aptitude. If we attempted to teach everyone fluting, some would excel, regardless of their fathers' abilities; others would do less well. Why? Some have musical natures (327b9). Analogously, some sons have natural aptitude for *arete* and others don't. All human beings have some capacity for, and thus can be taught some measure of, *arete*. However, since there is natural variegation of aptitude, some learn better than others and some can become teachers and help others improve. Protagoras counts himself as the best in doing just this (328b1–6).

Protagoras' view, as should now be clear, is slippery. What exactly does he teach? Is his subject, his *mathema*, analogous to techne or not? Sometimes he says yes (when he uses the punishment and natural aptitude argument); other times no (when he agrees with Socrates that the typical technai belong only to a few). I suggest that this vacillation is quite deliberate and that in his myth Protagoras systematically equivocates on the character of what he teaches. Protagoras' long story is a deliberate, and brilliant, attempt to disguise his subject. He wants to give it the appearance of being a techne, without having to accept the consequences that follow from such a claim. What he is doing is fully self-conscious. In an important sense, it is also coherent. As such, it constitutes a serious response to Socrates, who in this case is a representative of logos itself. To clarify what I mean, let's examine the myth more closely with an eye to exactly how Protagoras uses "techne."

Techne first appears in the myth in the phrase "technical wisdom" at 321d1. Epimetheus was in charge of distributing the "powers" to the animals. The species were given various attributes to allow them to survive. But Epimetheus neglected the human race. Unlike the birds, who were given wings, and the wolves, who were given thick skins, humans had no means to protect and save themselves. They were naked, unshod, bedless, weaponless (321c5). Prometheus, attempting to correct his thoughtless brother's error, intervened on behalf of humanity. He stole technical wisdom (*entechnon sophian*), along with fire, from Athena and Hephaestus. This provided humans with the wisdom needed for the maintenance of life (321d4).

"Technical wisdom" here means the very general intellectual ability to maintain life. It is the skill that would lead to building tools, houses, agriculture, etc. It is, to reformulate twice, "the fiery techne" (321e2–3), the ability to use fire to build tools, or "the productive techne" (322b3).

Human beings, on this account, seem to be by nature technical. But what does this mean? Is techne at this stage of the story analogous to, say, geometry or painting? No. Techne, in all three of the formulations cited above, refers to a very general and indeterminate ability to make things. When such an ability is systematized, when the fiery techne is made determinate by devising standards, procedures, and specific subject matter, then a "typical" techne would arise. Techne at this stage, then, is really "proto-techne," that natural ability to make things that is prior to the systematic acquisition and transmission of knowledge.

Proto-techne grants humanity a "portion of divinity" (322a3); it makes us like gods, specifically the craft-loving gods Athena and Hephaistus. It is that by which we construct religious altars and statues, that is, organized religion. It is that by which we devise language ("speech and words"), houses, clothing, shoes, beds, and food (322a3–8). It is the basis of all cultural phenomena. The key point is that for Protagoras, man is man the maker. Language, religion, the polis (322b6): none of these is "natural" in the sense of formally preexisting out there in the world before human activity. They are all made by human beings, and for one reason only; for survival, the only guiding principle of the Protagorean developmental story. As such, religion, language, and political community are analogous to the bird's wings and the wolf's thick skin: they are attributes of the human species that are best comprehended by their contribution to survival.

As noted above, "cities" (*poleis*) are produced by proto-techne for the purpose of survival (322b6). "*Poleis*" here refers to primitive communities in which humans gather to protect themselves from stronger animals. But these *poleis* do not function well. The war against the animals is being lost because humans "do each other wrong" on account of not having the political techne (322b4–8). Human survival is threatened. This time Zeus intervenes. He sends Hermes to humanity with "respect and a sense of right" (*aidos* and *dike*), in order that the bonds of communal solidarity can be forged.

Hermes asks whether these two gifts are to be distributed in the same way as were the technai (322c5). Zeus answers no. The technai were distributed only to a few who then administer to the needs of the many. One doctor, for example, treats many laymen. But *aidos* and *dike*, the primitive constituents of political life, are distributed to all.

As mentioned above, this part of the story implies that Protagoras agrees with Socrates that, in this regard at least, political life is disanalogous with techne. But the disanalogy cannot be total; if it were, Protagoras would put himself out of business. Therefore, at certain crucial points, the Sophist affirms the analogy in order to give his *mathema* the veneer of epistemological credibility. Consider, for example, the use of the phrase "political techne" at 322b5 and 322b8. Both contexts are negative: primitive humanity did not have it. This is why primitive communities failed. Later in the story communities succeed. The listener is thus invited to infer that humanity gained the political techne. In fact, however, Protagoras never quite says this. Instead, he says that *aidos* and *dike* were distributed to all. Once again the listener is invited to infer: *Aidos* and *dike* are political techne. Soon the phrase "political *arete*" replaces *aidos* and *dike* (322e2–3). Then, "*arete*" alone comes to the fore (323a3). The listener is thus led to believe that *arete* is synonymous with political techne, and indeed scholars regularly make this claim.[39] *But Protagoras himself doesn't.* And for good reason. Techne, in the strict sense that Socrates has suggested and Protagoras has agreed to, is knowledge of a determinate object. And Protagoras, for reasons to become apparent below, doesn't want to make such a determinate knowledge claim. On the other hand, he must maintain that his *mathema* is teachable and so he invites his listener to infer that political techne is present in his developmental account as a fact of human life.

All human beings, says Protagoras, must participate in the political *arete*, in justice and moderation (323a1–2).[40] To reiterate, this implies that techne and political life are disanalogous, since the typical technai are available only to a few. There is another point of disanalogy. "In the other technai, just as you describe, if someone says he is a good flutist, or good with respect to any other techne that he isn't good at, they either laugh at him or get angry" (323a7–b1). In other words, in the typical technai it is prudent to admit one's ignorance. If someone cannot play the flute, he is mad to say that he can. Why? He will be quickly exposed as a fraud when a flute is put into his hands. Since techne is knowledge of a determinate subject matter; it is easy to establish clear criteria to determine whether someone possesses a techne or not. By contrast, "in justice and the rest of political *arete*," if someone is unjust it is madness not to dissemble and pretend to be just. A person can afford to feign justice: there is no determinate test to disqualify the claim. Therefore, no one should publicly admit to being unjust.

Now we can see why Protagoras doesn't want the analogy between his *mathema* and techne to be strict. It would be mad for him to claim to play the flute: Socrates would put the flute into his hand and ask him to play. Analogously, if Protagoras were to claim a political techne with a determinate subject matter, Socrates would ask him to identify and explicate that subject. He would put the political analogue of the flute into Protagoras' hands in order to refute the Sophist's claim.

The techne-analogy, as suggested above, is a most effective tool with which Socrates can refute his opponent's knowledge claim. Protagoras, however, is far too intelligent to allow Socrates to pin him down in this fashion. Therefore, he systematically equivocates on the analogy between his *mathema* and techne. There is good evidence that he succeeds in fending off the Socratic offensive: Socrates soon drops the analogy and changes his tactics after Protagoras' story.[41]

To summarize: To the extent that Protagoras claims that what he has to offer is in fact teachable, he draws the analogy between his *mathema* and techne. He did this with the arguments based on punishment and the fact that fathers try to educate their sons, and the natural-aptitude argument. By making proto-techne pivotal in his developmental story, and by suggesting that the political techne makes political life possible, he implicitly invites the reader to draw the analogy. But Protagoras is far too clever to push the analogy too far. He realizes that his subject is not determinate in the sense that would please Socrates; he does not want Socrates to put the political analogue of the flute into his hands. He therefore denies the analogy. He explicitly contrasts his political teaching with the technai: the latter belong to a few experts, while his subject potentially belongs to all. He disanalogizes further by saying that in the other technai it is prudent to admit one's ignorance, while in political matters it is prudent to lie.

What are we to make of Protagoras' vacillation here? Are his views confused? Hardly. Protagoras, I propose, has quite deliberately made his conception of techne slippery. He has artfully toyed with the criteria implied by Socrates' use of the techne-analogy. Sometimes he has aligned himself to them and so appears to claim a techne; at other times, he seems to steer away from claiming a techne for himself. As a result, he succeeds in presenting himself as having something to teach while not being forced to render his subject matter determinate. He thus preserves his clientele and saves himself from Socratic refutation.[42]

If this interpretation is plausible, then is it possible to specify what Protagoras teaches? Yes: *arete*. But what is this? It is not an epistemological entity analogous to the objects of geometry or arithmetic, the paradigmatically determinate technai. So what is it?

I suggest we can answer this by reconsidering briefly the impact and strategy of Protagoras' speech. He has hedged, but to his greatest advantage. Given his claim that *aidos* and *dike* are distributed to all, he has transformed every one of his listeners (including Hippocrates) into potential customers: they all have a potential for *arete*. By means of the natural-aptitude argument, he has allowed for the possibility of an "elite," like himself, who can teach *arete*. At the same time, he has sufficiently distanced his *mathema* from techne and so avoided Socratic refutation.

What does this tell us? Protagoras has just *exhibited the very subject that he teaches*: rhetoric. He teaches his students how to become "most capable in political affairs." He himself, with his long story, seeks victory in the competition he is waging with Socrates for the soul of Hippocrates. This, and not the truth, is the goal of his discussion.

What makes Protagoras' story so interesting is that it not only exhibits his talent for rhetoric, but it also provides a background, a picture of the world, in which rhetoric would dominate. The Sophist's story provides the reasons, even gives a kind of justification, for why he so gracefully vacillates. Consider the following: Protagoras is a materialist. Mortal creatures were composed of earth and fire (320d). He does not mention a soul or any nonmaterial dimension of human life.[43] Furthermore, he puts human beings on the same level as all other animals: all were created in the same manner, all are guided by the same principle, namely survival.

Indeed, survival is the *only telos* allowed for in his story. It is, apparently, the highest good available to humanity. Needless to say, this sharply differs from Aristotle's view on the telos of the polis.

From such a starting point there emerges only one political value that is operative in a polis: social harmony. The citizens must cooperate in order that the polis become a strong enough community to sustain life. The problem with primitive communities was that humans harmed and thus weakened themselves. *Arete* is the ability to get along with others so that the polis is strong enough to win the battle for survival. But, given Protagoras' basic ideas here, does it really matter what type of community one belongs to? No. A communist regime may be harmonious as well as a democracy. As one commentator puts it, "This position is clearly unsatisfactory, as it leaves Protagoras no ground for moral criticism of the institutions of any state, no matter how cruel, unjust, etc., provided only that that state retains enough social cohesion to ensure its continued survival."[44]

It should be mentioned, however, that this position is unsatisfactory only if there are nonconventional standards that can serve to measure the various states. In other words, it is unsatisfactory only if relativism is false. And this, as yet, is still a matter of debate.

To continue with Protagoras' story: It should be noted that Epimetheus had to *persuade* Prometheus to allow him to distribute the powers (320d6–7). This implies that the two initially disagreed as to who should receive this honor. This first episode of Protagoras' myth sets the stage or tone for what is to follow. Prometheus and Epimetheus disagree; they then wage a battle of words in order to determine who is to distribute the powers; Epimetheus wins, and his victory determines the development of the story. By positioning it in the first episode, rhetoric is thus portrayed as primordial, as the preeminent and paradigmatic form of speech. It is the key to winning the struggle for power that is the essence of human life.

A similar point is also implied by Protagoras' description of language at 322a6: "Words and names" are the product of proto-techne. Man is man the maker and language is something constructed for the purpose of winning the battle for survival. Contrast this with the Aristotelian description of language cited above. There language was said to be for the purpose of uncovering the truth about natural beings existing in the world.

Protagoras' "worldview" starts to emerge. In an important sense it is similar to that offered by Callicles. Humans are material beings making what they need and fighting to enhance their prospects for survival. All cultural phenomena and institutions are products of proto-techne and contribute to this end. Therefore, no cultural phenomenon has any intrinsic value other than its ability to enhance the human prospect for survival. Since survival can be achieved in an indefinite number of ways, cultural phenomena can, for Protagoras, be legitimately manipulated, as long as such manipulation does not interfere with social harmony. For examples, consider language and religion. Neither has an inherent relationship to anything outside of the human community that uses them. Thus, there are no external restraints to govern their use. There is nothing, therefore, to prevent them from being manipulated. Why shouldn't a powerful and ambitious man like Callicles use language to distort the truth of a situation if he thinks it will benefit him? For Aristotle, whose conception of language implies that there is a world "out there" to provide an unyielding standard with which to measure any speech, Callicles falls short and is repugnant. By contrast, there is no basis given within Protagoras' worldview to criticize him.

A similar situation obtains for the Protagorean view of religion. For the Sophist there is no possibility of blasphemy. Human beings share, we are told, in a portion of divinity. But this means that they are like Athena and Hephaestus, the two gods who make things. Human beings make their own world. They even make their own religion; they "construct altars and statues." As such, there is nothing to prevent them from manipulating religion for their own benefits, from using it, for example, to give credibility to any public endeavor. In fact, Protagoras does exactly this at the end of his story. He encourages his students to go to a temple to declare what they believe Protagoras' instruction is worth (328a1). In other words, he uses religion to imbue his own profession with respectability.[45]

The view put forth by Protagoras is in fundamental opposition to logos. Logos, according to Protagoras, is a false and stultifying barrier to flourishing. In his view human beings are power seekers, political men seeking to enhance themselves. They are not driven toward a purpose except that of operating skillfully in the political realm. Logos, then, is a fraud according to the sophistic credo. Protagoras does not explicitly say this. But his deliberate manipulation, his artful deceit, his contempt for the Socratic question, imply it.

For Protagoras the only constraint on human behavior is that it not interfere with social harmony, the essential condition for human survival. But given that one stricture, if it can even be called that, the door is open to anything. As such, Protagoras' is an unstable world where human achievement depends on the struggle for power. And power is best

achieved through language, through rhetoric. If Protagoras himself vacillates on the question of techne, he does so deliberately in order to combat
Socrates: he does not want Socrates, the incarnation of logos, to pin him
down to a specific conception of *arete*. This is because he does not think
arete can or should be pinned down. It is not a matter of logos. Instead,
arete floats, it shifts with the changing currents of popular opinion. In a
similar fashion, his own story shifts ground continually. Its form mirrors
its content. If the world is in flux, so, too, is his story. Indeed, this is
exactly what Protagoras teaches: how to mold one's speeches to fit the
appropriate occasion; how to respond to the indeterminate set of circumstances that continually, and unpredictably, arise; how, in other words,
to win the battle for survival that occurs in human political life.

The world of human significance—of values, purposes, and meaning—
which for Aristotle can and should become an object of rational inspec-
tion, is for Protagoras a battlefield.

(2)   Descartes' Provisional Morality

Logos began by asserting its unconditional goodness. It was convinced
that it, and it alone, could heal, could make us whole and well. But logos
discovered that it had enemies. Since it is in its very nature to welcome
challenges to itself, logos entered into battle to defend its claim. And so
logos, in the person of Socrates, went to visit and interrogate Protagoras.
The Sophist responded to the Socratic challenge with an attack of his
own. He showed himself to be a relativist who teaches and practices
rhetoric. By offering his own "worldview," one that features man the
maker in a battle for survival, he conspires to usurp the throne logos had
occupied. Logos will soon angrily respond; this is certain.

Before proceeding to that, however, the challenge to logos, which has
come from a fellow Greek, needs reformulation. A continual aim of this
book is to demonstrate how modern ideas often mirror ancient ones. I
have already tried to indicate how Nietzsche, and by extension Derrida
and Rorty (each of whom attacks logos), actually reformulate basic themes
of Greek sophistry. Next I hope to show that the challenge to logos is not
isolated to this subversive fringe of contemporary thought. Instead, it is
intrinsic to the very basis of modernity.[46]

We turn now to Descartes, the great French philosopher and mathematician of the seventeenth century. He is one of the principal architects and
prophets of the modern scientific worldview. As such, he is a mainstream
modern thinker and hardly a "deconstructionist." Nevertheless, we will

find that, despite the fact that in one sense Descartes is a "hyper-rational-ist," he too attacks logos with a passion. Furthermore, the consequences of his attack are surprisingly similar to some of the basic ideas latent in Protagoras' great story.

In 1637 Descartes wrote *Discourse on Method*. It is in part an intellectual autobiography. This does not mean that the book faithfully reports all the many details of Descartes' life. Instead, in the form of a fable, Descartes describes certain pivotal moments that helped to formulate his basic stance toward the world.[47] He starts with his early education.

> I have been raised on letters from my childhood, and because I was con-vinced that through them one might acquire a clear and steady knowledge of everything that is useful for life, I possessed a tremendous desire to learn them. But, as soon as I completed this entire course of study, at the end of which one is ordinarily received into the ranks of the learned, I changed my mind entirely. For I was embarrassed by so many doubts and errors, which appeared in no way to profit me in my attempt at learning, except that more and more I discovered my ignorance (p. 4).

Descartes was raised in the best schools of Renaissance France. He eventually rejected his traditional or "scholastic" education, which here he calls "letters." In our terms, we might say he had a training in the classical liberal arts. His curriculum was based to a large extent on the writings of Aristotle as they had been assimilated and systematized throughout the medieval period. For the purposes of this chapter, it is enough to say that Descartes rejected Aristotle, or classical logos, when he "changed his mind entirely" about the value of his education.

Before we proceed to the reasons for Descartes' conversion, note well the words he uses to describe the original expectations he had brought to his education. He hopes to gain a "clear and steady knowledge of everything that is useful for life." It is not surprising to find that Descartes desires clarity, since this is something most of us strive for in our quest for knowledge. (Although it should be remembered that Aristotle, in his discussion of the degree of precision to be expected in various studies, believes that clarity is not equally forthcoming in every subject.) But what does Descartes mean by "steady" (*assurée*)? Presumably, that which is reliable, secure, without variance. Finally, Descartes also wants knowl-edge to be useful for life. But useful for what aspect of life? We will have to read further. At this point, only observe that in no way does Descartes argue that these three criteria—clarity, steadiness, and usefulness—are appropriate in the search for knowledge. He simply asserts and is guided by them from the outset.

Descartes is quite specific about his verdict on the subjects he studied at school:

> I realized that the languages one learns there [in school] are necessary for the understanding of classical texts; that the gracefulness of the fables awakens the mind and read with discretion they aid in forming one's judgment; that reading good books is like a conversation with the noblest people of past centuries—their authors—indeed, a studied conversation in which one discovers only the best of their thoughts; that eloquence has incomparable power and beauty; that poetry has a ravishing delicacy and sweetness; that mathematics contains very subtle inventions that can serve as much to satisfy the curious as to facilitate the arts and to diminish men's labor; that writings dealing with morals contain many lessons and exhortations to virtue that are quite useful; that theology teaches how to go to heaven; that philosophy provides the means of speaking with probability about all things and of being held in admiration by the less learned (pp. 5–6).

Each of the items on this list is briefly commented upon, and the comments seem positive. In fact, however, as the book unfolds it becomes clear that Descartes is being ironic here. For example, it sounds as if studying languages, the first subject mentioned, is a good idea: after all, they are necessary for "understanding classical texts." But what if, on the basis of the *Discourse* as a whole, it can be shown that Descartes rejects the value of classical texts? This would imply that the praise of languages he offers here is deceptive; it is a screen behind which he hides his true contempt for a subject that in his day was widely accepted as an essential feature of a good education. Or take the third item, reading good books. This is said to be like a "conversation" with the best minds of the past. But what if Descartes later formulates a method that is antithetical to conversation? Again, the apparent praise of the passage above would be undercut. I suggest that precisely this undercutting occurs in several of the items on the list.[48]

Descrates barely hides his contempt for "philosophy," by which he means that type of logos practiced by Aristotle. Philosophy teaches men how "to speak with probability (*vraisemblablement*) about all things." We will soon see that probability is a highly pejorative term for Descartes since, in his final analysis, it should be treated as equivalent to error. Thus, without sounding too harsh about a venerated master, with this single comment Descartes has heaped the worst blame possible upon Aristotle.

The only subject that meets with unaffected enthusiasm on the list is mathematics. Mathematics has two features to commend it, one theoretical and the other practical. It "satisfies the curious." When a solution is achieved to a mathematical problem, it is unambiguous. Mathematics broaches no doubt. Its answers are clear and steady and as such it is theoretically satisfying. Furthermore, many of these solutions can be applied. This is what Descartes refers to when he speaks of "the arts" (in Greek, "technai") which "diminish men's labor." He is thinking of "the mechanical arts" or what today we might call engineering. To a large extent such arts require the application of mathematical principles in activities designed to achieve some goal that is determined to be useful. In the introduction we have already noted the connection between mathematics and techne, and it is precisely this link that inspired Descartes in school. As he makes quite explicit later in the text, it was mathematics that would guide him throughout his career:

> I took especially great pleasure in mathematics because of the certainty and evidence of its arguments. But I did not notice its true usefulness and, thinking that it seemed useful only to the mechanical arts, I was astonished that, because its foundations were so solid and firm, no one had built anything more noble upon them. On the other hand, I compared the writings of the ancient pagans who discuss morals to very proud and magnificent palaces that are built on nothing but sand and mud. They place virtues on a high plateau and make them appear to be valued more than anything else in the world, but they do not sufficiently instruct us about how to know them (pp. 7–8).

Descartes here explicitly contrasts the certainty and firmness of mathematics with the "writings of the ancient pagans who discuss morals." The latter phrase comes close to referring to logos itself.[49] To highlight this contrast Descartes invokes a metaphor soon to become prominent in his book: architecture. Mathematics is founded on principles that are clear and distinct. Because of this "steadiness" it offers a firm foundation upon which an "epistemological edifice" grounded on mathematical certainty can be constructed. By contrast, the ancients built palaces on sand. They elevated the virtues to the highest degree, but never explained exactly (precisely, clearly) what they were and how they could be known. The ancient version of logos, in other words, was groundless, based on nothing firm. It did not know itself; it thought itself a magnificent palace, whereas in fact it was nothing but sand and mud. This is the heart of Descartes' prophetic tirade against logos.

Descartes despises logos and wishes to transform it radically. We have seen that Aristotle insists that logos can articulate the right and the wrong. We have seen the protreptic logos culminate in praise of the goodness of itself. Or, to use Descartes' phrase from above, the protreptic logos "contain[s] many lessons and exhortations to virtue that are quite useful." But useful for what? Certainly not for what Descartes has in mind. We have also seen Aristotle admit that his logos of values cannot attain the same level of precision as mathematics. The nature of the subject matter does not allow for it. This is what Descartes hates. This is why, when we strip away his polite language, he is really thundering against logos here: "You speak with such confidence about what is good, what is naturally the best; and yet you produce nothing clear and certain. You know nothing about yourself, not even where you dwell, and yet you dare to speak for us all."

To use Descartes' own, more measured, words, "I shall say only that, aware that philosophy has been cultivated over several centuries by the most excellent minds . . . there is nothing about which there is not some dispute—and thus nothing that is not doubtful" (p. 8).

To reiterate an earlier point, the three original criteria proposed for knowledge—clarity, steadiness, and usefulness—were taken by Descartes to be self-evident. They predisposed him to reject Aristotle. In the citation above we see him invoking a further criterion, certainty, which itself is a refinement of the notions of clarity and firmness. Armed with these weapons he bombards logos which, it is quite true, does not achieve mathematical certainty. Logos makes visible objects in the world. Because these objects vary in kind it does not consistently attain the highest level of precision. As Aristotle says about the results achieved in his *Nicomachean Ethics*, the treatise whose object of study is the political or social dimension of human being, "It will be satisfactory in this particular kind of study to show the truth roughly and in outline and, since we are speaking from and about something that only usually holds good, to make our conclusions in a similar manner."

In Descartes' view to admit the probability of one's results is equivalent to admitting failure. Probability, however, is only a defect if it can be argued, and not simply asserted, that certainty and the highest degree of precision are both possible and desirable in all subjects. But such an argument is not provided in the *Discourse*. Instead, Descartes states, "I took to be virtually false everything that was merely probable" (p. 8). As a result, he rejected logos.

Let me digress a moment to situate Descartes' complaint a bit more precisely within the context of classical thought. In Plato's dialogue, the *Phaedo*, Socrates addresses (among other things) a traditional philosophical subject, the immortality of the soul. Exactly as Descartes describes it, there is dispute, doubt, and a lack of certainty in this conversation that Socrates has with his friends. At one point, when the dialogue has hit a particularly difficult turn and the conversants are confused, Socrates digresses to discuss what he terms "misology," which means "hatred of logos." He offers an analogy between misology and misanthropy, which he says come about in the same way. The latter arises when someone who is excessively and unreasonably trusting in other human beings is continually disappointed in his relationships with others. After enough disappointments such a man finally ends up trusting no one and hating everyone. Analogously, when someone has an excessive faith in the capacity of logos to articulate the truth and is then sorely disappointed when logos repeatedly seems false to him, he runs the risk of becoming a misologist, one who believes that no logos can ever be truthful or secure. According to Socrates, for whom logos is our best hope for happiness, there is no greater evil.

To guard against misanthropy, Socrates continues, we require knowledge of human beings and must accept the fact that most are neither extremely good nor bad but somewhere in-between. A proper orientation toward human possibility will protect us from excessive disappointment and misanthropy. Similarly, knowledge of logos will protect us from the danger of misology. Socrates does not elaborate on the nature of this knowledge. I suggest, however, that Aristotle's teaching on the level of precision in various subject can be useful here. To remain "philologists," friends of logos, we must understand that given the nature of the different objects we study, the same level of precision is not to be expected in all subjects. If, for example, mathematical certainty is used as the standard to measure ethics then the logos of human values will indeed seem false and misology, at least with regard to this particular sphere, will ensue.

Descartes wants all subjects to achieve the same kind of certainty attained by mathematics. He is the prime example of one whose expectations of logos are enormous and, therefore, from a classical perspective, his understanding of the nature of logos is flawed. Since Descartes concludes that those "ancient pagans who discussed morals" failed to meet his standard, he abandons their enterprise altogether; he becomes a misologist. This does not imply that he abandons the quest for knowledge; it means that he relinquishes the desire of attaining knowledge in those areas where logos had once held sway, namely the realm of human significance and value. He comes to hate the "magnificent palaces" built only on sand, the claims of logos to articulate what is good and bad.[50]

To return to the *Discourse*: As a result of his unhappiness with the traditional curriculum, Descartes "dropped out."

> That is why, as soon as age permitted me to escape the tutelage of my teachers, I left the study of letters completely. And resolving to search for no more knowledge than what I could find within myself, or rather in the great book of the world, I spent the rest of my youth traveling . . . (p. 9).

As have young people of all generations, Descartes sought knowledge in his travels throughout Europe. But this experience was also disappointing.

> It is true that, while I spent time merely observing the customs of other men, I found hardly anything about which to be confident and that I noticed there was about as much diversity as I had earlier found among the opinions of the philosophers (p. 10).

The comparison Descartes makes here is extraordinary. He likens the diversity and conflict found in philosophical debate to that which he encountered in the world through which he traveled. The human world is rich, continually at odds with itself, surprising. People disagree and parade their differences in both speech and violence. There is no reprieve from the continual and contentious flow of life. Traditional philosophical dialogue, as Descartes says, is similar. Attempts to discuss the old questions about the value and meaning of life usually end in disagreement or lead to further questions. Such conversations are unpredictable; digressions are necessary, new issues emerge, objections are shouted. At best probable and tentative conclusions are reached. This was the basis for Descartes' disenchantment with logos. The living world through which Descartes traveled failed to satisfy him for precisely the same reasons. Philosophy, logos in the classical sense, mirrors life. To the exigencies of both life and philosophy he prefers the steadiness of mathematics.

Descartes was in Germany when his next great moment occurred.

> The onset of winter held me up in quarters where, finding no conversation with which to be diverted and, fortunately, otherwise having no needs or passions which troubled me, I remained for a whole day by myself in a stove-heated room, where I had complete leisure for communing with my thoughts. Among them, one of the first that I thought of considering was that often there is less perfection in works made of many pieces and in works made by the hands of several masters than in those works on which but one master has worked. Thus one sees that buildings undertaken and completed by a single architect are commonly more beautiful and better ordered than those that several architects have tried to patch up, using old walls that had been built for other purposes (p. 11).

Descartes reports that alone in his stove-heated room he devised a method with which to order his intelligence and construct his scientific edifice. What is perhaps more important than the details of his method itself is the way Descartes describes discovering it. He did it alone. He, quite happily, was free from all conversation. Remember what was said concerning a passage from Aristotle's *Politics*: Logos is natural and best for human beings. We are "meant" to talk with one another about what is right and wrong. Indeed, this is the soul of a political community. Such talk will never lead to absolute certainty and so will not dissolve all the questions and doubts we have about what constitutes a good and meaningful life. But such talk, the very activity itself, tells us who we are and can thus make us happy. Descartes rejects this view. Only when he is removed from the world, free from conversation, can he commune with his own thoughts.

The architectural metaphor is prominent here. A typical city is a motley patchwork of styles and buildings constructed over the years by many architects. Descartes envisions something better: a single architect designing a totally unified city. Such a design would be more like a mathematical proof than a rollicking conversation.[51]

The details of Descartes' actual method, as presented in the *Discourse*, are sketchy.[52] He states four of its "rules."

> The first was never to accept anything as true that I did not know evidently to be so; that is, carefully avoid precipitous judgment and prejudice; and to include nothing more in my judgments than what presented itself to my mind with such clarity and distinctness that I would have no occasion to put it in doubt.

> The second, to divide each of the difficulties I was examining into as many parts as possible and as is required to solve them best.

> The third, to conduct my thoughts in an orderly fashion, commencing with the simplest and easiest to know objects, to rise gradually, as by degrees, to the knowledge of the most composite things . . .

> And last, everywhere to make enumerations so complete and reviews so general that I would be sure of having omitted nothing (pp. 18–19).

The last three rules represent procedures similar to those used in any mathematical or axiomatic system. From a simple beginning more complex propositions are generated. Each step must be carefully stated so that checks can be made and error avoided. What is really of most interest is the first rule. The beginning must be beyond doubt; it must be totally certain. Only when that is achieved can the generation of propositions properly commence. This is why he says, "I thought that I ought, above all, to try to establish something certain" (p. 22). If Descartes can construct a firm foundation, then he can build the edifice of modern science which, unlike the palaces of the ancients, will endure.

The search for a certain beginning takes us to the famous dictum "I think, therefore I am" (p. 32). This self-affirmation of the mind's existence is utterly certain because, unlike all other statements, even in the very act of doubting it the statement itself is affirmed. Doubting itself is a kind of thinking; therefore, that "I think" cannot be doubted. Unlike thousands of introductory philosophy students, however, let us not concentrate on analyzing the validity of this famous argument. Instead, let us focus on the context in which it is presented; and that is the quest for utter certainty.

Descartes' systematic search for a first indubitable principle is guided by his admonition, "reject as absolutely false everything in which I could imagine the least doubt" (p. 31). But what does he sacrifice in order to achieve his goal or even just to commence his quest? To characterize that which is the least bit dubious as absolutely false is to declare war on logos. Logos is the commitment to articulating the real world, not only of material bodies in motion or of mathematical relationships, but of values, of purposes, of living ends. When it deals with these questions, which I have labeled the world of human significance, it does not attain certainty. Therefore, it is precisely these questions that must be sacrificed by Cartesian methodology.

It should be remembered that Descartes himself makes a comparison between traditional philosophy, the very act of asking questions about the realm of human significance, and his travels through Europe. The "real world" he visited is like philosophy in its ambiguities and disagreements. Therefore, not only does Descartes declare war on logos in order to achieve his scientific objectives, he declares war on human life. He severs life from his revolutionary conception of reason. He negates the hope of ever attaining knowledge, "real" knowledge in his prophetic sense, about the realm of human significance. This is made apparent, not only by his solitary happiness in a stove-heated room, but also in what he calls his "provisional morality."

> Now just as it is not enough, before beginning to rebuild the house where one lives, to pull it down, to make provisions for materials and architects, or to take a try at architecture for oneself . . . one must provide for something else in addition, namely where one can be conveniently sheltered while working on the other building; so too, in order not to remain irresolute in my actions while reason requires me to be so in my judgments, and in order not to cease living during that time as happily as possible, I formulated a provisional code of morals, which consisted of but three or four maxims (p. 22).

When it comes to knowledge Descartes is guided by the principle, if X is doubtful or probable, then X should be counted as false. If this principle were applied to actions taken in the world or to value judgments made about those actions, Descartes would become "irresolute"; his beliefs and opinions about these matters are at least partially dubious. There is, presumably, something about this "subject" of actions and values (the realm of human significance) that does not lend itself to certain resolution. Such irresolution, however, would not be convenient for the work that Descartes takes most seriously, namely the pursuit of certain knowledge. Therefore, some provisional form of morality must be devised to manage the unruly, and unwanted, vagaries of life.

The key point is this: The manner in which Descartes treats the human realm of action and value is exactly opposite to the manner in which he enters into his quest for knowledge. In the latter, if X is probable, X is rejected. In the former, probability is all there is. And what are Descartes' rules for action? Only the first two need concern us.

> The first was to obey the laws and the customs of my country, firmly holding on to the religion in which, by God's grace, I was instructed from childhood, and governing myself in all other things according to the most moderate opinions and those furthest from excess that were commonly accepted in practice by the most sensible of those people with whom I had to live . . .

> My second maxim was to be as firm and resolute in my actions as I could be, and to follow with no less constancy the most doubtful opinions, once I have decided on them, than if they were quite certain . . . (p. 25)

The provisional code is really quite simple: when in Iowa do as the most sensible Iowans do. When in New York, where the behavior is quite different, shift accordingly. Of course, this raises the question, how do we figure out who "the most sensible" really are? For Descartes, the answer seems to be by observing what most people are doing and what types of behavior are frowned upon. On the basis of such observations it is possible to imitate the accepted practices of the community.

The second maxim teaches us to adhere to a decision once it is made even if it is not certainly known that the decision is correct. If, for example, one observes that Iowans seem not to approve of overt displays of hostility and then tentatively concludes that he himself should avoid such displays, he should adhere firmly to this conclusion even though it is only probably correct; it is too inconvenient to vacillate. What is needed is a way of getting by in the affairs of life, not a way of discovering what is best to do.

To reiterate, what is most striking here is that the procedure for treating values is the exact antithesis of that used to attain knowledge. When it comes to values, we have to lie, to act as if there is certainty when there is not. Values, life, ordinary language, the entire realm of human significance, is drained of the hope for knowledge. They are relegated to the junkpile of the irrational.

We reach now the great affinity between Descartes and Protagoras, between the modern scientific view and ancient sophistry. Both drain from the world of human significance all hope of becoming a matter of knowledge. Both decertify logos, rob it of its authority, render it mute on the old questions (Is my life any good? What am I missing? What should I do?). Descartes fills the void created by the absence of logos with his provisional morality. Protagoras fills it with rhetoric. For the Sophist, life is a power struggle and rhetoric is therefore the privileged form of human speech. His great story describes human beings as strictly material creatures for whom survival and communal security are the highest goals. He does battle against Socrates who represents the urge to attain knowledge about what is a truly good human life.

Unlike Protagoras, Descartes is a hyper-rationalist. He wants to achieve mathematical certainty in his scientific work and understand the material world fully. But this work is severed from his life as a human being in the polis. The world of breathing humanity is abandoned by Descartes and left to fend for itself. His own stance is to adopt the provisional code. This means that finally he, too, adopts a form of relativism: when in Iowa do as the Iowans do.

The modern scientific worldview, with all its hope for clarity and precision, has a "flipside," a complementary set of views which it generates as its train. And this is its misology, sophistry, its abandonment of rationality in the world of human significance. There is thus a quite literal type of schizophrenia in the world bequeathed to us by the Cartesians. It is, on the one hand, hyper-rational; it seeks to extend the purview of mathematical physics throughout the universe. On the other hand, it relegates the world in which the physicist himself dwells, the unique world of humanity and its communities, to the junkpile of the irrational. We who know so much are prohibited from knowing ourselves.[53]

There are (at least) two possible objections to my reading of Descartes. First, the provisional code is, after all, *provisional*. It might seem, then, that once Descartes discovers his first principles he can add ethics to his scientific edifice. To shift metaphors, once the roots of knowledge are firmly in place, then a fruitful tree can arise, one of whose branches is "morals." I will not directly address this objection because its treatment would require too great an analysis of Descartes' other works (especially *The Passions of the Soul* and its discussion of "generosity"). I must therefore simply assert that I agree with those scholars who believe that "Descartes' definitive morality is the same as his provisional morality, which is to say that morality remains incomplete."[54]

The second objection to my account is this: Descartes does not sever reason from human life. He can reconnect the two; after all, one of the three criteria animating his quest for knowledge is usefulness.

> [T]hese general notions show me that it is possible to arrive at knowledge that is very useful in life and that in place of the speculative philosophy taught in the Schools, one could find a practical one, by which, knowing the force and the actions of fire, water, air, stars, the heavens . . . just as we understand the various skills of our craftsmen, we could, in the same way, use these objects for all the purposes for which they are appropriate, and thus make ourselves, as it were, *masters and possessors of nature* (pp. 61–62).

The knowledge, certain and precise, that Descartes hopes to achieve and then apply is mathematical physics. He is explicit here: Such application is like "the various skills of our craftsmen"; it is techne in its ubiquitous modern guise, namely the application of mathematical knowledge of the material world. With his techne, which will replace the "speculative philosophy taught in the schools" (in other words, logos), Descartes hopes to conquer nature, reduce it to a slave, force it to remedy human life with "an infinity of devices that enable us to enjoy without pain the fruits of the earth" (p. 62). His principal example is medicine:

> I am sure that there is no one, not even among those in the medical profession who would not admit that everything we know is almost nothing in comparsion to what remains to be known, and that we might rid ourselves of an infinity of maladies, both of body and mind, and even perhaps also the enfeeblement brought on by old age, were one to have a sufficient knowledge of their causes (p. 62)

It is easy to imagine words such as these being spoken by a contemporary medical researcher. Recent scientific work on the genetic basis of aging might even give some grounds for thinking Descartes right: there may indeed be hope that the enfeeblement of old age can be conquered by science. But even if Descartes was sincerely animated by the goal of using science to help human beings, even if his admonition to master nature is construed as a moral imperative, his solution still cannot satisfy. What can guide the Cartesian doctor? How should the knowledge gained in the Cartesian quest, how should techne, be applied? Should, for example, life always be extended by the application of medical technology? Descartes cannot answer; he provides nothing to guide the application process other than his provisional morality. If all the doctors in Iowa do X, then the Cartesian doctor should do X as well. Not because X can be demonstrated to be a good thing to do, but because others do it. Techne, in such a scheme, will run unchecked; there is no conception of knowledge capable of regulating it. The Cartesian doctor may know her physics well, but will be strictly prohibited from knowing herself as a member of the human community.

It should now be clear that Descartes' provisional morality parallels the subversive denial of the efficacy and goodness of logos. The subversives (at least those following Nietzsche) lack the Cartesian's faith in science.[55] Nevertheless, these two pivotal tendencies of the twentieth-century, one so apparently hyper-rational, the other so contemptuous of the proud claims of reason, are actually "flip sides" of a single coin. For Descartes, if X is probable, then X should be treated as false. If the realm of human significance cannot be cleansed of all probability (and much of what is to follow in this book is meant to show this) it can never be approached with the aim of attaining certain knowledge. That realm must, therefore, be relegated to the irrational. "All names of good and evil are images; they do not speak out, they only hint. He is a fool who seeks knowledge from them." Thus speaks Nietzsche's Zarathustra.[56] And Descartes would agree. By draining the human world of the possibility of becoming rational, Descartes carves out the space now occupied so noisily by the subversives.

As has been stated and implied throughout this chapter, such a stance toward the human world, which has been called relativism, is unacceptable. It transforms the questions of value and significance into irrelevancies. It denudes the human realm of all hope of knowledge and thus allows men like Protagoras and Callicles to enter the vacuum created by the banishment of logos and fill it with their sophistic strategems for gaining power. It replaces logos with rhetoric and so prepares the way for thinkers like Rorty and Derrida. It is dangerously offensive and must be fought.

(3)   Spinoza's Critique of Teleology

Logos has been attacked, first by Protagoras and, then, in a modern formulation, by Descartes. The attacks have different origins and motivations, but their consequences are surprisingly similar. Descartes rejects logos because it does not achieve the certainty he craves. He replaces it with his own conception of rationality, one modeled essentially on mathematics. He is a hyper-rationalist who wants to construct a well-grounded scientific edifice.[57] In wanting to do so he denudes the uniquely human realm of action of any hope of being made rational; mathematics, after all, is mute on the questions of human goals, values, and significance. As a result, Descartes comes to share Protagoras' view that the human realm is without rational purpose (except for survival or convenience). For the Sophist, life is a power struggle in which the forces of the intellect should be marshaled, not to discover the truth, but to defeat one's opponent on the political battlefield. Although he is not nearly as forthright about this, there is nothing in Descartes' *Discourse on Method* to oppose this sophistic teaching. His provisional morality indicates that the questions of life are to be relegated to the junkpile of the irrational. Once this move is made, there is no obstacle left to impede, to limit or regulate, the powerful desires of a man like Callicles.

A third variation on this theme now follows. We turn to Spinoza, a near contemporary of Descartes and a fellow-builder of the modern world. In a short section of his largest work (one whose title bespeaks the very issue we are now considering), *Ethics Demonstrated in Geometrical Order* (published around 1680), he expresses clearly his enormous hostility to teleology, which we have already identified as the lifeblood of classical logos. Spinoza is a critic forging a new vision of science, one that will arise on the ashes of an old world torn down. He, too, is a prophet predicting well the demise of the old king and the arrival of the new.

"All the prejudices I here undertake to expose depend on this one: that men commonly suppose that all natural things act, as men do, on account of an end" (Appendix, Part I, p. 439).[58] With these words Spinoza clearly states the basis of his assault. The old way, the way of logos, had assumed that nature, the world out there, was like human beings. We saw this well in Aristotle: his vision was of a familiar world in which humanity was at home and welcome. His was a world where ordinary language was ordinal and could faithfully reflect that of which it speaks. Nature, like us, "acted" purposively. Therefore, the goal of any study of a natural object (including human beings) would include the discovery of purposes (or "final causes"). This assimilation of the natural and the external to the internal and subjective is what Spinoza blames as the chief cause of error. Aristotle thought that the world was like us . . . and according to the most basic assumptions of modern science it is not.

What is interesting about Spinoza's analysis of this fundamental error is that he views it as emerging from what is typically thought of as human nature itself: "I shall begin by considering this one prejudice, asking first why most people are satisfied that it is true, and why all are so *inclined by nature* to embrace it" (p. 440; emphasis mine). Human nature, or at least human beings as they ordinarily suppose themselves to be, causes human beings to misunderstand nature. Why?

> [A]ll men are born ignorant of the causes of things . . . all want to seek their
> own advantage, and are conscious of this appetite. From these [assumptions]
> it follows, first, that men think themselves free, because they are conscious
> of their volitions and their appetite, and do not think, even in their dreams,
> of the causes by which they are disposed to wanting and willing, because
> they are ignorant [of those causes]. It follows, secondly, that men act always
> on account of an end, viz. on account of their advantage, which they want
> (p. 440).

Two facets of human existence are noted by Spinoza. We are ignorant,
and conscious that we are ignorant, of the causes of things. Second, we
desire what is useful. Since we are ignorant of the cause of our own
desiring, we think we are free. When we, for example, desire a drink and
"decide" to move toward the faucet for some water, we think that we, as
the locus of that desire, are the free originators of the action. Furthermore, since this action is the consequence of a desire, its aim is to achieve
what is deemed to be useful to us. Since we are as equally ignorant of the
"causes" of water as we are of our own desire, we might falsely suppose
that the purpose of water is to quench our thirst.

If we recall the protreptic argument offered earlier, we can see that
Spinoza agrees with it to a certain extent. He assumes that human beings
act with an aim in view; we aim for some benefit, something that is
taken to be useful and good. The protreptic logos assumed that this
phenomenon was inherently revealing of the way the world really is. For
Spinoza, this fact of human intentionality is but the misleading and
superficial appearance of our lives. We *seem* to be free and to move toward
what we think is useful. But, in fact, we are not free. Spinoza is a strict
determinist. He thinks we are not the free originators of our actions.
Instead, we are part of an enormous network of causes and effects over
which we have no control. Spinoza's vast explanation of this thesis in the
Ethics is well beyond the limits of this chapter. Instead, we need only to
consider what for many readers is surely a common enough thought:
our sense of being free is a consequence of our ignorance. We think, we
feel, we believe, we are free agents, but are not. We delude ourselves.

In a similar fashion we delude ourselves about the world out there.
Men,

> . . . necessarily judge the temperament of other men from their own
> temperament. Furthermore, they find—both in themselves and outside
> themselves—many means that are very helpful in seeking their own advan-
> tage, e.g., eyes for seeing, teeth for chewing, plants and animals for food,
> the sun for light, the sea for supporting fish . . . Hence, they consider all
> natural things as a means to their own advantage. And knowing that they
> had found these means, not provided them for themselves, they had reason

to believe that there was someone else who had prepared those means for
their use. For after they considered these things as means, they could not
believe that the things had made themselves; but from the means they were
accustomed to prepare for themselves, they had to infer that there was a
ruler, or a number of rulers of nature, endowed with human freedom, who
had taken care of all things for them, and made all things for their use . . .
Thus this prejudice was changed into superstition and struck deep roots in
their minds. This was why each of them strove with great diligence to
understand and explain the final causes of all things (440–441).

Spinoza here attacks the religious belief in a loving God who created
the world for the benefit of humanity. Such a belief is a far cry from any
that Aristotle would entertain. Nevertheless, in this paragraph we can
see how Spinoza's attack would apply, not only to religious "superstition,"
but to all teleological explanation and thus to logos in general. Any
philosophical enterprise that takes its bearings from ordinary language,
which is loaded with beliefs in purposes and values, is fundamentally
misguided and indeed is no more than superstition. Spinoza's goal is
methodically to replace teleological language with one that is purified of
all taint of anthropomorphism: the mathematical language of science.

Human beings, because of their ignorance of the world, believe that
since various objects are useful to them, such usefulness is part of the
nature of those objects. The sun sustains life; the eyes are useful for
seeing. Ignorant humans falsely infer from these facts that the sun was
made (by God) in order to sustain life and the eye was made for seeing.
Aristotle would deny that "God" made the sun. For a variety of reasons
intrinsic to his conception of teleology, he would not make even a truncated version of the first claim (the purpose of the sun is to sustain life).[59]
But (if we subtract God the maker) he would be perfectly happy with the
second: the eyes are for the purpose of seeing. Spinoza would disagree.
The objects of the world, including parts of living organisms, have no
purposes. They are all material beings obeying the laws of mechanical
necessity. To think these objects do have purpose is to confuse the way
we appear to act with the way the world really is; it is to be misled by
the surface shine of ordinary experience and language. Teleological
thinking, according to Spinoza, imposes a poorly understood, or ordinary, conception of human desire onto the larger tableau of a nonhuman
world: "What is called a final cause is nothing but a human appetite
insofar as it is considered as a principle, or primary cause, of some thing"
(p. 544).

Spinoza believes that his discovery of a world without purposes might
have remained "hidden from the human race to eternity, if Mathematics,
which is concerned not with ends, but only with essences and properties

of things, had not shown men another standard of truth" (p. 441). Precisely like Descartes, Spinoza takes his bearings from mathematics. Mathematics, ever mute on purposes, cleanses the imagination of all false notions of final causality. Therefore, by fixing our gaze on the necessary deductions of geometry, we can learn that "Nature has no end set before it, and that all final causes are nothing but human fictions" (p. 442).

The troika of characters who comprise this chapter can now be yoked. Spinoza's critique of teleology shares much with Descartes' provisional morality. Both deny that the values and purposes of human life are capable of being understood in their own terms by ordinary language. Since both men are rationalists they believe that values and purposes can be understood—but not as values and purposes. They can be understood as motions of material body parts such as the brain or heart; they cannot be understood as independent principles that guide and regulate free human behavior.

Like Descartes, Spinoza can be affiliated with Protagoras; that is, the consequences of his teaching for the world of human significance are sophistic. For Protagoras, man, made from earth and fire, is "man the maker." All cultural phenomena, including language, religion, and purposes, are "fictions." They are devices manufactured to achieve the end of communal survival. Purposes are subjective productions imposed upon a world in which they have no natural place. Protagoras is a rhetorician. He teaches his students how to become "big men" in the city, how to persuade others to accept those particular purposes they happen to champion. Although Spinoza seems to teach something far different, when it comes to interpreting the human world he arrives at a similar conclusion: It is a realm empty of rational hope, awaiting the strong desires of those who are powerful enough to take charge.

Spinoza's teaching leads to two possible outcomes for the human realm of purposes. First, that realm could become an object of knowledge. This implies that it could be fully assimilated to mathematical science. ("I shall consider human actions and appetites just as if it were a Question of lines, planes, bodies" [p. 492]). However, since mathematics is not itself teleological and human experience, as people are "inclined by nature to embrace it," is, then the Spinozistic vision would transform the human world into something far different from what it ordinarily takes itself to be. In other words, if mathematical science is the *only* paradigm of knowledge, and if the human world is something to be known, then it must become an object of mathematical science. But, as Spinoza himself seems to grant, we are not "inclined by nature" to think of ourselves as such objects. Our language, our ordinary desires and experience, all tell against such a mathematical interpretation of ourselves. (The evidence for such a claim? Simply ask, do you feel yourself, experience your goals, desires, hopes, loves, do you explain yourself, in mathematical terms?) Therefore, given Spinoza's conception of knowledge, to make the human world knowable would require reconstituting it totally, transforming it into something unrecognizable.

(The above is not in itself a successful argument against Spinoza. It would only succeed as such an argument if it further explained why ordinary experience deserves to be treated as a standard. What, in other words, privileges the ordinary in measuring claims to knowledge?)

The second possible outcome is that the human experience of purposes would be interpreted as bereft of all rational content. Again, Spinoza himself seems to believe that insofar as we pertain to ordinary language and to the surface appearance of our lives, human beings seem to make value judgments, assume they are free, seek purposes. But if human experience were to be properly understood in a Spinozistic manner it would be treated as devoid of all purposes. But what then would happen to that experience? It would have to be treated as an aberration, held in contempt as a form of self-delusion that denies the mechanical workings of the universe. It would have to be taken as something that needs to be subdued. Human experience would have to be excluded from that which can be understood.

Given either of the two options, then, modern science is quite literally dehumanizing.

(It should be mentioned that if the above is at all correct, then once again the link between modern science and the contemporary subversives has been clarified: both agree that the human world of purposes is not to be understood, is not to be regulated by a rationally determined Good.)

The triumphs of modern science are, of course, magnificent. The computers never cease to fascinate and the prospects for the manipulation of the genetic structures of animals and plants stagger the imagination. But what do we know of the scientist and the purposive world in which she experiences herself as dwelling? According to Spinoza, nothing. We either reconstitute that experience so that it can be expressed in mathematical terms—we turn human beings into objects that can be treated, or perhaps even engineered, by mathematical science; or we dismiss such experience as incomprehensible—we agree with Nietzsche that morality is not an arena in which reason plays a significant role.

Spinoza, like Descartes, is a thundering prophet. He mounts against logos a comprehensive criticism. He accuses logos of not knowing itself. Logos believes it is rationally self-sufficient, that it can defend, and not simply assert, its claim to goodness. But Descartes and Spinoza, who begin with criteria for knowledge such as clarity, certainty, steadiness, and usefulness, and end by making mathematics paradigmatic, launch a frontal assault on the self-confidence of logos. How does logos know that it does not, as Spinoza says, impose its own desires onto a world that is not really of its kind? How does it know that purposes are not fictions and that teleology, even of the sober Aristotelian variety, is not just superstition? Logos believes it is solid. How does it know that it is not just a palace built on sand? These are the questions that will be confronted next.

C The Response of Logos

(1) The Argument from Self-Reference

Logos has been three ways attacked. The Sophist charges logos with falsely parading itself as a spokesman for a stable and structured world. By promising to locate an enduring reality outside of the vital rush of life logos, says Callicles, denies the human power of action. By seeking to discover those "values" that reside in the nature of things, logos loses touch with the valueless, ever-changing flux that is life. The result is weakness and disease. The result is Socrates.

Descartes accuses logos of being without foundation. Like a palace built on sand, traditional philosophy was grounded on nothing firm. It chirped about all subjects, but in none did it achieve indubitable certainty. As a result, its talk never went beyond mere probability and so its only audience was the ignorant. Real knowledge, says Descartes, is modeled on mathematics. It is clear and steady. It is useful; it can, in its manifestation as technology, be applied to manipulate, even to master, nature.

Spinoza attacks teleology, one of the great hopes of logos. For him, Aristotle's beautiful vision is nothing but contemptible anthropomorphism. To "find" purposes in nature is actually to project human desire onto an inhuman screen. It is to fabricate purposes, not discover them. Logos, in Spinoza's view, is a perverse extension of a specific desire humans typically, perhaps even naturally, have: to see themselves in the world. To elevate such a desire to the status of reason is fundamental error and superstition.

Against such charges logos will react in sharp defense, for it has now been accused of the very crimes that it had once brought to bear against its own enemies. Remember, in section 1.A.3. a basic tactic (or moment) of logos in arguing for its unconditional goodness was through "The Indirect Argument." Here logos began with a premise directly contrary to its own belief: Logos is not unconditionally good. From such a beginning unacceptable consequences were generated and, as a result, the initial premise had to be rejected and logos's own assertion had to be accepted.

The argument was this: If logos is not unconditionally good, then it is (at best) only conditionally good. If this is the case, there must be some condition that is capable of negating the goodness of logos. But this condition, this X, is not itself susceptible to rational articulation. Since it is an essential and unique task of logos to ask the "what-is-it" type of question, if logos is suspended by X, then the question, what is X?, cannot be answered. As a result, X is beyond the pale of rationality. It dwells in silence. As a result, if the initial premise were allowed to stand, logos would lose its stature. The X would hover constantly, threatening to uncover the mantle of authority with which logos was accustomed to drape itself. Logos would no longer, for example, be deemed final judge and arbiter of disputes about values. Such disputes would have to be settled by some other means (force, persuasion, whim, political or religious consensus).

It was argued in I.A.3. that the position generated by the premise "logos is not unconditionally good" is relativism and that it is unacceptable because it denudes the critical question of value of all hope of rational resolution. Logos accused its enemy of being both false and pernicious, for relativism implies that value decisions are groundless; since they cannot be adjudicated by reason, they are based on nothing firm. Perhaps they are based on political authority or mere fancy. What X is, what that which conditionalizes and replaces logos is, cannot be articulated. And so, hidden from view, it shifts constantly. The result is a diminution of the human urge to know. The result is the groundlessness of value judgments and this, said logos, is disease; it is the distrust of the urge to speak about and know what is right and wrong. The result is chaos, for if value judgments are emptied of the hope of rational adjudication all that remains are individual desires competing against one another for power.

In section 1.A.3. logos sent out a call: "you who deny the unconditional goodness of logos pollute and must be banished. No one should admit you into their home. You are vile for you deny what is best about being human. You cheapen life, for you would plunge us all into the groundless dark. You make a mockery of the altogether typical and admirable urge to defend our values in rational dispute. You are shameful and should show your face no longer."

But in the next section, 1.B., logos was itself attacked with what is very much the same charge. Coming from Protagoras (and Callicles), Descartes, and Spinoza, logos was called false, unhealthy, groundless, and but one desire among many.

And so now logos is enraged: "How dare you say this! For it is I, not you, who want, more than anything, to be grounded on the firm foundation of truth. It is you, not I, who believe that desire alone should be a guide to life. You defame me with your charge. You are blind, three ways blind, to accuse me of what you yourself are so guilty."

In more measured terms, logos will bring arguments to bear against its accusers. First is the argument from self-reference, which is similar to the indirect argument given above.

Let us begin with the first of the three charges against logos, that brought by the sophistic relativism propounded by Callicles and Protagoras. The assertion here was that values and truths are relative; that there is no stable, non-human measure of the Good or the Truth; that there are only truths and goods relative to, dependent upon, the many human beings who uphold them.

(To reiterate two points: The procedure of capitalizing the first letter of "Good" and "Truth" to indicate the position of logos is borrowed from Rorty who, needless to say, prefers lower-case letters.[60] Second, the question of what type of relativism Protagoras holds is frequently a matter of scholarly debate. Is he a relativist only about values [an ethical relativist] or does he hold the same beliefs about knowledge and truth? [Is he also an epistemological relativist?] This type of question could be applied to Rorty and other Sophists as well. In this section I will follow Plato's lead, and take sophistry to be concerned with both values and truth.)

Assume that sophistic relativism is correct. If so, it seems perfectly fair to ask that this doctrine be applied to, or refer to, itself. If this occurs, however, we discover that relativism cannot coherently refer to itself. If relativism is true, then relativism cannot be true. After all, as a doctrine it is the denial that any doctrine is truthful. Since this denial should apply to, refer to, itself, relativism is a doctrine that negates itself.

Consider the proposition "truth is relative." If it is true, then it should apply to itself. If, however, the truth of that proposition is itself relative (to, for example, the person speaking it), then it is no longer true about the truth of all other propositions. Since the proposition does seem to make an assertion about the truth of other propositions, it suffers an internal breakdown; it cannot make sense of itself.

If Protagoras is right that all human beings are measures of the truth, then he himself is but one among many measures of the truth. And so when he says, "all human beings are measures of the truth," he is asserting, not the Truth, but only his own version of the truth. According to the very rules implied by Protagorean relativism, if one of the Sophist's opponents should then say, "You're wrong, Protagoras; only some human beings, those with knowledge, are measures of the Truth," Protagoras could not coherently object by saying that his opponent is wrong. For the Sophist, all statements are, with regard to their truth, equal. There is no measure of truth or falsity. Since all statements are equally true, there is no substantial difference between saying "all human beings" or "some human beings" are measures of the truth. There is no difference between truth and Truth. Protagoras' position cannot defend itself intelligibly without contradicting and thus destroying itself. The Sophist is blind to his own incoherence.

This blindness, this failure of self-reference, is the key to the demise of logos's prophetic accuser. As revealed in his great story, Protagorean relativism rests on a notion of materialistic flux. (This is also consistent with Socrates' analysis in Plato's dialogue, the *Theaetetus*.)[61] The world is in constant change and turmoil; it is a purposeless game in which the sole object is to survive. Language (always a possible translation of "logos") is but one of many human productions used to create some island of apparent calm in the midst of the storm that is real life. But if this is so, then language cannot legitimately purport to assert a Truth about real life. If Protagorean relativism claims to be True, it claims to be independent of this flux. If the world is flux, and language is part of the world, then language is flux; if so, then language cannot coherently refer to a stable, nonflowing Truth. But this is what Protagoras does.[62] As such, his doctrine fails the test of self-reference and merits the charge of incoherence.

A third way of expressing the dilemma is this: if Protagoras is right, then all human beings are, in one sense, equal. Since there is no Truth, no human being is closer to the Truth, more truthful, than any other. Since there is no Good, no human being is Better than any other. We are, in this regard, all the same. In one regard only is there difference between people: some have the power to enforce their particular version of what is good upon others. But such an understanding of values is ludicrous and untenable: people have convictions, typically think that they are, and can show that they are, Better than others.[63] There is an urge, strongly felt, to defend in public the values one champions. As his story shows, Protagoras himself believes that he himself is Better; after all, he offers to teach and thinks he can best Socrates in argument. His very tone of voice indicates the great sense of superiority he feels in himself. Callicles explicitly believes this as well.

Such beliefs, therefore, testify to a deep incoherence. It is possible, as we will see below, to be a coherent relativist. But it is not possible for the relativist coherently to operate under the auspices of reason in the attempt to defend the superiority of his position. His position advocates the equality (from the perspective of Truth) of all positions. As such, it is in principle indefensible. The relativist can, of course, argue in order to have this or that position adopted; he can also argue that this or that position is more in keeping with, for example, customary practice or with conventional religion; but he cannot argue that his position is really True as opposed to others that are False. Therefore, once the Sophist attempts to defend his position in a debate with Socrates, who is interested only in what is True, he is doomed to incoherence. Since Protagoras agrees to answer Socrates' question it becomes fair to ask that his relativistic position refer to itself; and this it cannot coherently do.

This point can be illustrated by briefly discussing Richard Rorty. Rorty wants to straighten traditional philosophers (or "Platonists") out. They have continually deluded themselves and outlived their usefulness with their all-too-serious quest for the Good and the True. To replace Philosophy (the Platonic quest for the Truth), he offers what he calls "conversation." Unlike Philosophy, unlike logos, conversation does not seek rational foundations. Instead, it is a civilized exchange of views, of truths, that takes place in a tolerant and convivial atmosphere. Rorty believes that the kind of questions asked by Plato should no longer be asked. His goal is not Truth; it is to engage in as many conversations as possible.

The above only summarizes Rorty's position.[64] The argument I propose is this: Let us assume that Rorty's version of conversation is compelling. If this were so, then there would be at least one person with whom Rorty could not converse: the Platonist. Such a person will always demand that the goal of a conversation be the Truth, the determination of who is Right and Wrong. Since Rorty denies that such demands are efficacious, interesting, or valuable, he should not argue against the Platonist. He should not try to prove that he is Right. He indicates this by closing his book with the following statement:

> The only point on which I would insist is that philosophers' moral concern should be with continuing the conversation of the West, rather than with insisting upon a place for the traditional problems of modern philosophy within that conversation.[65]

In other words, Rorty *insists* that *his* version of conversation should be adopted by philosophers. He insists that the Platonist should be spurned for he thinks his own doctrine, and not the Platonist's, is Right. If he didn't think this, why would he be so adamant that the Platonist not raise the traditional problems of Western philosophy? Something must be Wrong with those problems, with that approach to the world. Rorty *insists* that traditional philosophers open themselves to the conversation of the West as he depicts it. He tries to persuade his reader that his vision of conversational and tolerant philosophy is Right. (Of course he does; what else do any of us do?) In other words, he does something very traditional and exactly what he says philosophers shouldn't do. And this causes him to be incoherent: his own views should have inhibited him from making the statement cited above.

This does not imply that Rorty's views about conversation and Platonism are wrong. It only implies that, given his views, he has no "right" to insist that he is Right. Apparently, Rorty could not resist the temptation of claiming that he was Right, and this is the downfall of his relativism: it cannot refer coherently to itself.[66]

(2)   Techne and the Good

Logos next counterattacks Descartes, who may fairly be called a "technocrat" (one who thinks techne should rule) or a "technicist" (one who thinks techne is the highest good). We saw that his work aims at the goal of creating a useful and reliable techne with which humanity can be healed of its infinity of woes. Descartes has a vision which in its way is beautiful: For him, man, through the technology spawned by mathematical physics, can become master and possessor of nature. Medicine can flourish. Nature need not threaten. Techne will rule and it is good.

To achieve his goal Descartes redefines the criteria for knowledge. Above all else, he makes certainty, modeled on mathematics, foundational in the quest for knowledge. As a result of this most fundamental assumption, the questions of human significance are demoted in stature. Since their answers cannot be rewarded with certainty, human questions must be relegated to the irrational. The human realm is governed, not by knowledge, but by the ethical relativism expressed in Descartes' provisional morality. In other words, relativism is generated by and becomes the flip side of Descartes' technicism, his belief that mathematical techne is the highest good.

Descartes succeeded as few men in history ever have, for we live today in a thoroughly Cartesian world. But it is not a coherent world. Ethical relativism is generated as a consequence of Cartesian technicism, and these two notions simply do not cohere. Why? Because technicism declares that techne is the highest good. But if relativism (the denial that there is a highest good) is true, then such a declaration loses its meaning. That declaration, however, is precisely what initiated and animated the Cartesian project. To put this in other terms, it is of course possible to assert that techne is good. But to do so is immediately to deny technicism, for it is to invoke a standard higher than techne: there must be some "good," against which techne measures up as good. If such a standard is invoked, then technicism and relativism no longer make a coherent conceptual pair. Instead, they fall apart. (In much the same way that the world today, split as it is into its two predominant impulses, technicism and deconstruction, is falling apart.)

Techne is value-neutral. This means that it can be used for good or evil and that it can make no value judgments about itself or anything else. Therefore, it is inconsistent to assert that techne is the exclusive mode of knowledge *and* that it is known to be good. One or the other, and not both, of these two assertions can be made. If, for example, someone states that techne is the exclusive mode of knowledge, he has to be willing to admit that there is nothing that can be known about its goodness. Instead, techne "just is" and its progress must remain unevaluated, unfettered by any knowledgeable regulation. If, by contrast, someone asserts that techne is good, then various qualifications have to be added. This position would insist that techne can be good, but only if it is guided properly or regulated knowledgeably; only if, in other words, there is a higher and more comprehensive mode of knowledge capable of subordinating it.

There is an internal tension within technicism. Plato understands this well, and Socrates often exploits it when he finds it (or something like it) in one of his opponents. A good example comes from the first book of the *Republic*. Socrates, the representative of logos, the enemy of relativism, here argues against Thrasymachus, a professional rhetorician and (like Callicles) a student of Gorgias. Thrasymachus sells (teaches) his knowledge of rhetoric. Since he identifies himself as a teacher, and since techne is that type of knowledge which is paradigmatically (most easily recognized as) teachable, he thinks of himself as possessing a techne. As a rhetorician, however, Thrasymachus affirms a type of relativism. Socrates attempts to show that the combination of these two tendencies, the affirmation of both techne and relativism, is finally incoherent.[67]

When Thrasymachus is asked by Socrates, "What is justice?" (one of his typical what-is-it questions), he answers, "For my part I say that the just is nothing other the advantage of the stronger" (338c1–2). As mentioned in an earlier section, what Thrasymachus means by "the stronger" is the politically stronger, or the ruling body. Justice, in his view, is determined by, and so is relative to, the regime that is currently in power. It could, for example, be advantageous for a tyrant to outlaw freedom of the press and for a democratic regime to tolerate dissent. Neither policy is intrinsically good or bad; they are equal in the sense that they get their "value" from the regimes in which they are enforced. For Socrates such a (sophistic) position is unacceptable, and he uses an elaborate argument to refute it. First, he convinces Thrasymachus to agree to the following propositions:

(1) Justice is the advantage of the stronger.
(2) It is just to obey the ruling body.
(3) The ruling body sometimes errs; it makes incorrect laws.
(4) An incorrect law is one that is disadvantageous to the ruling body.
(5) It is just to obey all laws, both correct and incorrect.
(6) Therefore, it is just to do what is disadvantageous to the ruler.

Socrates then shows Thrasymachus that (6) contradicts (1). The entire series of assertions is inconsistent and the rhetorician's definition of justice must be rejected.

At this point, a man named Polemarchus celebrates Socrates' apparent victory over Thrasymachus by shouting "Yes, by Zeus, this is most clear!" (340a1). But another character, a man named Cleitophon, objects to such enthusiasm and says, "Of course, if you are witness for him" (340a3). Polemarchus insists that Socrates' argument is convincing. After all, Thrasymachus had agreed that sometimes the ruling body makes mistakes and so commands what is to its disadvantage; since it is just for those who are ruled to obey these orders, it is (sometimes) just to do what is to the ruler's disadvantage. Cleitophon explains that "Thrasymachus had posited that doing what is ordered by the rulers is just." Again Polemarchus repeats the argument: Since Thrasymachus agrees that it is just to do what the ruling body orders, and that the ruling body sometimes errs, his initial assertion must be abandoned since it is inconsistent with the other propositions he has accepted.

At this point, Cleitophon makes a little speech:

> But he [Thrasymachus] called the advantage of the stronger what the stronger *believes* to be advantageous to himself. This is what must be done by the weaker and this is what he posited as the just (340b6–8).

Cleitophon here alters Thrasymachus' position slightly, but significantly. What he has seen is that the initial definition, "justice is the advantage of the stronger," presupposes that there is real or true advantage as opposed to an illusory or false one. This is a distinction needed to distinguish correct from incorrect laws (proposition 3). Only if there is a true advantage is it possible to assert that a ruling body sometimes mistakenly chooses a course leading to its real disadvantage. One can make a mistake only if there is some standard by which correct and incorrect laws can be measured. In this case, the standard is real advantage.

Cleitophon has seen a tension inherent in Thrasymachus' position. First, there is Thrasymachus' relativism. He believes that values gain their validity or meaning solely through the ruling body that enforces them. When he states (proposition 5) that it is just to obey all laws, whether they are correct or not, he implies that justice is simply obedience to the laws posited by any given regime. This is relativistic because it offers no way of justifying laws except through the fact that they are laws of a specific regime. In this view, no law is good in and of itself; it is "good" only relative to the ruling body that makes it.

There is, however, a second, countervailing tendency in Thrasymachus' position. He relies on an objective standard, the ruler's real advantage, to differentiate correct from incorrect laws. If, for example, it would be advantageous for regime A to raise taxes, but due to an an erroneous analysis it does not do so, then obedience to the tax laws of the land would in fact be disadvantageous to the regime. In Thrasymachus' account, obedience to the laws of regime A would be both unjust (1, 4, 6) and just (2 and 5).

The point is this: As a rhetorician, Thrasymachus believes that he can teach rulers how to identify and then achieve what is *really* to their advantage. He believes he has a techne to do this.[68] He wants, in other words, to charge his techne with value; he thinks it good and well worth paying for. As a result, Thrasymachus retains a commitment to some measure of objectivity and to the notion that there are some standards of which only a few have knowledge. On the other hand, he is also committed to relativism: he does not believe that any law is in itself good or bad. Socrates' argument is meant to show that he can't have it both ways: these two commitments do not cohere.

Cleitophon offers Thrasymachus a way out of his dilemma by suggesting that the initial definition of justice be changed from "advantage of the stronger" to "that which the stronger believes is his advantage." These two formulations are critically different. The former affirms some objective standard by which to measure real advantage. The latter, which radicalizes the moderate relativism latent in the former, does away with such standards for it does away with the possibility of error altogether: if justice is simply what the ruler believes is advantageous, then the ruler is never wrong.

Thrasymachus ignores Cleitophon's friendly appeal. Again, this is because he thinks he possesses a valuable techne worth paying for. He wants to preserve the possibility of the ruler making mistakes because he wants to preserve his own position as a teacher of potential rulers. Instead of following Cleitophon's advice he takes an altogether different line against Socrates. The challenge for Thrasymachus is to explain how the possibility of error (the making of incorrect/disadvantageous laws) can be reconciled with relativism. He does this by saying that the person with a techne, insofar as he has a techne, simply does not err. Unlike opinion or mere belief, knowledge (and techne is surely that), in the most precise sense of the word, does not err. The doctor, as a doctor, does not make mistakes. When she does make a mistake she, at the very moment of erring, does not really (precisely) possess the techne of medicine. Analogously, if a ruler, who is presumed by Thrasymachus to have a techne, errs, at that very moment of erring, he does not really have the techne of ruling. This would remove the problem Socrates has detected by removing proposition (3).

Socrates is quite willing to go along with Thrasymachus' very stringent conception of a techne. He is glad to see Thrasymachus affirm his allegiance to techne because, as the next argument will show, precisely such an affirmation will eventually cause the Sophist's downfall.

(1)   The doctor (the one in precise speech, the one with a techne who does not err) cares for the sick.

(2)   The pilot of the ship cares for the sailors.

(3)   Therefore, all technai are directed toward the advantage of their objects.[69]

(4)   Therefore, no techne considers its own advantage.

(5)   Justice is a techne.

(6)   Therefore, justice does not consider its own advantage (341c5–342e8).

Again, the initial definition of justice, the advantage of the stronger, has to be rejected because it leads to inconsistent results.

The point of these refutations is this: Thrasymachus' initial definition of justice is a formulation of relativism. At the same time, Thrasymachus is a kind of technicist.[70] He describes justice as a type of techne so that he may teach potential rulers how to rule. Socrates will not allow him to be both a technicist and a relativist. The first argument pins him down on the issue of incorrect laws. It shows that he is not a thorough relativist; a dimension of evaluative objectivity remains in his position. The second exploits a basic principle about techne: it is oriented to an object other than itself. Medicine, for example, studies the workings of human bodies; it does not study medicine (or the doctor). Carpentry studies the properties of wood; arithmetic studies number. Techne is not "self-reflexive;" it is "objective," directed to an object other than itself. Because it cannot reflect upon itself or its possessor, because it knows nothing about the human context in which its results appear, it is value-neutral. Thrasymachus defines justice as a techne that can secure the ruler's advantage. This implies that a techne can be charged with value. Socrates' argument is meant to show that it cannot.

Socrates has a similar argument with Thrasymachus' teacher, Gorgias (in the *Gorgias*). First, he makes sure that the famous rhetorician admits that he has a techne (449a). Then, he persuades him to agree that a basic characteristic of a techne is that it have a determinate object. Gorgias is quite reluctant to do this, but Socrates is persistent, repeatedly asking him to identify specifically what his techne is about (449d1, d9, 451a6). Finally, Gorgias relents and says it is about "the just and unjust" (454b7).

The next move that Gorgias makes, the one that will seal his doom, is to assert that techne is value neutral. His example is wrestling. A person who learns how to wrestle can use his knowledge well or use it to beat up his mother (456e). If he chooses to do the latter, neither the teacher nor the techne itself should be blamed (456d–457c). The techne, after all, is neutral on the question of use. A similar situation obtains with rhetoric. If Gorgias teaches a student the techniques of artful persuasion which the student then employs to argue for an unjust cause, neither Gorgias nor rhetoric should be blamed.

The problem with Gorgias' position is that justice, the professed object of his own techne, is by definition not a neutral item. A student who studies with Gorgias will learn justice. Such a man will be just and cannot be unjust. Gorgias' claim to a techne, which is value-neutral, whose object is justice, doesn't make sense (460a–461b).

These Socratic refutations are instructive. Many people, especially professors, profess to be relativists. At the same time, they want to be rewarded, or congratulated, or recognized, for their knowledge. They want to write books and be paid to give lectures that will win applause. To do this they almost invariably have to conform to the dictates of techne, the most easily recognizable form of knowledge. As a result, there is a tension within their work that can be exploited by a man like Socrates in order to bring about their downfall.

Of course, the refutations do not prove that relativism is false. They only show what happens when a Sophist's relativism is formulated and professed in a certain manner. If the Sophist is clever and strong enough, he can avoid Socratic refutation. Much of what was discussed in section I.B.1. about Protagoras and his relationship to techne was meant to suggest this. Protagoras is a more advanced thinker than either Thrasymachus or Gorgias. He understood well Socrates' strategy. Socrates began his assault on the Sophist with the techne-analogy. He wanted to pin Protagoras down in the same manner that he pins Thrasymachus and Gorgias down. But this he failed to do, for Protagoras never allowed himself to be caught in the Socratic trap; *he never clearly claimed to have a techne whose subject is arete.* He understood the nature of his own relativism well enough to realize that capitulating to Socrates' repeated insistence that he do so would lead to his defeat. Thus he hedged on the techne question: he aligned himself with techne, but only superficially in order to give his *mathema*, his subject, the veneer of being something teachable. When he was pushed, he distanced himself from techne and, as a result, avoided the kind of tension that Socrates finds in Thrasymachus. Protagoras hedged, but beautifully and to his greatest advantage.

By examining the strategy with which Socrates places his opponent's claim into an analogy with medicine, arithmetic, and so forth, we can see the pivotal role techne plays in his thinking. Socrates believes techne can be good. He is not a technicist because he also believes that there is some good that can be known by some (presumably) nontechnical form of knowledge. This latter knowledge is "higher" than techne; that is, it is capable of making knowledgeable judgments about techne, about the use of its products, its value, its meaning, its human significance.

Socrates is quite pleased when a sophistic opponent such as Thrasymachus or Gorgias professes to have a techne. (In a similar manner, I was quite pleased when Rorty *insisted* that he was right.) By professing this the Sophist implicitly claims to know what is good. Therefore, by claiming a techne, the Sophist sets up within himself an obstacle to his own relativism. Relativism is the real enemy, and the fact that some relativists affirm the goodness of techne can be exploited in the fight against them.

(3) Poeticism

Protagoras, Descartes, and Spinoza finally agree on one crucial point: Human beings *make* their own values, meanings, and purposes. They agree that the human world is *produced* by human activity. As such, they can each be called "poeticists." This word comes from the Greek "*poiein,*" meaning (among other things) "to make" or "to produce." The most familiar English word derived from *poiein* is "poet," which for us has a very narrow meaning: It refers to a writer of poems. The Greek word can have a similarly narrow meaning: Homer was a *poietes*, a poet. But the Greek can also be much broader and refer to all who make, to productive activity in general.

"Poeticism," as I use the term, is the doctrine that the human world is manufactured by human "poets" or "producers." Since human beings vary from time to time and place to place, poeticism implies that the human world is in a state of flux. It is, therefore, a variation on the theme of relativism.

The poeticism in Protagoras' story is quite apparent for it clearly describes man as man-the-maker. Proto-techne, the intellectual capacity to produce, is what allows human beings to survive and become unique among the animals. Language, the polis, religion, and all the cultural phenomena that occupy the uniquely human realm of significance, are produced. Protagoras himself alludes to the kinship his version of sophistry has with poetry (in the narrow sense) by saying that Homer and Hesiod were in fact disguised versions of Sophists (see 316d).

Descartes and Spinoza are quite different from Protagoras in that they are hyper-rationalists; they view the world of matter in motion, which came to be known as the physical world, not as a result of human production, but as something "out there" to be analyzed by the tools of modern mathematical physics. But, as has been argued, there is a flip side to their view. In addition to being proponents of modern science, they are Sophists as well: their hyper-rationalism generates in its train the notion that the human world, the world of cities and values and purposes, is governed only by the rules of provisional morality. According to Descartes, we "make do" with the conventions that have been sanctioned by custom and law. Such conventions are not to be scrutinized or evaluated under the categories of true, false, better, worse; they are to be used to supply a comfortable survival to the Cartesian scientist who does not want to be interrupted in his quest for the laws of physics.

Spinoza, by rejecting teleology as completely as he does, by interpreting the ordinary human urge to discover purposes in nature as erroneous anthropomorphism, states that such purposes are made: "Final causes are nothing but human fictions," he says. As such, both he and Descartes finally must confess to a very sophistic, poeticist, view of the human world.[71]

The true quarrel, the real conflict, animating this story is between logos and poeticism. This is something Plato understood full well. In the *Republic* he mentions "the old quarrel (*diaphora*) between philosophy and poetry" (607b5). (Philosophy here can substitute for "logos.") The reason that this dispute is so old, so fundamental, is that it is between two of the most basically different and extreme views of the human world that can be held. Is the world made by human productive energy, or is it somehow structured by entities that exist independently of human choice? Is man the measure? If so, then the human world is subject to endless shifts and changes. Human freedom and the power to create become the most cherished of gifts. Or is the world constituted by a stable set of objective standards that somehow reside in the world outside of human agency and thus function as natural goals by which we can measure our activity?

The history of Western thought, as complex and elaborate as it is, is so often just the debate on this single question. That certainly is true today. Rorty and Derrida, as complex as their views seem to be, finally can be described as poeticists. For them, there are no enduring nonhuman structures accessible to human reason. Instead, the structures that exist are temporary things, fleeting, changing, ever different, present and then absent. They are a product of "conversation," says Rorty. They are a product of "writing," says Derrida. The human world according to the subversives is fabricated and final causes but fictions.

A remarkable thread unifying today's subversives is the fact that they share a common enemy: the ancient philosopher Plato who is identified by them as the champion of logos, the purveyor of a world of eternal, unchanging, forms. A good example of the extent to which Plato has been vilified was already noted in the Prologue. There a remark from a recent book titled *After Philosophy* was quoted. Speaking of the many contributors to this volume, the editor states, "all are agreed in their opposition to the 'Platonic conception of Truth.' "[72] "The Platonic conception of Truth" here means the belief that logos should seek to articulate the stable, nonproduced, structures and values that give shape to the human world. It is condemned as life-denying, as contemptuous of the creative plurality of voices that constitute human history. The ancient dispute thus takes the form, even today, of a battle between Platonism and poeticism.

As will become apparent in the following two chapters, I think the subversives are wrong in their understanding and evaluation of Platonism. In general I think they have too thoroughly assimilated Plato to Aristotle. It is indeed true that Plato stands opposed to the subversive's poeticism. But he does not do so in the same way as his student. Aristotle is the great theoretician who articulates a vision of a world in which natural and stable structures can be rationally discovered. His is the most optimistic and richest view of the possibilities of logos. Plato is quite different. Most telling is the fact that he writes dialogues that are themselves a kind of poetry. We will see that for him logos is a more questionable, less assertive, and in this sense less happy affair than it is for Aristotle. When viewed from the perspective of the contemporary subversive or Cartesian, it is indeed true that Plato and Aristotle are united in their defense of logos. But this does not imply that they fully share a conception of what logos is.

The meaning of "logos" thus has started to shift, away from Aristotle and toward Plato. I hope that as this story further unfolds the Platonic conception of logos will be understood as different, not only from what is typically taken to be "the Platonic conception of Truth," but also from the Aristotelian vision that was discussed in the first section of this book.

Logos argues that all three of its accusers are led to poeticism. It screams that this is finally unacceptable. Why? Because poeticism leads to nihilism, the rejection of all value. Poeticism interprets all values as the product of the creative energies of the value-makers. And these change. Values finally become a matter only of which creator has the most power to impose his particular version of value on the rest of us. There is nothing (*nihil*) with which such creativity can be measured or regulated. Anything goes; everything is in principle legitimate; it doesn't matter what values are created, only whether or not they can be successfully imposed.

Poeticism implies that the human world is nothing but a flowing stream of ever-changing values. The flow never ceases, it takes with it all hopes and goals. This is madness, nihilism, and the degradation of human life; this is pollution. And logos is enraged. Are we to succumb to the flimsy and fickle whims of creativity, or to something more stable and enduring that can give our lives meaning? That is the question: and the reader can now predict the response of logos.

CHAPTER 2

IS LOGOS
UNCONDITIONALLY GOOD?

A CLEITOPHON'S ACCUSATION

Even after having undergone the attacks leveled against it, logos can still assert (with confidence, with vigor), "I am unconditionally good. I represent what is best about being human. Without me you are left only with poetry and doomed to a life of insignificance, unhappiness, and disease." Logos has weathered its storm.

And yet . . .

We have seen cracks, potentially vulnerable openings in the shield of logos. (The techne-analogy that Socrates foists upon unsuspecting opponents . . . and Protagoras' artful dodge of it; the fact that logos failed to clarify, and perhaps even begged the question on, its guiding premise in the protreptic and indirect arguments; the defensiveness that has characterized logos's response; and finally, Cleitophon's suggestion to Thrasymachus.)

The confrontation between logos and its accuser, this throwing back of charge and countercharge; is it but a squaring off and a screaming of two separate and hostile voices? If so, there would be nothing particularly distinctive about it; people with opposed views yell at each other all the time. But this particular confrontation is unique for two reasons. First, it represents two fundamentally different ways of looking at the world, both of which deserve to be taken seriously. Second, as we will slowly see, this is a dispute that neither party can win.

Plato, more than any other philosopher, understands the nature of this most fundamental of disputes. He understands that both sides of the ancient quarrel are powerful and have merit. Plato is indeed a champion of logos; Socrates is his hero. But, perhaps surprisingly, Plato is not the single-minded proponent of the "Platonic conception of truth" that the subversives make him out to be. The Platonic conception of logos (of which this book is finally intended to be an exhibition) acknowledges and then incorporates within itself the voice of its accuser. Plato understands the terrible precariousness of logos' assertions. Rather than simply declaring its unconditional goodness, he is willing to ask, "is logos in fact unconditionally good?" Platonic logos is willing to look at itself critically, suspiciously. And the result is a form of logos unlike any other, one that has neither the calm assurance of Aristotle, nor the utter distaste for reason found among the subversives. Both of these are univocal, singularly voiced. But Plato's voice, always expressed in the form of a dialogue, is complex. It praises and then seeks the Truth, but it does not claim to know it. It recommends the life of logos, but does not suppress or forget the voice of its accuser.

Some indication of what I am talking about can be gathered from Plato's very short dialogue, the *Cleitophon*. Here the same character who in the *Republic* offered Thrasymachus a way of avoiding Socrates' refutation is the major speaker. What follows is a translation of the dialogue in almost its entirety.[1]

Plato's Cleitophon

406a   *Socrates:*   Someone has just now told me that Cleitophon, son of Aristonymos, when he was conversing with Lysias, condemned the time he spent with Socrates, while he praised his association with Thrasymachus to the skies.

Cleitophon: Socrates, this fellow did not correctly relate to you the conversations I had about you with Lysias. For while it is true that with respect to some matters I did not praise you, with respect to others I did. And since, even though you pretend not to care, you are obviously blaming me, I would gladly recount these conversations to you myself so that you don't think that I am badly disposed to you. After all, the two of us are alone. For it's possible that you didn't hear the story correctly and so you're harder on me than you should be. So, if you allow me the chance to speak frankly, I'd accept it gladly and be willing to speak.

407a   *Socrates:*   It would be shameful of me not to accept your offer. After all, you're eager to benefit me. For it's clear that once I know in what way I am worse and in what way better, I will pursue and exercise the latter and flee the former to the best of my ability.

Cleitophon: Please listen. Socrates, during the many times that I've associated with and listened to you, I've often been astonished, for in comparison with the run of men you seemed to speak so beautifully. Whenever you rebuked men you sang like a god on the tragic stage saying, "To where, men, do you think you are going? Don't you know that whoever among you invests his entire energy to making money does not do what he should? For your sons, those to whom you will

pass on your wealth, you do not provide teachers of justice who can teach them how to use their wealth properly— assuming, of course, that justice is something that can be taught. And if justice is something to be practiced and exercised, you do not provide your sons with those who will exercise and practice properly with them. Finally, you have not attended to yourselves in this regard. But when you see that you yourselves, as well as your sons, are sufficiently knowledgeable
407c about grammar and culture and gymnastic, which subjects you suppose to comprise a complete education in excellence (*arete*), and yet you are no less vicious concerning money, how is it that you do not despise your current education and seek someone who will help you overcome this lack of real culture?"

"Indeed, it is on account of this dissonance and indolence, and not on account of some problem you might have playing the lyre, that brother deals inharmoniously with brother, and cities fight without measure and do and suffer the worst possible things to one another. . . .

407e Socrates, when I hear you saying these things, I admire them greatly and I praise them wonderfully. And I also praise you when you utter the follow-up to this speech, when you say that the ones who exercise their bodies and disregard their souls are disregarding that which ought to rule and taking too seriously that which ought to be ruled; and when you say that if someone doesn't know how to use something it is better for him to give up using that thing. For example, if someone doesn't know how to use his eyes or ears or any other part of his body, it is better for him neither to hear nor see nor put any other part of his body to any use whatsoever.

408a This point is especially true concerning techne. For whoever does not know how to use his own lyre clearly does not know how to use that of his neighbor; and whoever doesn't know how to use the lyre of others, does not know how to use his own. And this applies to the use of any other instrument or possession.

This speech (*logos*) of yours also ends beautifully when you say that it is better for one who doesn't know how to use his soul to keep his soul quiet and not to live and act on his own. And if such a man has to live, it is better for him to spend his life as a slave rather than as a free man. He should hand over the rudder of his intellect, just as if it were the rudder of a ship, to someone else who knows the techne of steering human beings. This techne you, Socrates, have often called "the techne of politics," saying that it is the same as judging and justice.

I must say that I have hardly ever spoken a word against these or any of your similarly fine speeches. You claim that *arete* is teachable and it is necessary for us most of all to be concerned with ourselves.

408c Nor do I think that at some future point will I say anything against these most beautiful and protreptic speeches. Just as if we were sleeping, they wake us up.

Next, I was determined to hear what follows these initial remarks. At first, however, I did not ask you, Socrates, but your contemporaries and fellow enthusiasts, or comrades, or whatever these fellows should be called. First I interrogated those among this group who are held in highest regard by you. I asked, "what is the logos that comes next?" I imitated your manner and asked them, "Best of men," I said, "how do you interpret the protreptic speech in which Socrates exhorts you toward *arete*? Do you think that this speech alone is all he has and that it is impossible for us to comprehend and grasp the issue completely? Will this be our life-work, to "protrepticize" those who have not yet been "protrepticized?" And will these latter men simply follow suit and protrepticize others? Or should we ask ourselves,

408e 'what comes next?' We might agree that men ought to do this very thing . . . but what comes next? How do we explain how the study of justice should begin?"

"It's as if someone noticed that we were just like children who had no idea what gymnastic and medicine were and then protrepticized us to be concerned for our bodies. This person would censure us by saying that it is shameful to be so concerned about wheat and barley and vineyards and however many other things we do and possess for the sake of the body, while at the same time to have neither a techne nor a procedure by which the body might become as good as possible.

409a For such a techne does exist. And if we were to ask the man protrepticizing us, 'what are these technai?' he would probably answer that they were gymnastic and medicine.

In an analogous fashion, we now ask, 'what is the techne concerned with the *arete* of the soul?' Let it be explained."

The fellow who seemed to be most vigorous in this group responded to these questions and said that this techne is the very one that you hear about from Socrates; it is none other than justice. To this I said, "Don't just tell me its name, but answer me in the following way: someone might say that medicine is a techne. That which issues from this techne is two-fold. On the one hand, there is the continual production of doctors in addition to those who already existed. On the other hand, there is health. The latter, what we call health, is not itself a techne, but is the product (*ergon*) of that techne which both teaches and is taught.[2] The techne of carpentry is similar. Houses are its product and the techne of carpentry is its teachable content."

"Now, let justice be analogous in one respect: it produces just men as do each of the technicians mentioned above. But can we identify the other element, namely that product which the just man is able to produce? Tell me."

409c   As I recall, this fellow answered, "the advantageous." Another one said, "the proper;" another, "the beneficial; and another, "the profitable." I then went back a step and said, "But these names, 'act correctly, be profitable, beneficial, etc.,' are found in each of the technai. But to what all these names refer each techne will articulate a unique something. For example, carpentry will use 'well, beautifully, properly,' specifically with regard to the production of wooden artifacts, which are not themselves the techne. Let the product of justice be articulated in a similar fashion."

Finally, Socrates, one of your comrades who was reputed to speak in the most refined manner, answered me and said that this was the unique product of justice: to create friendship in the cities. When this fellow was asked, he said that friendship is good and never bad. Furthermore, he said that although we apply the name to them, the "friendships" of children and beasts are not genuine friendships. For it had occurred to him that such relationships are more often harmful

409e   than good. To avoid the untenable conclusion that would follow, he said that these relationships were inappropriately described as friendships. For the most truly genuine friendship is obviously likemindedness. When asked if likemindedness means having like opinions or knowledge, he first of all debunked like opinions, for it is necessary that many harmful like opinions arise among men. By contrast, he agreed that friendship is entirely good and the product of justice. The conclusion, he said, was that likemindedness and knowledge, and not opinion, are the same.

410a   At this point we were at a real impasse in the logos, and those who were present were ready to strike at that man and say that the logos had run around in a circle and returned to where it began. They said, "medicine is also a type of likemindedness as are all the technai. Furthermore, the other technai are able to articulate what it is they are about. Whatever the subject matter is of justice or likemindedness, about which you've been speaking, it has eluded us and it is unclear what its product really is."

Finally, Socrates, I raised these questions with you yourself. You told me that justice is harming your enemies and helping your friends. But later it seemed that the just man, since everything he does is for someone's benefit, never harms anyone.

I endured and persisted with these questions, and not just once or twice, but a great many times. But finally I gave up. For I reached the conclusion that of all men you are able most beautifully to protrepticize others into being concerned for *arete*. However, I decided that one of two alternatives had to hold: either you were able to do

410c   only this and nothing more. This is a situation which could come about in any other techne. For example, someone who is not a pilot of a ship could study carefully and compose a eulogy about the great worth of piloting to humanity. This could happen with any of the other technai as well. Someone could perhaps lay upon you the same charge about justice, namely that even though you praise justice beautifully, you are not the least bit knowledgeable about it. Of course, this is not my opinion.

As I said, one of two alternatives has to hold. Either you do not know or you're not willing to share your knowledge with me. Therefore, I think I'll go over to Thrasymachus, and whomever else I can, since I am at such a loss. It's as if I had been protrepticized to study gymnastic and not to disregard my body. Directly following the protreptic logos, you would tell me what sort of regimen my body, which has a particular nature, requires. If only you would desist from your protreptic speeches and give me an analogous account of justice.

410e   Now let it be stated that Cleitophon agrees that it is ridiculous to be concerned with extraneous matters while disregarding the soul, that for the sake of which we go through all our labors. And suppose also that I agree with all the consequences that follow from this initial statement. And while I am speaking I am in no way asking you to behave differently, so that I will continue to praise you in some respects to Lysias and others. But in other respects, I will blame you. Because, Socrates, I will declare that for the man who has not yet been protrepticized, you are most worthwhile. But for the man who has already been protrepticized, you are virtually an impediment in the quest for complete *arete* and happiness.

What is unique, and surprising, about the *Cleitophon* is that it is almost exclusively a *criticism* of Socrates. This fact led many scholars of the past to claim that it was not written by Plato himself, that it was "spurious."[3] After all, they asked, why would Plato write a dialogue in which Socrates, his great hero, the champion of logos, falls silent in the face of the charges leveled at him by Cleitophon? I propose that these critics missed something essential about the Platonic conception of logos. Incorporated within it is a dimension of profound self-criticism. Included within it is precisely Cleitophon's accusation.

Cleitophon states that he both praises and criticizes Socrates. He praises him for composing the finest of protreptic speeches. He enjoys listening to Socrates rebuke other men for not caring enough about *arete* or excellence. Instead of asking, how can I live the best possible life?, most men spend their time trying to make money. Instead of seeking a real education, most men simply accept conventional wisdom and do not probe seriously the value and nature of their lives. No one is better at encouraging such men to cease relying on traditional and thoughtless opinions than Socrates. No one is better at turning men toward the project of logos. Socrates provides rousing, pointed speeches and Cleitophon admires them. Apparently, he shares with Socrates a deep dissatisfaction with traditional wisdom and is willing to step beyond the dictates of convention in order to seek actively the good life.

Cleitophon, however, has been consistently disappointed with "what comes next." Socrates is wonderful at waking men up and encouraging them to pursue *arete*, but he fails miserably when it comes to actually explaining to Cleitophon what justice, what the good life that he praises so beautifully, really is. It is as if someone constantly exhorted him to take care of his body, but failed to teach him or explain the technai of medicine and gymnastic. Without such explanation the exhortation becomes empty: even if he is "converted" and decides to care about his body, how would he know how to do so properly? Analogously, men can be turned by Socrates toward the project of caring about the well-being of their souls, but without some techne to direct this caring, Socrates' protreptic is incomplete. Cleitophon employs the very techne-analogy Socrates himself is accustomed to use: As medicine is to health so justice (interpreted as a techne) is to X. Socrates cannot identify the X, the determinate object or result (*ergon*) of the purported techne and so, as Cleitophon says in conclusion, his value is limited. Socrates is fine, but only for those who are asleep and not yet protrepticized; he can wake these people up. For those who have already been persuaded to question conventional wisdom, and actively seek the good life, he is worthless; he cannot properly identify the techne to which he apparently points.

In sum, Cleitophon admires Socrates' ability to encourage his listeners to ask questions about living a good life. Finally, however, he rejects Socrates because he provides no definite, no technical answers to these questions. As a result of his dissatisfaction, Cleitophon has decided to give up on Socrates and turn toward Thrasymachus; he has given up on logos and turned toward rhetoric.

In an important sense, Cleitophon's accusation is similar to that leveled by Descartes: traditional philosophy, logos, is *nothing but protreptic*. The ancient philosophers, says Descartes, "place virtues on a high plateau and make them appear to be valued more than anything else in the world, but they do not sufficiently instruct us about how to know them" (p. 8). Like Descartes, Cleitophon holds to a singular standard of what counts as knowledge. For him it is techne; clear, certain and reliable knowledge.[4] Socrates' protreptic speeches, while stirring, are for him no more than a passionate description of the goodness of logos. They promise much, but teach nothing. As a result, they are like palaces built upon sand. Socrates praises speeches that he promises will come later. "Pursue logos," he urges, "for it is the source of the good life. Seek the logos of justice itself, goodness itself, beauty itself. Care about your life, your soul; don't just obey orders. Leave the herd and enter into philosophy. Ask questions. Speak and speak some more."

"But where are these further speeches?" asks Cleitophon. "What comes next? Why can't you straightforwardly tell me what justice is? What can't you give me the techne by which I can guide my soul in conformity with reason? I want answers and not just more questions." Socrates urges others to want knowledge about values, about justice. His praise of that desire is beautiful and stirring. But that is all. Instead of teaching he only redirects, or even manipulates, the desires of his audience. He seduces them to philosophy. Philosophy is the desire for being able to say what justice is. If, however, the answer to this question is never given, a desire is all that philosophy is.

Cleitophon implies that there is a basic similarity between sophistry and philosophy: both manipulate their audiences' desires. (Descartes implies this as well by saying of philosophy that it "provides the means of speaking with probability about all things and of being held in admiration by the less learned" [pg. 6].) There is, however, one crucial difference between them: the Sophist acknowledges this (either overtly, as does Callicles, or covertly, as does Protagoras). He admits that his goal is not the truth, but the production of opinions in others. The philosopher, on the other hand, dissembles, or simply does not understand himself. He purports to seek the truth, to be able to articulate what justice is. This, however, he does not actually accomplish, for his speeches are really only protreptic. The philosopher urges his audience to pursue an impossible goal.

Given this similarity and this difference, Cleitophon finds sophistry more attractive. It is, in his eyes, more honest and promising. Since he will never accomplish anything of substance with philosophy and Socrates, he turns to sophistry and Thrasymachus. At least here, armed with the weapon of rhetoric, he will be able to pursue effectively what seems to be his own self-interest.

Socrates falls silent in the face of Cleitophon's charge. Why doesn't he refute, or at least respond to, it? Answering this question, I suggest, will tell us much about the nature (and the limits) of logos. Cleitophon is a powerful interlocutor, and to understand fully his accusation we should turn back to his short speech in the *Republic* which was discussed above.

Thrasymachus, it may be recalled, was a victim of Socratic refutation. He was defeated by Socrates because he (incoherently) maintained both a positive evaluation of techne and his own version of relativism. Cleitophon made a short appearance in that dialogue. He proposed to Thrasymachus that he substitute "what seems to be the advantage to the ruler" for "what is the advantage to the ruler" in his definition of justice. In other words, he proposed that Thrasymachus get rid of all vestiges of objectivity in his account of justice and become a "radical" or thorough relativist. This tactic would have saved Thrasymachus from refutation, for it would have removed one of the two contradictory poles that Socrates detects and then exploits. Thrasymachus, however, rejected Cleitophon's friendly advice. He is, after all, a professional teacher who wants to claim for himself a techne.

What happened to Cleitophon in the *Republic*? He fell silent. He was heard neither from nor about again.[5] Such silence, I propose, is significant. One reason why is that *Socrates' behavior in the* Cleitophon *is the same as Cleitophon's in the* Republic. There is an uncanny mirroring effect between these two dialogues. In the dialogue named after him, Cleitophon is frustrated by what he perceives as Socrates' inability to move beyond protreptic speech. Cleitophon himself has already been "protrepticized" to the extent that he is able to identify conventional wisdom and values as mere opinions. He has been persuaded to rely, not on the traditional standards of the polis, but on his own powers of reason and discourse in order to achieve happiness. But instead of pursuing real wisdom, a truthful account of what is good, as a replacement for the conventional wisdom he has abandoned, he has turned to rhetoric. Rhetoric, at least as Plato understands it, is intimately connected with relativism. Its purpose is to teach men how to speak effectively regardless of what aims they hope to attain. It assists men in pursuing what they *believe* to be to their advantage; it does not teach what truly *is* advantageous.

In the *Republic* Cleitophon asserts his relativism and then falls silent. In the *Cleitophon* he explains why he is a relativist: he is not convinced that logos can transcend its merely protreptic stage or that knowledge can replace opinion. In this dialogue it is Socrates who falls silent. There is a gap between these two men, one that logos does not seem able to mend.

In the *Republic* Cleitophon suggests that the just is what *seems* advantageous to the ruling body. The ruler might decide that it is just to murder everybody over the age of ten or to make philosophers into kings. There is no rational or moral difference between these two acts if justice is strictly a matter of seeming. To put this point in stronger terms, if justice is only a matter of seeming, there is no reason to discuss the respective merits of these or any other conflicting actions. If logos is the attempt to differentiate the true from the false, and the good from the bad, logos is, given Cleitophon's proposal, pointless noise.

Cleitophon dramatically incarnates a fundamental human possibility for Plato. His long speech in the *Cleitophon* shows why he turns away from logos: he is persuaded that Socrates can do no more than exhort his listeners to pursue philosophy and the study of justice. Since Socrates does not seem able to ground such exhortation, Cleitophon sees no difference between him and Thrasymachus. As such, the relativism (the denial of grounds) of the Sophist is preferable. In the *Republic* Cleitophon actually states his thoroughly relativistic proposal. His silence thereafter is fully consistent with his statement. No analysis or rational discussion of his position and its merits would, on his terms, be fruitful.

In neither of these two dialogues is Cleitophon refuted by Socrates. It is in this sense that Plato incorporates Cleitophon's accusation within his own conception of logos. Plato, I suggest, knows that there is a gap here that logos cannot mend. Socrates can refute only those with whom he can converse, and thorough relativists such as Cleitophon can refuse or ignore conversation and yet remain consistent. Philosophical dialogue of the sort Socrates wishes to engender depends upon an unconditional affirmation of logos, a value that for it is "axiomatic." An axiom must be presumed before further arguments can commence. Since all arguments or proofs require that axioms be used, axioms cannot themselves be proven or defended by the arguments they generate. To attempt to do so would beg the question: in the very attempt to prove the axiom the axiom would be assumed.

Precisely this impasse plagues logos and constitutes the gap between Socrates and Cleitophon. Logos must presume that it is good in order to argue that it is good. Therefore, it cannot demonstrate that it is good because such a demonstration would have to assume what it purports to prove, namely that logos is good.

There is no refutation of a thorough relativist for he can, while remaining quite consistent, refuse to acknowledge the goodness of philosophical dialogue, of logos, and then refuse to argue at all. Unfortunately (for logos) there is no argument that can, without begging the question, establish the goodness of argumentation. Socrates can only refute those who, like Thrasymachus, affirm the goodness of such dialogue. (This Thrasymachus did by including within his own position the possibility of attaining knowledge about real advantage. Since he stated that it was possible to differentiate between correct and incorrect laws, he implies that it is reasonable and good to have discussions about value.) By contrast, Cleitophon (like Callicles) is not a teacher but only a practitioner of rhetoric. As such, he feels no obligation to include a comparable affirmation of knowledge in his "position." He cannot be refuted for he does not acknowledge the fundamental axiom presupposed by all argumentation.

Thorough relativism, the enemy of logos, is a deeply serious problem because it testifies to the fact that rational argumentation depends upon a value judgment: that it is good to pursue the argument, to strive to replace opinion with knowledge. It is precisely this judgment that animates Socrates' beautiful speeches. But because it is a value judgment it is subject to rejection by someone asserting that values are relative to the ones upholding them. As a result, the very project of logos now seems dependent upon a judgment that cannot itself be secured by argumentation. In other words, this project is initiated, and perhaps sustained, *not by a demonstration of its value, but by protreptic.* In a certain, frightening, sense, Descartes was right: ancient philosophers do no more than encourage and exhort; they do not actually teach or know.

Cleitophon's presence in the *Republic* is a surd, an irrational interruption, that is never truly removed, even if it remains silent. Indeed, Cleitophon's silence here, and Socrates' in the *Cleitophon*, hint at a terrible truth about logos. Silence looms as an irremediable possibility. It hovers on the horizon of philosophical dialogue, both limiting and threatening it.

I do not only, or even primarily, refer to silence in the literal sense. Instead, I refer to any form of speaking that does not, and cannot, conceive of a reason for itself to continue. Any form of speaking that cannot answer, or at least address, the question "Why should I speak rather than fall silent?" is itself equivalent to "silence" in the sense I use the term. One could, for example, believe there is no reason to speak, but continue to do so for the sake of habit or manners or for the physiological sensation it produces. If, however, there is no reason to speak, no reason to be reasonable, then speaking is finally indistinguishable from, and simply a noisier version of, silence; it is purposeless chatter.[6]

There is a gap, a chasm, that looms between Socrates and Cleitophon.[7] Socrates cannot refute this opponent; and Plato does not disguise this fact. Instead, he integrates it into his dialogue. The whole dialogue, then, becomes a peculiar and complex blend of positions and characters. The most prominent feature of most of Plato's dialogues is their protreptic sheen: "Love and pursue logos," they tell us again and again, "for here lies your happiness." But in many of the dialogues, such as the *Republic*, there is a softly stated but unmistakable presence, one that conditions, that qualifies, that tarnishes the bright luster of the protreptic. This is Cleitophon, a man who rejects the basic axiom of logos and who knows enough about himself to resist the temptation to argue for his rejection. Plato's shortest dialogue is titled after this character (whose name, perhaps ironically, literally means "illustrious voice"). I propose that despite its length it is a work of disturbing importance. Socrates' silence testifies to the precariousness of logos for it forces us to ask, Is it really true that logos is unconditionally good?

B   EROS AND LOGOS

Logos: "My mind begins to wander, to whirl; I think I may go mad. Can this be? I no better than Thrasymachus because I cannot refute Cleitophon? I cannot break beyond this fact. I . . . one voice among many and not a king who with only his words shapes the world? I . . . not unconditionally good? I am but a desire and all desires emanate from the same source, the human beings who desire; and this source, this vast mass of struggle, cannot possibly sustain the claim of being unconditionally good. I fear the old prophet had eyes; I fear I have said too much. Am I guilty of the very crime of which I accused others?"

Logos trembles . . . and well it should. It recalls those moments of discomfort: the begging of the question, Protagoras' artful dodge, the space Cleitophon carves out for himself; an inviolable space immune from Socratic refutation. It is just this immunity that may drive logos mad, for it reveals a weakness not before divined.

Logos, the commitment to finding the truth, has now recognized a most painful truth: It cannot refute the radical, the consistent and self-conscious, relativist. Therefore, logos must admit that, like the relativist, it itself is essentially a matter of desire. It *wants* to say what is right and wrong, true and false. It exhorts its listeners to want the same. But it cannot ground this desire. That is, it cannot prove that as a desire it deserves any privilege or is in any way definitive of being human. Such a demonstration would require that logos prove, without begging the question, that relativism, the "claim" that all desires are ultimately equal in their baselessness and that the realm of human values is therefore no more than an arena for the struggles of power, is false. And this, as we have seen, it cannot do. Therefore, the classic assertion, that logos is unique and more than one desire among many, the vaunted claim that logos is unconditionally good, is called into question.

And yet . . . logos is not yet prepared to relinquish its throne. It has, however, recognized the force of Cleitophon's charge. (This it did in the form of Socrates' silence.) Therefore, if it is to defend itself, it must do so on a different footing than that it initially used. It must part ways with Aristotle who, with clear and happy spirit, articulated a beautiful vision of a world "out there" in which logos was at home. Aristotle's was a theoretical vision of an objective world. Now the emphasis must shift to a world "in here." Logos must take its bearings and build its case from the fact that it is a desire.

What logos will next argue is that, yes, it is but a desire, but that, no, desires are not all equal. Human desire has an ordered structure with logos at the pinnacle. This conclusion will be similar to that offered by Aristotle who stated (in his *Nicomachean Ethics*) that desire is "not empty and vain." Because of this assumption, Aristotle concluded that there must be a "highest good." In other words, he claimed that because desire was not empty and vain, because life was not meaningless, the objects of desire have an order. Some objects must be higher than others and, finally, this sequence must terminate in that which is desired for its own sake. If this were not the case, the objects of desire would proceed indefinitely; nothing would be intrinsically satisfying and desire would be empty and vain.

Aristotle's implicit argument was valid: *If* desire is not empty and vain, if it is not indefinitely expanding or utterly without structure, then some objects of desire are higher than others. But this doesn't say much. Aristotle simply assumed (against potential opponents like Callicles and Cleitophon) that life was "meaningful," that desire had a termination point. But what if he was wrong? Now logos must do more. It must actually demonstrate, rather than simply assume, that desire has a structure. What follows will attempt that task; it will be a "subjective analysis," an analysis of desire itself. What follows is a discussion of a passage from Plato's dialogue, the *Symposium*.[8]

The setting is a drinking party in which the guests entertain themselves with speeches. The topic, they decide, will be eros, a word which in both Greek and English means "love," particularly that love expressed in sexual passion. The task that Socrates and his companions give themselves is to praise eros as fully and accurately as possible. Socrates is the last official speaker and he begins his talk in typical fashion, by interrogating the speaker who immediately preceded him, a poet named Agathon.

Agathon had gone along with a conventional view, that eros is to be praised as a god. Eros, he said, was the most beautiful and beauty loving of all the gods. By examining this assertion, Socrates elicits the following four characteristics of eros. First, eros (says Socrates) is always "of something." Assume P loves. If so, then P loves or desires some A. (The addition of "desires" will be explained shortly.) Eros must have an object. In this regard it is like consciousness. When sensing or thinking, it is impossible not to sense or think of something; similarly, when loving, it is impossible not to love something. To put this in somewhat technical terms, eros is "intentional." (To verify this, one needs only to try an experiment: Try to think without thinking of something. It seems impossible. Now try to love without being directed toward, without loving some object; try simply loving. It is, it seems, impossible. To love is to love something.)

The second characteristic of eros is this: the something, the A, that is loved by P is *not* possessed by P. When I am hungry and desire food, it is because my stomach lacks food. When my stomach is totally full, I feel no hunger. If I am weak or sick, then I desire to be strong or well. The general statement "If P loves A, then P does not possess A" thus seems to hold. Eros is "negative."

Ths statement above, however, cannot quite stand as formulated, for there is an obvious counterexample to it. If I now possess health, I may still desire to be healthy. Socrates explains this by saying if P loves A, and P possesses A, then P desires to possess A in the future. Since this third statement contradicts the second (because it allows P to love and to possess A), we should amend the second: If P loves A, then P does not possess A permanently and completely. If I am healthy and still desire health, it is because health requires continual maintenance to be preserved.

These few remarks (which occur from 199c to 201c) decisively shape Socrates' later discussion, for they disclose the third characteristic of eros: It is essentially temporal. Human beings are caught in the flow of time. We are incomplete, or finite, and aware of our incompleteness. We are continually lacking and so we are continually loving. We love and want what we lack, and our lives are spent in perpetual striving to overcome incompleteness (or finitude). Aristophanes, the famous comic poet and an earlier speaker, had touched upon this theme earlier when he had said, "The desire and the pursuit of the whole is called eros" (192e10). For Aristophanes, however, wholeness was found only in sexual union with a well-matched partner (accompanied by a healthy dose of religous piety). In other words, Aristophones, like most comedians, retained the ordinary meaning of "eros." Socrates does not. For him, Aristophanes' was an insufficient account of eros because, as we will see, human beings can never be fully satisfied, can never achieve the completeness we crave, through intercourse with other human beings.

The first three characteristics all rest on the fourth, which is simply assumed throughout Socrates' discussion. Eros is a desire, a going after its object. Eros is a motive force: it impels the one loving to pursue, to move toward, an object. The Greek word for desire is *epithumia*. Let us, therefore, describe eros as "epithumotic."[9]

Armed with these four characterizations of eros, Socrates refutes Agathon who had said that eros was the most beautiful and beauty loving of the gods. Since eros is of what it lacks, if it is the love of beauty it lacks, and so cannot itself have, beauty. Indeed, it is clearly implied by Socrates' analysis that if eros loves beauty, then it cannot be a god (for in general the gods do not lack anything and so they surely should not lack beauty). Agathon quickly admits that his own account cannot be sustained. Socrates then dispenses with him and tells a story.

He had once, he says, been instructed in erotic matters by a priestess named Diotima. She had put him through an interrogation in much the same way that Socrates himself had examined Agathon. Socrates too had once believed that eros was a god, both beautiful and beauty loving. When he learned that eros could not be such he was at a loss. If eros was not good and beautiful, he asked, was it then ugly and bad? If eros was not an immortal god, was it then mortal? Diotima rebuked him sharply for thinking only in these extreme terms. Socrates, she says, had ignored the possibility of the "in-between." Eros is inbetween a human and a god, the mortal and the immortal. It is a "daimon," a spirit (201e–202e).

Diotima devotes the rest of her speech to articulating the structure of this daimon, this "spiritual" force that shapes human lives. She is most concerned with explaining the objects of eros. This makes sense: if eros is intentional, then it is precisely the capacity to enter into relationships with objects. Therefore, to explain the structure of eros means explaining the nature and order of its objects.

The first statement Diotima makes is that eros has as its object "beautiful things" (204d3). Quickly, and without argument, she substitutes "the good" for the "beautiful" (204e1). (This substitution is not quite as arbitrary as it sounds: the Greek word for beautiful, *kalos*, has "moral" overtones.) If P loves, P loves and desires to possess A. If P loves and desires A, it is because A is felt or believed to be good (to be attractive, beautiful). P expects that attainment of A will result in a state of affairs better than the one not including A. This can be reformulated (in terms used earlier): the object of P's eros is the attainment of "happiness" (*eudaimonia*: 204e7), that state of affairs achieved when good things, beautiful things, are possessed. It is, therefore, what we all want.

All this may sound quite "idealistic." But in fact it is not. From the thief to the best of women, all action is directed toward some goal that is thought to bring advantage. This notion of advantage, here called the good or the beautiful, can be conceived in an indefinite number of ways. But the point is that human beings always go after what they take to be good. In other words, Diotima has added a fifth characteristic to the list: Desire is "teleological" in the sense that the object for the sake of which, toward which, human beings move must be "judged" to be good by them. This process of judging is rarely made articulate. The thief who steals the car rarely bothers to attempt to articulate why he believes (incorrectly) that such an action is good. But he does believe, however inarticulately, that what he does is for his good. If he did not, he would not do it. Diotima's point is that, in principle, every action propelled by desire could be made articulate. If P desires to move toward A, it is because P "thinks," however inarticulately, that A is good. If P did not think A were good, P would go elsewhere. In sum, "human beings love nothing other than the good" (205e7–206a1).[10]

The next stage of Diotima's analysis begins with a crucial transition. If P loves A, A is thought or felt to be good and so P desires A to be his own in order to be happy. Furthermore, P desires A *always* to be his own (206a9). The desire for what is good is the desire for the permanent possession of what is good. Soon this is reformulated even further: eros is eros of immortality (207a3), in the form of the immortal possession of the good.

At a first hearing this description sounds farfetched, even mystical, and far from the ordinary lives of human beings. Does it make any sense to say that we want to be immortal? If it does, it is because of the earlier discussion Socrates had with Agathon. There it was agreed that eros is epithumotic and necessarily contains within it a negative moment: we desire what we do *not* have. Eros is teleological: we desire what is good. Eros is essentially temporal: we desire good things whose possession extends into the future. Ultimately, what we do not have is immortality. Immortality, therefore, is the ultimate object of desire. It is what we all want whether we say, admit, know it or not.

Think of it this way: If you ever got totally what you wanted, you would cease to desire. Since desire is a necessary condition of life, if you ever got totally what you wanted you would cease to be alive as a human being. This can mean one of two things: Either you would be dead or you would become immortal. Rarely do human beings want to die. Therefore, insofar as you desire to get totally what you want, you desire immortality.

Perhaps Diotima's position can be made more clear by considering a possible objection to it. Assume a woman desires some object (A) even though, or just because, it is an object only to be temporarily possessed. A woman might desire to scale a mountain even though she knows she must return to the plains. She might argue that mountain climbing is made even more attractive just because she must return to the plains. Diotima's response could take the following form: Assume A is an object that fulfills a desire. If the woman desires to possess A on a temporary basis, there must be some reason why the woman does not desire A on a permanent basis. There must be some desirable object B that supplements, replaces, or conditions the desirability of A. But A has been assumed to be fulfilling and so it should not require any supplementation. Therefore, either A is not fulfilling, in which case some other object (B) is more desirable, or A must be desired as a permanent possession. (If the latter option is chosen, then the same analysis would be applied to B.)

The mountain climber might say, "You're crazy. Immortality is the furthest thing from my mind. I want to climb a mountain, but I do not want this as a permanent possession; part of the thrill of the mountaintop is that I know I must return to the plains." If the woman says this, she actually denies that what she wants is to climb a mountain. The mountaintop (call it A) only seems to be the object of her desire; in reality, she desires to have a complex feeling that includes both the thrill of the mountaintop and the security of the plains (call it B). What she wants is the complex object A + B (call it C). This, not A, is what she wants. If she argues that she wants C only temporarily, some other object, D, will arise, and then we will have to say that she really wants C + D, or E. And if she thinks about it she will have to admit that, finally, it is E that she wants . . . and wants as a permanent possession.

An opponent might object: "What if there is no termination point; what if we desire an indefinite array of objects, none of which we desire permanently?" On this account, we love the seeking of pleasures and goods and neither permanence nor total satisfaction. For the opponent, the fact that the objects of desires neither are orderly nor terminate is not a problem but a pleasure. Again, however, the opponent cannot explain why any object is not in itself totally fulfilling. Why is there a need to return to the plains at all? Why not perish on mountaintops? Human beings are restless and never quite satisfied; we move on. We do so, not because all objects are equally unfulfilling, but because we seek an object that is completely fulfilling. If this weren't the case (if this weren't the belief that implicitly is operative in us), then there would be no motive force to keep us going from one object to the next.

It is our temporality, the fact that we are in and of time, that makes Diotima's account compelling. It is the awareness of our temporality that shapes and pushes forth our actions. Only because we are aware of the flow of time in which we are caught do we move, strive to achieve, push ourselves forward.

I wake up and realize that this morning feels much the same as yesterday's. I realize that soon this morning will disappear and become tomorrow, that I am caught in a flow that cannot be stopped, cannot be reversed. That even my youngest child will soon age. I look back at yesterday's morning and realize it is gone, vanished; only a memory, usually dim, remains. And I understand that this very morning will soon be an equally dim yesterday. I imagine my dying and realize that just before its moment this very morning will be as insubstantial as yesterday's morning is now. I imagine my grandfather, soon to die, and understand that his looking back at his past is no different than mine. We are all caught.

This is a very common feeling. We think about dying and the flowing away of our lives. Often it is easy to feel swept away in the current of time and sympathize with the famous lines of the deranged Macbeth:

> To-morrow, and to-morrow, and to-morrow,
>   Creeps in this petty pace from day to day,
>   To the last syllable of recorded time;
>   And all our yesterdays have lighted fools
>   The way to dusty death. Out, out, brief candle!
>   Life's but a walking shadow, a poor player
>   That struts and frets his hour upon the stage
>   And then is heard no more; it is a tale
>   Told by an idiot, full of sound and fury,
>   Signifying nothing.

If Diotima is wrong, then Macbeth is right. If there is no way to get out of time, then time is but a succession of "syllables" pacing toward their end. Diotima tells us that we desire life to be more than a petty path of yesterdays leading to dusty death. Macbeth has lost that desire; and he is a madman. We desire to escape, to stand outside, the flow of time. When Diotima says this she is not being overly idealistic or mystical. She is being realistic about ordinary human experience. We want to jump out of time. Only by understanding this desire can we hope to understand, and affirm, who we are.

But of course there is a basic problem. How can we, ever aging, "jump out of time?" What sense could this phrase possibly make? How can we gain access to or make contact with that which is not finite? At this point a metaphor takes command of the passage: Human beings are pregnant. Our lives are spent in giving birth to that which will remain when we are gone. The parent's child, the family legacy, the fame earned on the basketball court, the poet's poem . . . all represent the human urge to overcome finitude. As Aristophanes had put it, even in sexual embrace the soul desires something else that it cannot articulate, but only intuit, namely wholeness (192d). Diotima supplies the articulation that the comedian leaves out. She is willing to explain how it is that finite beings desire and attempt to give birth to that which is immortal.

It is here that Diotima launches into what has become known as the "ascent passage" (210a–212a). Here she supplies the analysis of desire, of eros, as a hierarchical structure. By so doing, she permits logos to agree with its accuser that it is a desire *and* to deny the further and most damaging charge that it is on a par with all other desires. If desire is structured hierarchically, then logos, through a psychological argument, can still make a grand bid to occupy the pinnacle.

The Ascent Passage

210a4   He who is to proceed correctly in this matter [the initiate] must begin, when young, to go toward beautiful bodies and first, if the one guiding guides correctly, he must love one body [stage 1] and there engender beautiful logos [stage 2].[11] Next he must realize that the beauty found in any single body is kindred to that found in any other body, and if it is necessary for him to hunt the beautiful in form, it is silly not to suppose that the beauty in all bodies is one and the same. Having had this insight, he must become a lover of all beautiful bodies and slacken his excessive love of one by being contemptuous and counting it something small.

210b6   After this, it is necessary [for the one proceeding correctly] to suppose that the beauty in souls is more honorable than that in body [stage 3]. The result of this is that even if someone is but slightly attractive, if he is fine in his soul he will be satisfying and the one proceeding correctly will love and care, and seek and give birth to such logos that makes the young better. As a result, he will be constrained to behold the beautiful in institutions and laws and to see that the beautiful is all bound together in kinship [stage 4]; and so he will suppose the beauty of the body to be something small.

210c6   After institutions it is necessary [for the one guiding] to lead [the initiate] to the sciences in order that he might see the beauty of the sciences [stage 5]. And looking at beauty on a grand scale, no longer is he a trivial and worthless slave who loves only an individual, either the beauty of a child or of some man or one institution, but turning towards and seeing the great sea of the beautiful he gives birth to much beautiful and magnificent logos and many thoughts in the abundance of philosophy [stage 6].

210d6   This [the intiate] does until being strengthened and nourished he looks upon one particular sort of knowledge, which is of the following sort of beauty. Try to pay attention now as closely as you can. For whoever has loved properly up to this point, and has seen the beautiful things in proper order and has thus reached the telos of the erotic journey, suddenly sees a beauty amazing in its nature.

210e4   And this, Socrates, is that for the sake of which all the previous labors were. First of all, it always is, and it neither comes to be nor passes away; nor does it increase or diminish; nor is it beautiful in one way, but ugly in another; nor is it sometimes beautiful and sometimes not; nor is it beautiful relative to something, but ugly relative to something else so that it is beautiful to some but ugly to others. Nor in turn will the beauty appear to him like a face or a hand or anything else that partakes of the body; nor is it a logos or a science; nor does it exist in any other place, for example in an animal or in the earth or the heavens or anywhere else; but itself together with itself it is always singularly formed and the rest of the beautiful things in some way participate in it. Unlike any which come to be and pass away, it neither becomes more nor less, and it suffers nothing.

Diotima's account is not an idealistic or "other-worldly" story of mystical transcendence. Instead, it is an analysis of what happens during the development of a hypothetical (and accessible) human desire. Not surprisingly, the "initiate," the one being initiated into the mysteries of eros, begins with the love of a single body. What is surprising is the fact that this first stage, this first and most familiar desire, soon slackens and its object is counted as "something small." Why? Is Diotima a prude who finds bodies distasteful? I don't think so. After the very first stage of loving individuals "beautiful logos" is generated. Eros, Diotima rightly explains, does not remain mute. We speak to our loves, call them "beautiful," tell why we love. Bodies, in and of themselves, simply do not satisfy for very long. For whatever reason, the urge is soon felt "to give birth" to logos which supplements, and soon comes to overwhelm, touch.

Our hypothetical initiate has felt the urge to speak. He generates a beautiful logos. As a result, he comes to realize that the individual body beside his is not totally satisfying. And so he moves to stage 2, love of all beautiful bodies. It is not obvious what Diotima means here. Does she allude to a bisexual Don Juan? Probably not. More likely she indicates that the production of logos leads to the realization that the extension of the word "beautiful" far outstrips any single body. What comes to the fore here is what she calls "the beautiful in form." Because of our talking we come to realize that what we love when we love even a single body is not what it seems to be.

The initiate says to his beloved, "I love you because you are beautiful." This is a logos, a speech produced by eros. The speech provides a means for the initiate to come to a realization: The word "beautiful" he has used does not exclusively refer to the body lying beside his. It refers to all bodies that can be described as "beautiful." There is a movement implied by logos, a movement from particularity (this beautiful body right here) to universality (to the form of beauty shared by all beautiful bodies). Language drives us upward, away from particularity. It forces us to realize that what we want is not an individual; we want more.

This first transition of the ascent passage, from stage one to two, is paradigmatic of the whole process of ascent. It is because we talk that the objects of our eros change. Logos, which is produced by human erotic energy, provides a means for having a "realization." Logos functions like a lens through which we see the objects we love. When there is a disparity between what we are saying and what we are loving, then a need is felt to move on. A single beautiful body simply isn't satisfying to one who speaks, for speaking refers to the beautiful in form. By speaking the initiate realizes (sees) that the single body does not fully satisfy and in this sense must be counted as something small.

(A warning: It is obviously not necessary that every person who loves come to this realization. It is possible that someone can spend an entire life loving only particular bodies. What Diotima wishes to explain is the structure of the process that is engendered by dissatisfaction at the various stages. The motive force animating such dissatisfaction is eros and it finds its expression in logos. Once the initiate comes to realize that there is a discrepancy between the logos used to comment upon his beloved at a particular stage and that beloved itself, he feels a lack and is driven forward, upward. He is driven to harmonize his logos and his eros. That the initiate feels so dissatisfied is a contingent matter; it need not occur. Diotima's objective is to explain what follows when it does occur.)

The initiate goes on to stage three, the love of souls. Here there is another realization, namely that the object of eros is not bodily at all. A body is necessarily particularized and the initiate's love is now for the beautiful in form, for the universal. Therefore, he must redirect his eros to the soul, which he takes to be the locus of universality. The soul, not the body, is the origin of logos, and it was the generation of "beautiful logos" that sparked the initial drive toward universality. Our initiate now realizes that genuine satisfaction comes through talking. As a result, he can be attracted by someone (like Socrates) whose body is ugly but whose soul is beautiful.

This realization brings with it stage four, the love of institutions and laws or, we might say, the love of the polis. Here eros is not concerned with individuals at all, for the polis is not simply an aggregate of particular bodies. It is a unified entity capable on its own of commanding the loyalty and passions of its citizens. The political person loves, not individuals, but the "soul" of the polis, its principles, ideals, history. These are disclosed through logos, which is (or at least used to be) the medium of political life.

Although she is quite vague about this stage, it is possible to make sense of what Diotima is talking about here. The process of wanting more, sparked by our talking, takes us beyond individual bodies to souls. Again, this is not idealism or prudishness; it is a description of what happens to people with powerful desires. They want something more than individuals. They want to be talked about. They want their words to reach far. They want to be recognized by the polis, and not just by their individual beloveds. Such recognition can take many forms; one might desire fame, political power, literary influence, the good feeling of deeds applauded as well done. Diotima does not spell any of this out. But her basic point, that because of logos the objects of eros progress upward, is clear and compelling.

Diotima is virtually silent about both the fourth ("the political") and the fifth stage of the ascent. The latter is only described as "the beauty of the sciences." She appears eager to arrive at the sixth and highest stage in the development of eros, philosophical logos. Politics and the sciences are briefly mentioned and then soon left behind. We are not told why. An obvious inference is that it is because neither is fully satisfying, and the ascent passage presents the structural development of a soul in search of genuine satisfaction. But why are these two human activities unsatisfying? First, to politics.

(I label stage four as "the political" even though I just acknowledged that there are many ways of interpreting what Diotima means here. I do this for two reasons. First, "political" is a very broad term. It refers to all public activity directed not toward the privacy of individuals, but towards the polis. Second, I think that when she says "institutions and laws" Diotima has politics [in a rather straightforward sense] in mind. The Athenians were an intensely political people, and it was a given that the most ambitious among them would seek political recognition. [In Greek, the word for "ambitious" is *philotimos*, loving of honor.] In what follows, then, I am presenting in skeletal form a Platonic critique of political activity.)

In concrete political terms, the polis always suffers from factionalism. It is riddled with contention and can never become either fully harmonious or just. This is due precisely to the erotic nature of human beings. There are always individuals (like Callicles) who seek "to have more" than their fair share.[12] There is among some of the citizens an urge to tyrannize, a desire for power. This is simply a specific application of Diotima's general teaching: eros is the desire for completeness, for total satisfaction. And one variant of such a desire is political. As Socrates puts it in the *Republic*, "eros has from old been called a tyrant" (573b6). Eros drives, it pushes; those with the strongest desires desire all. Political eros, therefore, issues in the desire for complete rule, for tyranny.

The polis is a conglomerate of competing desires, of competing speeches. Each politician speaks to the public (or, in a system less democratic than the Athenians', to his competitor), but only to advocate a specific political program. The goal is not realization of a universally just city, but the fulfillment of a particular desire. Eros cannot be controlled, these speeches cannot be purged of their particularity, and so the city cannot be made either fully just or secure.[13] Political logos, therefore, is necessarily limited and unsatisfying. The political realm is a cauldron of competition. If a politician's goal is total satisfaction, he has gone into the wrong business.

This point can be reformulated: Earlier we saw that eros seeks that which is immortal and so nonhuman. Since the city is strictly a human affair, eros cannot be satisfied through politics. Upon realizing this, the initiate must again metamorphize the object of his eros. He turns to the sciences.

Diotima is almost totally silent here about stage five. Presumably the vision of beauty gained through the study of the sciences is a form of intellectual satisfaction. Imagine the following scenario. For years our hypothetical initiate was driven by a desire to make a career in the polis. He directed his considerable ambition toward political activity. But he finally became frustrated. Politics, he learned, always requires compromise and capitulation and less than perfect solutions to its problems. The political man is forever pitted against others of his kind. His logos must, therefore, continually take into account what these others will say. Politics finally becomes ugly and after a while our initiate realizes that he desires something clean, something complete. In response he turns away from the city and toward any one of the particular sciences such as history, mathematics, or biology. Here he engages an object free from the hurries of human interference. The object doesn't vary, doesn't tantalize. The logos his science affords him need not direct itself to other human logoi that aim to thwart it. There is no need to compromise. He studies and learning pleases him.

But soon even this experience becomes unsatisfying. We wish Diotima had said more about why. It must be because, like politics, the sciences are partial and eros desires completeness. The problem is specifying the exact nature of their incompleteness. Perhaps this is a result of the fact that the sciences proceed on the basis of unproven assumptions (axioms), or categorical distinctions that are not made explicit. Perhaps the individual sciences are unable to give a full account of their foundations and what exactly it is that makes them sciences. Perhaps it is because they cannot give an account of their own goodness. In any case, they are partial, they "cut off" a portion of reality and study it. Biology, for example, studies only one small subject: living beings. Mathematics is only concerned with abstract magnitudes. Our initiate, a man driven by eros, wants more. He wants a logos of all things. He turns toward philosophy, the love of wisdom. The initiate turns away from, for example, biology, mathematics, or history, and toward "the great sea of the beautiful" where "he gives birth to many beautiful and magnificent logoi and thoughts in unstinting philosophy."

What is the object to which the initiate finally turns? To what does this philosophical logos refer? Typically this is called by scholars "the Idea (or Form) of the beautiful," although this phrase itself is not used here. At the pinnacle of the ascent, the initiate sees a "certain beauty" which is unchanging, complete, absolute (that is, nonrelative). This is "beauty itself," and it is the only object capable of satisfying fully human desire. Beauty itself is that which makes possible the beauty found in all particular objects; all these objects "participate" in it. It is perfect beauty found not in any particular manifestation, but only in the "Idea."[14]

Philosophy, the attempt to articulate the vision of beauty itself, is the attempt to satisfy the highest human desire. The only object capable of accomplishing this is the one that allows for no limitation. Only beauty itself, understood as an object of human eros, an eros that speaks, will produce a satisfying logos. Diotima describes philosophy as "unstinting." Unlike all others, philosophical logos does not run out. At every other stage of the ascent frustration had to occur. At stage one, for example, there was a discrepancy between the speech that expresses the love the initiate had for his beloved, and his beloved. His speech used the word "beautiful," a word that would describe all beautiful objects. But the object of his eros at that stage was a particular body: His logos and the object of his logos did not harmonize. Only at the highest stage of the ascent, in philosophy, is there a harmony between the logos and its object. Because its object is complete, perfect, singularly formed, philosophical logos addresses that which is commensurate with its need for total satisfaction. According to Diotima, philosophy is the highest human activity, for it and only it has as its object that which is unchanging, immortal; that toward which eros can direct all its energy without fear of its object failing to satisfy.

Diotima is a kind of inverse Freudian. She would say that latent within sexual attraction is the love of wisdom, of beauty itself; that Don Juan is a repressed philosopher. What we *really* love when we love (when we speak about what we love) is nothing particular. We really want to articulate what is permanent and unchanging within our experience. Diotima urges human beings to desire what we really desire. She urges us to know ourselves and thus to acknowledge the desire for immortality. Such self-knowledge, knowledge of the subjective constitution of human desire, confirms the goodness of logos. We are what we love and this, if understood properly, is wisdom. Therefore, only philosophy, the love of wisdom, adequately expresses the restless urgings of an eros that speaks.

The objects of eros can be structured hierarchically. All human beings are erotic; we want, we love. We begin in the love of individual bodies. Virtually all of us begin to talk and thus produce (or "give birth to") a logos. Insofar as the logos attempts to express or comment upon the loving relationship, it forces the lover to count his beloved "something small." For logos bespeaks more than individuals. The discrepancy between the object of eros and the logos about it drives us forward, toward the city, toward science, finally into philosophy. Logos is the vehicle of this erotic ascent. Therefore, logos is good insofar as it, and only it, allows for the complete expression of desire.

All this implies that Cleitophon was wrong—or, at least, not totally right. It is true that Socrates' protreptic speeches, like those of the Sophist, address themselves to the desires of his audience. But unlike the Sophist, Socrates urges men and women to actualize the proper nature of their desire. Because the objects of desire can be ordered hierarchically (a contention the Sophist would deny), Socratic protreptic is not empty or vain; it is efficacious in urging us to pursue with logos the proper and most satisfying object of our desire.

Logos has been humbled, but not defeated. It still has the strength to claim its throne. It may be a desire, but it is the highest desire. Logos still stands. It has confronted its accuser and seen within his very accusation a basis for hope. Through its subjective or psychological argument, it has weathered the storm of Cleitophon.

C THE PHILOSOPHER AND THE POET

But there are problems. For anyone who has followed the course of this book, for all those potential accusers, these are predictable. First, one could argue that Diotima's analysis of eros simply recasts Aristotle's assertions about human nature and the highest good (discussed above in I.A.1.) into metaphorical terms. Even though her treatment is a subjective one that takes its bearings from the human being who desires, she approaches eros as if it were an object in the world to be analyzed. By so doing she is open to the same set of objections previously directed at Aristotle. How does Diotima know eros is structured as she says it is? Her speech is a set of assertions about an object. She speaks as if her access to this object were unimpeded, as if language can with ease articulate this "thing" in the world as it is. But what if it can't? Diotima speaks as if there were a "human nature" that is teleologically structured. But is there? Do people really love the way Diotima says they do, or is she just reiterating the "classical assertion" and foisting upon an unsuspecting audience her own conception of how a human being should love? Does Diotima deny and repress the polymorphous wonder of human eros?

There are other objections. As admitted above, the transitions between the various stages of the ascent passage are contingent. For example, it is easy to imagine someone not moving from love of bodies to the love of the polis, and then leaving politics to study a particular science: there is no necessity that binds the movement between these stages. If this is the case, then in what sense can eros be said to have a structure? It is of course possible that someone *might* go through the development Diotima proposes. But the fact that someone might do so hardly certifies the further claim that this is the very nature of eros. And if this latter, very strong, claim cannot be substantiated, then Diotima does not actually advance the cause of logos any further. Logos remains but one desire among many, and not the culmination of a hierarchical structure.

Another version of the accuser's objection would focus on Diotima's contention that eros has a termination point, a highest object. Did Diotima beg the question in order to reach this conclusion? Did she assume what she purported to prove, namely that eros has a hierarchical structure? If so, she simply repeated the classical assertion of Aristotle and is thus subject to the same objection he faced; she assumed, rather than proved, that desire is not "empty and vain."

No doubt there are other problems with Diotima's account of eros. There is, however, a way of summarizing these many difficulties faced by the ascent passage (faced by the second attempt of logos to resecure its throne). In the *Symposium* Socrates is confronted by (at least) three types of people. There are sophists, a technician (in the form of a doctor), and poets.[15] As has been argued throughout this book, these three types share a basic conviction, namely that the human world of significance is produced. (The Sophists and the poets are explicit proponents of this position; the technician embraces it as the "flip side" of his view.) In other words, all three types of opponents are "poeticists." What this means is that at least in terms of its characters the *Symposium* presents a version of the "ancient dispute" between philosophy and poetry. This is, however, more than just an observation about the dialogue's dramatic background; it is the perspective of the poeticist that best encapsulates the objections to be brought against the ascent passage.

The poeticist would object: "Diotima, there's one enormous problem with what you describe, and it has to do with the various objects of eros that you propose. How do we know that this initiate of yours didn't *make them all up?* Your analysis of eros speaks only from the side of the subject: you tell me what the initiate wants. But you don't tell me whether what he wants actually exists. And if you can't tell me this, then your story is in big trouble. Isn't it possible that the 'Idea of Beauty,' which finally is the telos of your entire account, is just a 'fiction'? After all, you yourself admit that this is a psychological argument. Why, then, should I believe that all these objects of desire aren't just figments of a hyperactive imagination? Furthermore, and worse, if these objects are all made, then no one of them is higher than any other; they all share the same essential stamp of human production. The making is all, and any standard one would use to measure such objects would itself be made; the making goes on and on. Don't misunderstand. I love the productive imagination. Your problem is not that you made up the Idea of Beauty; rather, it's that you pretend that the Idea of Beauty isn't made at all, that it just exists out there, itself by itself, to be seen by the philosopher. You pretend that you're different from us, but in fact you're just like us—you manufactured the Idea."

The ascent passage can only succeed in defending the goodness of logos, can only argue that logos is the pinnacle of desire, if it can establish the fact that the Idea of Beauty actually exists independently of human being and is not a fiction. (For if this is not the case, then there is no reason to privilege philosophical logos.) The passage, however, does not comment on the reality or nature of the objects the initiate desires. Instead, it is a psychological analysis, an account of eros. (And since the stages it postulates are not necessary, even as a psychological account it provides at best only a probable story.)

Consider this: grant Diotima the assumption that human beings desire immortality. Even if this is true, it does not imply that anything immortal actually exists. Human beings may be (as Spinoza suggests) predisposed to delude themselves, to want objects that do not exist. What we want is not necessarily what is. The ascent passage finds the initiate wanting that which is beyond the individual, namely the universal. But what is the status of these universals? Are they real, or are they fabricated by the initiate himself? The ascent passage does not say.

To reformulate the poeticist's objection: Throughout the ascent passage there is continual interplay between the metaphors of giving birth and of seeing. For example, the initiate, in the transition from stage one to two, gives birth to a logos which in turn lets him see (or "realize") that individual bodies are unsatisfying.[16] The initiate sees the discrepancy that obtains between his logos, which beckons toward the universal, and the object of his eros, which at this early stage is only particular. Logos is the vehicle that propels human eros toward a more universal object. But logos is a human production. Therefore, the question should arise, how is it possible to distinquish between what logos allows us to see and what logos produces? In other words, how do we know that what we talk about exists "out there" to be seen and is not just a product of our verbal imaginations? How do we know that there is anything out there whose impressions we receive untainted by our productive apparatus? Do we see and discover, or do we make?

Contrast the highly metaphorical ascent passage with the quite straight-forward statement from Aristotle cited earlier:

> Spoken words are symbols of the affections (*pathemata*) of the soul, and written words are symbols of spoken words. And just as written words are not the same for all men, so spoken words are not the same for all. However, those first things of which these spoken words are signs, namely the affections of the soul, are the same for all, and the things of which these [the affections of the soul] are likenesses are also the same (*De Interpretatione*, 16a3–8).

Aristotle's is a confident and unperturbed vision of the real. He broaches no doubt that the "first things," the psychic affections of which spoken words are signs, are universally present in human experience. And this is because these affections are reflective of a set of invariable objects in a common and constant world out there with which human beings successfully interact. Plato, at least insofar as he speaks through Socrates' story of Diotima, is more honest: he gives the subject more of its due. That is, he grants that the origin of logos is in the human subject, understood as an erotic agent, and not the world. To say this does not in itself preclude logos from viewing, without distorting, objects in the world. But it does raise a problem to which the opponent of logos will point: what is the ontological status of those objects? Is beauty itself an entity that exists independently of the human subject, or is it a mental or linguistic construct and thus dependent on the subject? Diotima's account cannot answer this question, for the Idea of Beauty—in the final stage of the ascent—is broached only insofar as it appears as the ultimate object of desire. The ascent passage speaks only from the side of the subject. As suggested above, the statement "You desire immortality" tells us only about you and not whether there actually exists any immortal object.

Logos originates not in a cognitive capacity for the apprehension of objects, but in the desire to give birth to beautiful speeches. Like a child, it is born from passion. Its object never simply shows itself. Instead, it shows itself only through the lens manufactured by the erotic energy of the initiate. The lens is like neither a window nor a mirror; it is more like a kaleidoscope (from the Greek: *kalos*, beautiful, *eidos*, form, *skopein*, to view). It sees what it wants to see, namely what is beautiful and most satisfying.

These conclusions are really quite strange (and the key point, one that will become paramount in Chapter III and will establish Plato as the hero of this book, is that Plato himself, the supposed champion of logos, is the author of this strangeness), for now the question must be asked, *What differentiates philosophy/logos from poetry?* How is it possible to determine when the desiring agent makes it all up and when he sees what is really out there to be seen? The interplay of the two metaphors of birth and sight can now either be denounced by the poeticist as incoherent or announced as evidence that Diotima is herself a poeticist. By contrast, poetry can still be denounced by the philosopher as nothing but embellished sophistry. The ancient dispute still rages.

How should we confront this dispute that plagued Plato and even today frames our most pressing debates? Logos is at stake. It no longer knows who it is. And we, the spectators, do not yet know who will triumph, the philosopher or the poet. How can the ancient dispute be resolved?

I propose the following: Let us trace the dispute back to its earliest (Greek) roots and examine it in its most primitive manifestation. Let us consider the differences between the very first philosopher of the West, Thales, who lived around 585 b.c.e., and the first fully self-conscious poet, Hesiod, who lived even earlier. By juxtaposing these two archaic voices we will see that the very origin of philosophy cannot be understood without a (hostile) reference to poetry. The dispute is thus essential in constituting the manner in which philosophy conceives of itself. Furthermore, by scrutinizing its earliest formulation we will come to understand the basic terms of the dispute, terms that reappear in its subsequent manifestations. To illustrate this second point, I will digress later in the chapter to compare Hesiod with Derrida. We will see again how today's subversives were prefigured in antiquity by the Greek poeticists. The ancient dispute, originally waged in Greece, still helps us situate today's most influential thinkers.

Standard versions of the history of philosophy invariably state that Thales of Miletus, who lived around 585 b.c.e., was the first philosopher. Quite simply, "Every history of philosophy begins with Thales." The reason Thales has maintained this durable appellation is that, unlike all before him, he "evidently abandoned mythic formulations: this alone justifies the claim that he was the first philosopher, naive though his thought still was." Thus, it has long been assumed that the year 585 was as significant as any other in Western history. Before that, thought was constrained by its expression in myth; it was only after 585 that the "first completely rationalistic attempts to describe the nature of the world took place."[17]

There are two features of this familiar claim that make it more extraordinary than it may initially appear. First, we have no writings whatsoever that can be definitively ascribed to Thales. All knowledge of his thought is based upon a limited "doxography," reports about him made by ancient commentators, some of whom are themselves unreliable. It is even possible that Thales himself wrote nothing at all. This was, at least, "a persistent tradition in antiquity."[18] Thus, the unanimously titled first philosopher is in the peculiar position of having no written texts that can undeniably be called his own.

Second, given the absence of such texts, the claim that Thales was the first philosopher can only be made negatively. Since there is no corpus that can be employed to identify him positively, the determination of who Thales was can only be made by asserting who he was *not*. As the citations above indicate, he was not a mythmaker. "*Muthos*" in Greek means "story." The mythmaker made up stories to tell about the world. He was, in other words, a poet, a maker. As a result, the first philosopher can be identified only by the declaration that he was *not a poet*.

The precise relationship between mythic poetry and early Greek philosophy is an issue fraught with scholarly controversy. Questions as to what Thales "really" said or to what extent the mythic tradition actually exerted an influence on the philosophers from Miletus have repeatedly been asked.[19] They are not the issue here. The concern of this book is not "philological" or historical in the narrow sense. Instead, its goal here is to reflect on the extraordinary fact that the history of Western philosophy originates with Plato's "ancient quarrel," with a distinction between philosophy (logos) and poetry (*muthos*).

Thales, a name with no texts attached to it, has become a repository or mirror for the tradition's understanding of itself. Thus "he" has become a uniquely revealing illustration of the demarcation that logos constructs between itself and that which is "different." It is just this difference that (as our reading of the ascent passage showed) encapsulates the basic opposition from which our drama is composed and upon which we will now reflect.

In order to engage in this reflection the Thalenic logos, or a reconstructed version of it, will be compared with that of Hesiod, a purely poetic or mythic "thinker" who flourished around 700 b.c.e. (and with whom the Milesians are often compared.) Hesiod "sang" rather than spoke rationally. His was the archetypal *muthos*, a story of the doings of the gods. It was inspired or given to him by the Muses, the divine daughters of Zeus and Mnemosyne, and was not the conclusion of argument or observation, two "methods" frequently ascribed to Thales. Hesiod wrote, not in the declarative prose sentences in which traditional philosophy has invariably expressed itself, but in the dactylic hexameter of poetry.[20]

The standard reconstruction of the Thalenic logos finds him writing in prose, in words that were "*psiloi*," "bare" of poetic embellishment. As such, despite its primitiveness, the Thalenic logos is akin to the traditional model of logos, of legitimate rational speech: he simply told his audience what he believed was the case, making no recourse to divine mediation, using unaided reason to discover and unembellished language to express the nature of things. By contrast, Hesiod's was a "mus-ical" discourse: he was inspired by the Muse, and poetry was his only voice. This, the opposition of bare, truth-telling, prose, and mus-ical poetry, is the ancient dispute.

The following is the beginning of Hesiod's poem the *Theogony*:[21]

> From the Heliconian Muses let us begin to sing, who hold the great and holy mount of Helicon, and dance on soft feet about the deep-blue spring, and the altar of the almighty son of Cronos, and, when they have washed their tender bodies in Permessus or in the Horse's Spring or Olmeius, make their fair, lovely dances upon highest Helicon and move with vigorous feet. Thence they arise and go abroad by night, veiled in thick mist, and utter their song with lovely voice, praising Zeus the aegis-holder and queenly Hera of Argos . . . and the holy race of all the other deathless ones that are for ever. And one day they taught Hesiod glorious song while he was shepherding his lambs under holy Helicon, and this word first the goddesses said to me—the Muses of Olympus, daughters of Zeus who holds the aegis:
>
>> "Shepherds of the wilderness, wretched things of shame, mere bellies, we know how to speak many false things as though they were true; but we know, when we will, how to utter true things."
>
> So said the ready-voiced daughters of great Zeus, and they plucked and gave me a rod, a shoot of sturdy laurel, a marvellous thing, and breathed into me a divine voice to celebrate things that shall be and things that were aforetime; and they bade me sing of the race of the blessed gods that are eternally, but ever to sing of themselves both first and last.

These lines (as well as the next 75 or so) constitute a prelude to the rest of Hesiod's poem and are an invocation to the Muses. Hesiod, who is a shepherd, begins in this fashion for it is from the Muses that he both learned what to sing and received the power actually to sing it. As is well known, the Muses are responsible for the production of poetry in general and through them human beings forget their troubles and find rest from sorrow (line 55). That they are truly indispensable is shown by the famous lines that I shall cite again:

> Shepherds of the wilderness, wretched things of shame, mere bellies, we know how to speak many false things as though they were true; but we know, when we will, how to utter true things.

A human being is a "mere belly," a body of appetites with no innate ability to transcend his appalling natural condition. It is only upon intervention by the Muses, who provide speech and song, that human beings attain some reprieve from the ceaseless pursuit of the satisfaction of appetite. Humans can sing, forget their sorrows, and speak with (what is felt to be) knowledge, if and only if the Muses choose to bestow their gift. Presumably men can, through some unspecified means, make judgments about what the Muses say and discriminate between their true and their apparently true (but false) sayings, for we are told that they say both what is true and what is false. By deciding to communicate their message to a general audience, Hesiod "implies a faith in the Muses' wish to tell the truth," a faith that may or may not be reasonably grounded.[22]

What this means is not yet clear. For the moment we can be content only with this: For Hesiod, human beings are mere bellies in need of mus-ical intervention in order to articulate and speak knowledgeably about things, in order to rise above the level of perpetual gastronomical dissatisfaction.

And what is it that the Muses teach Hesiod to sing? How the holy race of the deathless gods came into being. But not only that. The *Theogony* is the account of the generation of the divine, physical, and human cosmos.[23] The story tells of the coming into being of all the gods as well as the various components of the world (rivers, lakes, hills, dreams, etc.). The telos of the myth is the attainment of power by Zeus. In other words, it is the coming into being of the entire world that is under the sway of traditional Greek religion. It is not necessary, however, to worship pagan gods to appreciate Hesiod, for the real telos of the myth, as we will see, is the coming into being of the ordinary world we all, even now, experience. For our purposes here, it is only the very beginning of this story that is of interest:

> Indeed at first Chaos came to be, but next wide-bosomed Earth, the ever-sure foundation of all the deathless ones who hold the peaks of snowy Olympus, and dim Tartarus in the depth of the wide-pathed Earth, and Eros, fairest among the deathless gods, who unnerves the limbs and overcomes the mind and wise counsels of all gods and all men within them. From Chaos came forth Erebus and black night . . . (116–123)

The world began in *chaos* (which I here italicize to indicate that this is a Greek word). The meaning of this all-important first word is a matter of controversy. While the translator above uses the English cognate "chaos," another suggests "void."[24] Etymologically, *chaos* goes back to "gap" or "chasm," a looming empty space in between. As such, the cognate is actually misleading. "Chaos" to our ears suggests an unordered mass of parts. *Chaos*, however, has no parts. It is empty, formless, and undifferentiated.

It is from *chaos* that the ordinary (or phenomenal), the organized and intelligible, world in which we all live emerges. The most basic feature of the ordinary world is that it is intelligible; it makes sense. The reason that it makes sense is because it is characterized by "differentiated multiplicity." This means that it is filled with *many* objects which can be understood as *different* from one another. The desk in front of me is intelligible in that I can distinquish it from the lamp placed on top of it. I don't confuse the lamp with the desk; I have no problems telling the difference between the door and the wall. As a result, my ordinary activities proceed quite smoothly: I don't attempt to turn on the desk in order to receive light, and I walk through the door and not into the wall.

The *Theogony's* plot has a basic direction to it. It moves from *chaos* to intelligibility. It is the story of progressive articulation and organization. From *chaos* comes, through unknown causes, Earth, Tartarus (the lower world), and Eros. From these primordial beings comes, in genealogical order, a huge sequence of beings that constitutes the totality of the experienced or ordinary world. In sum, Hesiod teaches that the intelligible multiplicity that informs our experience originates in an undifferentiated primal chasm, which itself, because of its total lack of any differentiation, is unintelligible. More on this crucial notion will follow below.

A key point to be kept in mind about Hesiod's poem is that, despite its manifold transformations, *chaos* never quite leaves the scene in the *Theogony*. This is due to the presence of Night. Night is born straight from *chaos* (line 123), and she herself gives birth to Death, Sleep, Fate, and others. These births, however, are strictly autogenetic: Night has no mate. Therefore, with no cross-fertilization to weaken its "genetic" heritage, Sleep functions as a direct transmitter and representative of primal *chaos* within human affairs.[25] We fall asleep, and dreams often invade us with their shapeless terrors. For all that there is of light and clarity within human experience, there is also that which is dark and devoid of distinction. It is this cosmological fact of the retained presence of *chaos* that accounts for Hesiod's general stance of caution and moderation in facing up to the prospects of ordinary life. (This attitude comes out quite clearly in his other poem, *Works and Days*.) Behind the appearance of order and familiarity that characterizes our everyday experience lies that which is utterly unfamiliar, amorphous, and therefore threatening . . . *chaos*.

It is easy to see that one can derive "bare" philosophical propositions from Hesiod's poem. For example, Aristotle interpreted Hesiod's inclusion of Eros as one of the three primal entities as his stumbling effort to arrive at an "efficient cause," an answer to the question From what does motion or genesis of the world arise? Aristotle also claimed that by making earth the first of the corporeal beings to be generated Hesiod was among those early thinkers who are often described as "materialists."[26] From another angle altogether, a conception of the "human condition," one not too distant from what might be called an "existentialist" view, can be elicited from the *Theogony*.

That we can extract philosophical statements from poems is not surprising, for surely we are informed about ourselves, we draw out lessons from reading the great poets. Nevertheless, we do not call them, or Hesiod, philosophers. They are poets. In order to extract philosophical propositions from their poetry we must first commit an act of violence: we must translate their poetry into "truth-functional" prose (bare propositions trying only to tell things as they are). We must strip the poet of his Muse before analyzing the content of his work. We must expose the Muses for what they are: figurative representations of that mysterious affection, inspiration. We must then (if our commitment is to these bare, truth-ful propositions) condemn the poet for relying on so unreliable a source for his productions. The validity of inspiration cannot be tested and so should not replace rational substantiation of a "thesis."

In this sense Hesiod is a paradigmatic poet, for he is fully self-conscious of these limits of his song. He knows himself as a poet for he acknowledges his dependence on the Muses. He confesses that the truth of what he sings is not demonstrable. When his Muses say "We know how to speak many false things as though they are true," Hesiod makes explicit what is implicit in most poetry: He has no rational basis for his faith in the goodwill and competence of the Muses. The poet is in the grip of the Muse and cannot see beyond what she reveals to him. Unlike the practitioner of logos, the poet cannot defend, cannot argue for the goodness of, his poem; he can only sing.

When traditional wisdom tells us that Thales was the first philosopher because he abandoned mythic thought, it means that his great accomplishment was his repudiation of the Muse.

There is another way of approaching Hesiod's call to the Muses. The *Theogony* asserts that the origin is *chaos*. (Hereafter, I will use the Greek word *arche* instead of "origin." *Arche* means "source, origin, first or ruling principle." It is a word typically associated with early Greek philosophy, and I use it here in order to prepare for the contrast I am about to propose.) This implies that the *arche* is essentially unknowable or even unthinkable. As mentioned, whatever its precise meaning, *chaos* is undifferentiated and formless. The activity of the mind (often called its "discursive" activity) consists precisely in *differentiation*. Thinking is like talking: it is based upon making clear the differences between individual words. Without difference, there would be no intelligibility. Thinking is distinquishing among forms, structures, ideas, classes, or concepts. As such, thinking necessarily implies intelligible multiplicity. In other words, thinking presupposes that there are *many* forms, concepts, ideas, and so forth, and that they can be told apart.

Because of the above, it is, quite simply, impossible to think *chaos*. Using other translations, it is impossible to think "the void" or "nothingness." To be able to think *chaos* would mean being able to take "it" up as an object of thought; to think or articulate it would be to articulate it as an intelligible "something" that is distinct from other "somethings." But the void is precisely not a thing; it is a "no-thing." Thus, it cannot be thought. This point can be clarified by a simple experiment:[27] Try to think of nothing. Try to think the void. See what happens. It can't be done. When you think, you think of something. If you are thinking of nothing, how would you know you were thinking at all?

(Even if *chaos* is translated as "gap" it cannot be thought. We can conceive of a gap, but only as a space in between and bounded by two other objects. We cannot think of a gap without its two boundaries, and so we cannot think of it in and of itself.)

The Hesiodic *arche* resists explication by discursive reason or articulation by rational speech. As a result, implied in Hesiod's poem is a *radical discontinuity*, a fundamental difference in kind, between the *arche* and the human mind that thinks (or the voice that sings) it. There is a gap or chasm between the two. No discursive bridge can be erected between the ever differentiating mind and the shapelessness of *chaos*. As a result, in order to know or to bespeak the *arche*, in order to mend that gap, Hesiod *must* invoke some nondiscursive means. There is, one might say, a logical need for the Muses: their presence is mandated as a needed means of passage between the mind and *chaos*. Without them Hesiod would have been incoherent. That is, if he had attempted to explain the process through which he had obtained discursive knowledge of the *arche*, if he had attempted to justify his position in a traditionally rational sense, he would have refuted himself; since the *arche* is unthinkable he would have failed the test of self-referentiality. With the Muses, Hesiod acknowledges precisely the epistemological or cognitive status of his enterprise. Given the content of the Hesiodic *arche*, the invocation to the Muses, which is tantamount to a self-conscious affirmation of the limits of poetry, constitutes a well-crafted and coherent pro-logue.

To put this in slightly different terms: Hesiod's poem does contain a direct or positive claim: the *arche* is *chaos*. As such, the *arche* is implicitly present in his poem. But *chaos* is just that which can never be made present for thought. It is indeterminate and so forever absent from the explicit workings of reason. Therefore, Hesiod includes a disclaimer immediately upon making his claim: It is not his human thought that is responsible for his poem; it is the Muses. His poem is mus-ical, it includes a supplement, an external aid . . . and so it must. The result is graceful and coherent.

Let me digress: The "view" just sketched above and attributed to Hesiod—that the *arche* is *chaos* and the Muse is therefore required for song—is, I propose, quite similar to that now offered by the great deconstructionist, Jacques Derrida. It is worthwhile to expand on this observation in order to illustrate how the ancient dispute can still define the contours of today's most pressing debates. The real issue has never changed much; with all our sophisticated texts and subtexts it is, however, rather easily lost. By returning to the Ancient Greeks we give ourselves a chance to examine an issue unencumbered by contemporary fashion and language. By briefly suggesting a comparison between Derrida and Hesiod, this is what I would like to show.

A single insight often seems to animate Derrida's work. By exploring texts written by Plato, Aristotle, Rousseau, and others, Derrida concludes that traditional philosophy is "phono-centric." What he means with this term is that among the varieties of verbal expression, and especially as compared to writing, the voice (in Greek, *phone*), has been granted privileged status by the Western rationalist tradition.

> When I speak, not only am I conscious of being present for what I think, but I am conscious also of keeping as close as possible to my thought, or to the "concept," a signifier that does not fall into the world, a signifier that I hear as soon as I emit it, that seems to depend upon my pure and free spontaneity, requiring the use of no instrument, no accessory, no force taken from the world. Not only do the signifier and signified seem to unite, but also, in this confusion, the signifier seems to erase itself or to become transparent, in order to allow the concept to present itself as what it is, referring to nothing other than its presence. The exteriority of the signifier seems reduced. Naturally this experience is a lure, but a lure whose necessity has organized an entire structure, or an entire epoch.[28]

Speaking seems to allow the signifier, the words that are voiced, to function as a transparent medium that permits clear access to that which is signified. When I speak there is apparently nothing, no instrument, no accessory, between me, the speaker, and that which is spoken. I, the author or parent of the speaking, am present to make clear my speech. I am there to present that of which I speak and to protect it from being misunderstood, from going astray or even being stolen (misinterpreted).

In speech there is a proximity to the signified that is so great that it might seem possible for the signifier simply to erase itself, to become an unobtrusive medium whose only function is to allow the signified to be signified.

Imagine trying to explain why you did what you did last Saturday. If the person to whom you are speaking is right there with you, you will be able to answer her questions, continually reformulate, make sure she understands what you're talking about. Contrast this with writing an essay about last Saturday. It's risky. You might not use exactly the right words to express your meaning. You might, therefore, be misunderstood. Your written piece goes off into the world on its own and thus runs the risk of being misinterpreted. By speaking you are present as a mediator between your words and your audience. You, the parent of the words, are there to say and to protect what needs to be said. By writing, you absent yourself from your written work. Its fate, therefore, depends not on you, but on those who read.

According to Derrida, this comparison between speaking and writing has been fundamental in shaping the thought of an entire epoch (that begun by Plato and challenged by Nietzsche): speaking, as opposed to writing, has been made into an ideal. The goal of all communication, all forms of language and thought, has been transparency and the ability to make present, without distortion, the object to which the signs refer. The goal has been to erase all traces of the signifier and to let the signified simply be seen. As a result, traditional Western rationalism has been guided by a "phono-centric" set of values—truth, presence, correctness— all of which derive from the privileging of the voice. The tradition has hoped to achieve just those characteristics that seem to belong to speaking.

It is precisely these phono-centric values that Derrida calls into question. He asks his readers to deconstruct, to rethink, the traditional hierarchy into which writing and speaking have been placed, a hierarchy that "organized an entire structure, or an entire epoch." He asks us in particular to reconsider the place of writing. Writing compromises the proximity of the voice, for the written text, upon completion, is severed from its author and its destiny becomes a matter of chance as it circulates in a world of readers. The text is subject to endless interpretations, and its parent, its author, is absent, no longer there to defend it by clarifying its intention and meaning.[29]

For Derrida the essential characteristic of writing is its "iterability," its ability to be repeated, for with this comes its ineluctable potential for misinterpretation. Reading is made possible by the fact that written signs can be repeated in the absence of their author. The author perhaps intended to give voice to some original content, that which is signified, but when he commits his work to the page he creates the structural possibility of differentiation between signifer and original signified. The irremediable feature of writing, of the "grapheme," is its "structural possibility of being severed from its referent or signified."[30]

To pose a question in terms that Derrida himself would not favor, what if writing, and not speaking, were granted privileged status? What if philosophers took their bearings from writing and made it the authoritative version of all expression? (Derrida wouldn't say this because he opposes all such hierarchies.) It would follow on Derrida's account that values such as truth and presence would lose their weight. Since writing necessarily implies the possibility of endless interpretations of the written text, knowledge (making present in speech, without distorting their nature, objects in the world) would no longer function as the paradigmatic goal of intellectual activity. Interpretations would replace knowledge. (In Rorty's terms, truths would replace Truth.) No longer would there be the hope of, for example, finding a correct and authoritative reading of a text. Instead, there would only be readings, many readings, of many texts. Indeed, the world itself would become a text, incapable of sustaining a truthful account, shot through with *chaos*.

By reading a wide variety of texts of the past Derrida shows how speaking has been elevated over writing. Then he suggests that this dichotomy, this hierarchy, has no ground. In other words, the altogether crucial distinction between writing and speaking, one upon which the entire tradition is based, is itself baseless (is itself written). As a result, those dichotomies that have guided Western thought, truth/falsity, presence/absence, good/bad, correct/incorrect, are exposed as baseless. They are, in other words, deconstructed.

There is an affinity between Hesiod's call to the Muses and Derrida's analysis of writing.[31] It may be recalled that in the early lines of the *Theogony* the Muses tell Hesiod that they know how to tell both false things that sound like the truth, as well as true things. The Muses' true saying would give expression to things as they are, while the false would both resemble and deflect from reality. Only the Muses know for sure which version they are supplying to Hesiod. As a result, the poet sings as if he is revealing things as they are, but at the same time he admits that the truth is out of his reach. His call to the Muses acknowledges this bind. As suggested above, it is Hesiod's self-consciousness of his status as a poet, of his relationship to the Muses, that is the *Theogony*'s most startling achievement. And his relationship to the Muses resembles the all-important role to which Derrida would assign writing.

When Hesiod states that *chaos* is first of all things, he makes an assertion whose claim to truth he must immediately disavow: *chaos*, after all, is inaccessible to discursive thought. Only the intervention of the nondiscursive Muses makes possible his singing of the poem, and Hesiod admits that he has no way of knowing if they are telling him the truth. Hesiod's statement about the beginning of things could be written as follows: *chaos* is the *arche,* that which makes possible the intelligible world. But this proposition can never be simply presented as the Truth. For, if *chaos* is the *arche,* there is no Truth. The entire world is conditioned by its beginning and its beginning is a chasm, a gap, that cannot be rendered discursive. The poet must reflect this in his poem, and this he does by invoking the Muses. Hesiod never simply states the Truth as such. Instead, by attributing authorship of his poem to the Muses he absents himself from his poem and thus negates his own claims precisely at the moment of making them.

Derrida too negates his own claims. Since he is out to deconstruct the traditional hierarchies that have held Western reason in their thrall, he does not wish to replace them with a new set of dichotomies. He does not, for example, want to assert that writing is higher than speaking. Doing so would perpetuate the very tradition he hopes to overcome. Instead, by using a variety of devices he attempts to write "playfully," to give voice to his own version of *chaos.* This means he attempts to find a way of simultaneously asserting and retracting what he writes. As a result, he deliberately tries not to be serious. Since, *on his own terms* he should not make serious or substantial claims about the nature of things, Derrida requires a new, *playful,* form of expression—one that does not employ the traditional dichotomies.

(Consider as an example this statement made by one of Derrida's followers: "My way is to make ideas appear, but as soon as they appear I immediately try to make them disappear . . . nothing remains but a sense of dizziness, with which you can't do anything.")[32]

"Play" is a crucial notion in all subversive thought, and it will be discussed at some length in Chapter III. For the moment, let us only say this: Derridean playfulness, his writing that makes no serious claims, is like Hesiod's call to the Muses. Both give voice to *chaos* and so are negations or repudiations of the possibility of making present the Truth of things. Both are antithetical to logos.

Derrida conceives of himself as writing during "the eve of philosophy," after Nietzsche has successfully defeated the Platonic tradition. Hesiod wrote before its dawn. Of course, the two epochs are similar, for both are dark, without the benefit of the sun's light.[33]

To return, finally, to the subject of this section: The tradition insists that only with Thales did philosophy proper begin and that Hesiod was a "mere" poet. I have suggested that Hesiodic poetry contains a view, namely that the *arche* which both originates and abides in the world is *chaos*. Furthermore, the mode of expression employed by Hesiod, a singing inspired by the Muses, is intrinsically appropriate and uniquely adequate to its task. In other words, the form of Hesiod's song, his poetry, harmonizes with its content, his view of the world. (If the *arche* is *chaos*, then mus-ical poetry is the best way of saying so.) Therefore, in order to read Hesiod without doing violence to his thought, one must avoid the traditional treatment afforded to the poet, namely the effort to disabuse him of his Muse and to translate his verse into bare propositions. Such translation would disrupt the internal coherence of the *Theogony*. What is most characteristic of poetry is not its metrical or lyrical embellishment but its reliance on the precarious beneficence of the Muse, whose presence implicitly declares the impossibility of the poet's ever fully justifying and clearing the ground from which he speaks. The presence of the Muses dictates that translation of poetry into bare propositions devoid of music is disfiguring violence.

A parallel point about form and content can now be made about Thales (and the whole point of this chapter is to draw parallels: the ancient dispute involves two positions that can be placed alongside one another without intersecting.) The Thalenic view of the world, one radically different from Hesiod's, is equally in harmony with the form of the logos that expresses it. As we will see, given his understanding of the *arche*, nonmusical prose is the necessary form of Thales' logos. If I succeed in showing this, then the confrontation between Thales and Hesiod is between two self-contained and competing possibilities of thought, each with its unique content and an attendant form. Indeed, it is between two, perhaps the two, most basic human possibilities.[34]

To reiterate an earlier point: There are no writings whatsoever that can be definitively ascribed to Thales. Even in antiquity his name had attained the aura of a legend. For example, his was one of only four names that regularly appeared on the list of the "seven wise men of Greece."[35] "Thales" became a word used to label anyone with superior intelligence, as in Aristophanes' line "The man is a Thales." To Thales were attributed major advances in geometry, astronomy, enigineering, practical wisdom, and a journey to Egypt. Some of this doxography dates from around 500 a.c.e., over a thousand years after Thales lived and so is clearly unreliable. What occurred (most likely) was that ancient authors, in search of a pedigree, imposed upon Thales, a name with no texts, the role of progenitor without having any sure knowledge of who he was. Thales was, and still is, the missing father figure sought for, created by, a tradition in want of a genealogy.

As mentioned above, according to one tradition, Thales chose to write nothing at all. It is only with Anaximander, another Milesian and possibly Thales' student, that any written fragments remain. As one scholar says, "it was he [Anaximander] who first wrote down his views [about nature] . . . and thereby established a new literary form—the first in which prose was employed—which was to serve as the written basis for the new scientific tradition."[36] The reconstructed version of the Thalenic logos has regularly been assimilated into the tradition that Anaximander might be said to have actually founded, that of philosophical prose writing about nature. I will adhere to this tradition and present the following prose statements as representative of Thalenic thought:

(1) Of those who philosophized first, the majority believed that the only *archai* of all things were in the form of matter . . . But Thales, the founder (*archegos*) of this kind of philosophy says it is water.

(2) And some say that the soul is mixed up in the whole, for which reason perhaps Thales also believed that everything is full of gods.

(3) Mind (*nous*) is the quickest of all things, for it speeds everywhere.[37]

Even on the basis of just these few statements, Thales seems, when compared to his predecessors, to inhabit a new world, the most salient feature of which is the disappearance of the Muses. Especially with (1), the most reliable and widely accepted fragment, we are no longer befuddled by gods and stories. Thales here straightforwardly asserts that the *arche*, the origin, the first principle of all things, is water. It is often said that Thales' great accomplishment was his invention of empirical science. This was, at least, Aristotle's opinion. He speculates that Thales arrived at his famous conclusion by means of empirical observation: "Presumably he reached this conception from seeing that the nutriment of everything is moist, and that heat itself is generated from moisture and depends upon it for its existence."[38]

Every living being requires water; water, therefore, is the *arche*. So reads Aristotle's Thales, the first philosopher who, with no aid from the Muses, using his powers of observation alone, concluded that the *arche* was a unity underlying the apparent multiplicity of things. And this unity was intelligible, articulable, accessible to human thought: it was water, a typical and determinate substance found in all animate, and many inanimate, things.

It is, however, too narrow to describe Thales' great achievement as the "invention" of empirical science. Instead, I would formulate it this way:

Thales was the first thinker in the West to believe that the *arche* was intelligible. Consider the second and third fragments from above: Soul is mixed up in the whole, and mind is the quickest of all for it flows everywhere. What I suggest these statements imply is that the world is fully intelligible, that there is a *continuity* between the mind and the whole world out there that the mind thinks. The mind is at home in the world. It is "quickest" because it has the capacity to think all things. I can bring the concept "house" to mind and then quickly shift to "barn." By so doing, my mind speeds to both as they each become objects of thought. To turn Thales' dictum about water into a metaphor, the world is a series of determinate forms or "vessels" ("house," "barn") into which the mind can flow. Just as water adopts the shape of the vessel that contains it, so with equal fluidity does mind take on the form of that which it thinks. "[Mind] thus imitates water, by being able to run through and take on the form of all things . . . There is a remarkable affinity, a similarity in nature, of mind and the structure of the whole."[39] The world is, despite its appearance of multiplicity, essentially homogeneous. It is unified by its *arche*, water, which, as a determinate substance, can be thought by the mind.

In his assertion about water, Thales was of course wrong. Nonetheless, his achievement is historic. The Thalenic logos is an extraordinary departure from Hesiod's poetry because it posits a *continuity* between the mind and the *arche*. As a consequence, it does not require a nondiscursive passage to connect the two. Thales has no need for, and so he banishes, the Muses and replaces dactylic hexameter with simple prose. Thales nonpoetically makes his knowledge claim, and provides (in latent form) the condition that makes that claim possible—namely the affinity in nature between the mind and the *arche*.

To summarize: Hesiod's poem sings what it takes to be the truth that the *arche* is discontinuous with the human voice that sings it. As such, the invocation of the Muses is not an irrational and primitive appendage to a colorful poem, but a declaration of self-consciousness: Hesiod knows what he's doing. The Muses are a necessary condition for the poet's being able to overcome the essential discontinuity of the mind and the *arche*. The critical point is this: Hesiod differs fundamentally from Thales. But it is impossible to declare that Thales is somehow legitimate and Hesiod not. Their difference is that they *begin* differently. Thales begins with a conception of the mind and the *arche* as continuous. Hesiod begins with a conception of them as different. Upon such beginnings each bases his view and creates a mode of expression.[40] As a result, both the Hesiodic *muthos* and the Thalenic logos are adequate to express, they make good sense given, their respective beginnings.

If the above is correct, how do we measure which of these two fundamental antagonists is right? On the basis of what can we declare allegiance to Hesiod or Thales? This is to ask, is the *arche* intelligible or is it *chaos*? Upon this question hinges all, for answering it determines whether poetry or logos is the form of human speech that best does justice to the world in which we dwell. Unfortunately, it is extremely difficult, perhaps impossible, to answer this question. This is because it is fundamental. It is a question that must be answered *before* any other inquiry can commence.

This is what I mean: The question before us now is, Which form of expression is to be preferred—the poet's or the philosopher's? A bit more crudely, who was right, Hesiod or Thales? (The deconstructionist would object that this question already brings with it its own answer.) This is equivalent to asking, Is the *arche* intelligible (continuous with the mind) or not? How do we begin to go about trying to settle this issue? We could begin by approaching it rationally. That is, we could examine this dispute using the methods of traditional rationality. We could inspect each "position" for logical coherence, examine the respective consequences and presuppositions of each, and so on. But to begin this line of inquiry, is already to assume that Thales was right, that logos, not *muthos*, is the preferred form of our discourse. Why not begin by invoking the Muse? "Sing to me, O Muse, of the battle once fought between the philosopher and the poet. Tell me its story, declare its outcome." Such a beginning also is unfair: it, too, would simply assume that Hesiod was right.

The point is this: In a dispute as fundamental as that between the philosopher and the poet, there is no means of fair adjudication. We all have to begin somewhere. This means that we all have to decide, to take sides, and our doing so cannot be defended.[41]

The juxtaposition of the two voices that comprise this chapter finds two self-contained, self-begun, forms of thought. We cannot adjudicate between these two basic human possibilities. They are the primitive beginnings of the Western tradition of philosophy and poetry. And what we have discovered is that Plato was quite right: This is an ancient quarrel. The history of philosophy, of logos, begins with a dispute between competing beginnings. Thales vanquished Hesiod and defined an epoch that lasted until the emergence of Nietzsche. But logos did not supplant poetry reasonably. It did not win its throne on the basis of fair play. Instead, it took the throne away. Far from being the fair-minded, open-minded king it thought it was, logos now realizes that it was once a usurper; that it is a tyrant and not a king. Its birth is now rapidly coming to light. Logos is learning who it is.

CHAPTER 3

LOGOS IS
CONDITIONALLY GOOD

For I, men of Athens, have received my
reputation through nothing other than a
kind of wisdom. And what sort of wisdom
is this? That which is, perhaps, human
wisdom

—Plato, *Apology of Socrates*

A   THE IMPOSSIBILITY OF PHILOSOPHICAL DIALOGUE

(1)   Philosophical Dialogue

Logos seeks its origin. Unlike most, logos wishes to certify itself and its
rule with the full blessing of a reasoned defense. And so it seeks out
occasions for self-testing, for finding out whether its claim to authority
has any merit. Why should it rule? Why should it, and not Cleitophon,
and not the poet, be king? Because unlike its competitors logos can
explain and justify its occupation of the throne. It can (so it thinks)
demonstrate that its rule is grounded and not merely a manifestation of
its desire or rhetorical prowess.

But logos has suffered terrible defeats. It discovered first that it could
not refute the radical relativist. Then it recognized that it could not refute
the poet. Logos now stands accused, more alone than it ever has been.
And it hears a voice:

"Hunt no further. You've discovered too much. You now know who
you are not: you are not the pure-bred king. Your rule is bastard. Let
this interrogation alone. The charges against you, while hard, have not
yet fallen you. Stay on your feet and move. Dismiss your inquiry."

Such a voice is tempting. But of course logos does not concede. Its very
nature impels it towards further discovery. It cannot rest content on a
throne of falsehood. Logos is, perhaps above all else, honest—and so it
is driven to find out who exactly it is, what its defeats mean. "Let break
what will: I go forward to know."

There is one last, slim, avenue of hope for logos to regain (legitimately)
a portion of its throne. This is found in its belief in philosophical dialogue.
It has learned that Cleitophon and the poet (Rorty and Derrida) are
formidable enemies, each with their own self-contained presentations of
themselves. It has learned that it cannot unilaterally refute them, that

there are powerful reasons why it cannot demonstrate conclusively that they are false. But logos still believes it can talk with them; it still has faith in dialogue (dia-logos), the effort of two people holding opposing views to communicate and compare their differences, rather than polemically juxtapose them. Logos disagrees fundamentally with Cleitophon and the poeticist. The recognition that it could not irrevocably refute either of its two opponents hurt, nearly crushed. But logos still has the strength to say to its opponents, "Come, let us reason together. Let us examine our differences, talk in the spirit of openness and compare our positions. Between Socrates and Cleitophon there was silence; between Hesiod and Thales a gap. But why? There's no need for uniformity. Let us keep our differences alive but talk them through."

Armed with such a hope, logos can still press forward, no longer with its previous assertiveness, but at least with some confidence. Unfortunately, one last scene of pain remains to be enacted. For we will next see that philosophical dialogue of the sort in which logos now invests its hope is impossible. This scene is particularly painful because such dialogue is typically thought of not only as possible, but also as highly desirable. The exchange of opposing ideas, the testing of thoughts, the friendly play of competing views have long been encouraged. Indeed, in a democracy that guarantees the freedom of speech, philosophical dialogue seems paradigmatic of tolerance and free inquiry. Part of the seductiveness of philosophy is that it seems to promise just such dialogue. After all, our founding father, Plato, wrote nothing other than dialogues—and these have been taken to be a spectacular impetus for our intellectual tradition.

I agree that Plato's dialogues are spectacular and that I am happy to be a member of the tradition he helped to found. Nevertheless, there are serious questions about the nature and the very possibility of something we too often take for granted. What is a philosophical dialogue and is it in fact possible?[1]

Philosophy, as we have seen in our earlier discussion of the *Symposium*, is the love of wisdom. Wisdom is knowledge of the highest, most fundamental, most comprehensive or simply the most important things. (This is, I realize, a vague description. I will attempt to clarify it as I go on.) Philosophy is an *erotic* activity; it is the striving to gain this knowledge through logos. It is the commitment to discuss the most important and fundamental issues in the hope of attaining knowledge.

What, then, is dialogue? The original word comes from the Greek: *dialegesthai* means "to converse." Philosophical dialogue is a kind of conversation about fundamental issues. But what kind? The distinguishing feature of such dialogue is that it involves an "exchange between basically

different outlooks."[2] In other words, it implies fundamental disagreement or controversy. If there is no disagreement, a conversation may still
occur—but it is not a philosophical dialogue (as it is defined here). Instead, such a conversation will be one that is grounded upon some fundamental agreement and is "insular." Examples of this are instruction or
some sort of joint research venture.

Clearly, the type of dialogue logos now hopes for, that between itself
and Cleitophon, or itself and the poet, qualifies as philosophical, for
there is fundamental disagreement. The easiest way to illustrate this is
simply to state that logos believes in the ultimate intelligibility of the
world (of the *arche*), a contention with which neither the poet nor the
radical relativist would agree.

A philosophical dialogue would be this: a conversation in which two
equally articulate people disagree about positions they hold on a fundamental issue. It is an attempt to resolve the issue in question. I include
the portion about equality to eliminate the possibility of, for example, a
student arguing with a teacher. What is in question here is a disagreement
between two mature adults, each with a well-conceived position they
believe is defensible. I include the portion about the attempt at resolving
the issue because, given the definition of philosophy as embodying the
hope of and commitment to attaining knowledge of that which is important, the disagreement the two parties enter into must include the motiva-
tion to settle it. The issue over which they are at odds is fundamental.
Knowledge of it is the goal. The dialogue must be serious; that is, it must
be sincerely directed toward achievement of the goal. This is the specific
mode of conversation that I claim is impossible. The argument I will now
present in support of this claim is relatively simple and, of course, not
truly original.[3]

In order to take place, all conversation requires an agreed-upon "common ground." This is constituted by a common vocabulary and agreement upon the rules that govern the conversation and determine what
counts as "significant" or meaningful discourse. ("Rules" would refer to
those of grammar but also, and more importantly, to a more informal
and various set of principles. Examples will be provided shortly.) In the
case where the participants disagree and attempt to resolve the disagreement there must also be agreement upon what can, in principle, adjudicate the dispute. Without this there is no way to determine if progress in
the conversation has taken place. All this will be explained further below.
For the moment, simply accept the following: Philosophical dialogue is
a kind of conversation. As such it requires a common ground in order
to take place. A philosophical dialogue is about fundamental issues. As

we will see, however, agreement on such issues is precisely what constitutes the common ground needed for the controversial conversation to take place. Therefore, if there is a disagreement about fundamental issues, and there certainly can be, the result is not *dialegesthai*, but either *polemos*, polemical speech, or silence—either of the friendly (mutually tolerant and respectful) sort or not. Philosophical conversation is possible *only* in its insular variety. Both the silence between Socrates and Cleitophon and the gap between Hesiod and Thales are as necessary as they are lamentable.

One ambiguity in what has just been said lies in the notion of a fundamental issue when that phrase is used to define philosophy. Soon there will be an example. Before that, however, consider the following: What happens if, as is likely, a particular reader disagrees with my definition of philosophy. You could, for example, agree with my general definition, but disagree with the list of fundamental issues that I later propose. What you consider to be an issue might not be on my list. At first blush you and I, as philosophers, have nothing to say to each other. We've agreed that philosophy is about fundamental issues, but we don't have one in common. On the other hand, you might say, "We don't have an issue in common. Let's talk about that. What do you think a fundamental issue is? I don't agree. Defend your list."

Here it seems that you and I might disagree about our list of issues, but continue to discuss our disagreement. This would entail our entering into a "meta-philosophical dialogue," a dialogue about philosophical dialogue. We would each suspend our loyalty to certain fundamental issues and instead discuss what it is we should discuss. Having done this we would, it seems, have entered a neutral realm of discourse in which no stand would be taken on what issues should be discussed. Even here, however, there would still be a need for a common ground to make the conversation possible. We would still have to share a common vocabulary and set of rules. We would also have to agree that "it is good to suspend one's presuppositions about what constitutes a fundamental issue."

This latter agreement, however, can exemplify the problem. Assume for a moment that the statement in quotation marks expresses a judgment on a fundamental issue. It is clear that there can be no dialogue about it. If you think it's true that it is good to suspend one's presuppositions and I disagree with you, then we cannot argue. You disagree with me as to what constitutes a fundamental issue (an issue worth talking about) and to argue with you I would have to suspend my presupposition, which in this case happens to be that one ought not to suspend one's presuppositions. Consequently, to argue against you I would have to agree with you. The question, Should these presuppositions be suspended? cannot be debated without being answered. To debate the question requires a common ground which, upon being established, immediately renders the debate superfluous.

You might object and say this is a rather drastic view or that my example of a fundamental issue in the preceding paragraph was not appropriate. However, even if we dispense with the example, there are other problems. If you and I enter into a meta-philosophical dialogue we must agree, first, on the rules governing it and, second, on the criteria for adjudicating it. How do we legitimately argue for our chosen issue? Are we allowed to use foul language, cite poetry, or scream hysterically? Are there a list of informal fallacies that cannot be broken? Must the Principle of Noncontradiction be obeyed? Is vagueness to be counted as a liability? Is the sound of our words to be factored in as part of our performance? Should our positions be measured on the basis of their ability to move an audience?

These are just examples of what I mean by "rules." We cannot enter into a meta-philosophical dialogue unless we agree on them. Furthermore, we must agree how to determine when progress has been made in the course of such a dialogue. As Rorty puts it, we need "a set of rules which will tell us how rational agreement can be reached on what would settle the issue on every point where statements seem to conflict."[4] Unless there is some vision of what it means to agree, a conversation that involves disagreement cannot progress. Even if you and I disagree on the question, Would Dukakis have been a better president than Bush? we would share a sense of what agreement would be like. But what if we hold divergent views on the question, is *chaos* the *arche* or not? Given our views, that sense of agreement might be impossible to attain.

These rules are fundamental issues on which agreement is needed in order to constitute the common ground making the meta-philosophical dialogue possible. (The best example is the Principle of Noncontradiction, which will be discussed below.) As a result, the hope that there can be a dialogue about dialogue that operates free from judgment upon what a fundamental issue is, has been quashed.

In a similar fashion, another quashed hope would be that invested in the notion of a "method." Someone could say, "If two partners in a discussion disagree on first principles but share a common commitment to the same method for resolving the dispute, philosophical dialogue is possible."[5] This is wrong since commitment to a method implies commitment to a set of rules and criteria, to an entire conception of rationality. Agreement on a method thus implies agreement on fundamental issues.

To summarize: Assume two people agree that philosophical dialogues are about fundamental issues. Assume they disagree about what these issues are. There are two possible outcomes. Either they immediately stop talking, or they attempt to adjudicate their disagreement through a meta-philosophical dialogue. But the latter option has been shown to be impossible, for it recapitulates the dilemma involving fundamental issues. Therefore, in both cases philosophical dialogue is impossible.

Rather than disagree with my list of issues, you could instead disagree with my very characterization of a philosophical dialogue. This is the tack taken by Rorty. As mentioned above, he differentiates Philosophy, the traditional, or (as he would say) Platonic, quest for Knowledge of Truth and Goodness, and philosophy, the attempt "to see how things, in the broadest sense of the term, hang together, in the broadest sense of the term."[6] Without the capital *P* philosophy means "conversation" about a host of issues none of which should be called "fundamental." Rorty envisions as "all-purpose intellectual of a post-Philosophical culture" one who "passes rapidly from Hemingway to Proust to Hitler to Marx to Foucault to Mary Douglas to the present situation in Southeast Asia to Ghandi to Sophocles. He is a name-dropper, who uses names as these to refer to sets of descriptions, symbol-systems, ways of seeing."[7]

Rorty would accuse my definition of being Platonic. The question now is, can Rorty and I get into a dialogue in my sense of the term? Can we get into a "conversation" in his sense of the term?

The answer to the first question is no. I think there are fundamental issues and he does not. Two outcomes are possible. Perhaps Rorty will discuss my choice of an issue in the name of tolerance and collegial assistance. Although I am a Platonist he will assist me, for example, when I get stumped on the problems involved in the "theory of Ideas." Is this a philosophical dialogue? No, for there is no real, no "serious," disagreement about the issue in question. Rorty should not take a position on this issue (at least not a serious one), for it is a traditional issue and so he thinks it has outlived its usefulness. What Rorty wants is to change the subject; he is devoted explicitly to the elimination of fundamental issues from the philosopher's repertory. Again, he might talk with me, but our conversation would be on a par with the one he had about Rembrandt with the local art historian or the one about *L.A. Law* with his neighbor. In other words, all conversations are equal in that none is truly Better or more Truthful, none is more important, than any other. As a result, Rorty will not make a serious commitment to resolving the issue I present: he does not believe it is worth pursuing.

Can Rorty and I get into a dialogue on this question: Are some issues fundamental or not? No, for this question is itself fundamental. A positive or a negative answer to it would constitute a Philosophical position and would thus represent an old-fashioned, and therefore objectionable, claim to the Truth.[8] Someone who denies the possibility of fundamental issues surely cannot discuss this denial philosophically, for immediately upon doing so he would have contradicted himself.

The answer to the second question, Can Rorty and I get into a "conversation" in his sense? is also no, and for many of the same reasons. A Rortian conversation implies that no issues are fundamental. I believe some are. Therefore I, as a Philosopher, cannot participate seriously in a conversation which, in my view, is and always will be less than fundamental. What would be the point? I would, of course, attempt to persuade him that some issues are fundamental, but if Rorty is consistent then he will not seriously defend his denial.

(It should be apparent that the word "serious" is becoming increasingly important. Its opposite is "play" and will be discussed shortly.)

To summarize again: I offered a definition of a philosophical dialogue. We might agree that it is accurate. If so, then we will either agree or disagree about the list of fundamental issues. If we agree on this, there is no dialogue. If we disagree, there is no dialogue. Finally, we might simply disagree about my initial definition of a philosophical dialogue. If so, there is no dialogue.

This may all seem exaggerated; you might angrily respond, "Why be so extreme? Of course we can talk about these issues, even if we disagree. You listen to me and I to you. There will be mutual respect and attentiveness." So we talk. After having listened, you might say, "That was interesting. I totally disagree, but I've enjoyed and even benefited from listening to you. Thanks."

Was that a philosophical dialogue? No. Several points are relevant. First, there is a mutually agreed-upon respectfulness here. There must also be enough of a common vocabulary and a shared conception of what is significant discourse so that both parties can understand each other. This itself might constitute fundamental agreement. Even if it doesn't, what we really have here is tantamount to "philosophical silence" between the interlocutors. We each affirm the other's right to have and express views on various issues and so we are not faced with literal silence. From a philosophical perspective, however, we have not entered into a convation challenging the other on his ground while retaining our own. We distance ourselves from each other and so acknowledge the gap between us. By contrast, a philosophical dialogue, since it is erotic, requires a commitment to pursue the same goal, adjudication of the dispute. If there is merely a friendly distance and not a shared attempt at resolution of the issue, there is no dialogue. The fact that you say to me (and even say sincerely) "thanks," the fact that you actually benefited from listening to my presentation does not imply that we had a philosophical dialogue. You might be using my position as a means for testing your own. These types of converations often do occur and they are genuinely beneficial, but they are not, given my definition, philosophical dialogue.

There is another possibility here. After having listened you might say, "You know, you're right. I'm wrong. I'll come over to your side. Thanks." A less extreme version of this would be, "You know, you're right about that point. I'll modify my position to take your point into account. Thanks."

Is either of these a philosophical dialogue? Each certainly seems to be. In fact, neither is. The first represents didactic persuasion, or simply instruction. What occurs here is an evolution and a transformation on the part of one of the interlocutors. The conversation begins in disagreement. But in the course of listening to me you decide (or realize, or see) that my position is superior to your own. For this to occur there must be some point of agreement. Once this point has been reached, the dialogue—if there actually had been one—ends. But was there a dialogue before that moment? No. You were listening as I stated my views. You were silent and then realized that I was right. Is this whole conversation—the conversation before the point of agreement—the point itself, and the subsequent conversation a philosophical dialogue?

No. The question is whether it is possible for representatives of two "basically different outlooks and approaches" to converse. The case of didactic persuasion is very possible and highly desirable, but it is not a philosophical dialogue. What is at issue here is whether two people who disagree with each other can continue to converse while maintaining their fundamentally divergent positions.[9] In a didactic conversation the divergence at some point vanishes. The fact that we have such conversations gives us all the more reason to talk to each other. But this is not to say that philosophical dialogue is possible.

In the second case, where I modify my position to take into account the good points you have made, we again fail to have a genuine dialogue. This situation is very much like the one described above—namely that of self-testing or, more drastically, of honing one's weapons for future use.

There are at least two potential objections to what I have argued. First, someone might claim that I have stipulated a definition of philosophical dialogue that is so narrow as to reduce it to triviality. Put into other terms, the thesis offered here is tautologous and I am running around in logical circles. To a certain extent, that's true. (If a philosophical dialogue is so defined as to be impossible, then it is easy to show that it is impossible.)

If the definition is even somewhat accurate, however, this is not equivalent to philosophical triviality. When there is disagreement about fundamental issues, and then an attempt is made to engage in dialogue, big problems do emerge. Such confrontations are quite real. There are breakdowns in arguing against certain kinds of people and positions. At some point, there just isn't any reason to keep talking. This isn't an accident or one person's fault; it's the result of fundamental disagreement and represents the troubling side of human conversation. It is precisely this type of disagreement that has animated this book. As logos has interrogated its three accusers it has confronted those who differ on the most fundamental of issues. It is for the purpose of focusing attention specifically on this type of confrontation that the definition of a philosophical dialogue has been made so apparently narrow.

The second objection is that it might be possible to agree on one fundamental issue and, nevertheless, continue to disagree about others. (This is a restatement of the first objection that the definition was too narrow.) Can an agreement occur on one level and then become the common ground making possible a fundamental disagreement on another level? No. The reason for this is that issues are hierarchical with respect to their fundamentalness. Genuinely fundamental issues are those that, and only those that, establish common ground. (Now, I realize, this sounds completely circular.) Thus, if dialogue were to occur there would have to be agreement on fundamental issues, which is a contradiction. If such agreement does occur, any subsequent disagreement will be over an issue less than fundamental, and therefore dialogue about it will not qualify as philosophical. To make this point more clear I need Aristotle's assistance.

(2) Aristotle and the Principle of Noncontradiction

The name Aristotle gives to that discipline which studies the most fundamental of issues is "first philosophy," or sometimes just "wisdom" (*Metaphysics* 1026a24, 982a2). As opposed to all other forms of knowledge that "cut off" some portion of being (or reality) and then study it, this discipline is not partial. Mathematics, for example, cuts off one slice of reality, the abstract notion of magnitude, and studies it. Mathematics is not concerned with anything else; it narrows its focus and then concentrates only on its object. By contrast, first philosophy is truly fundamental, for it attempts to get to the bottom, to the cause or the principle, of *all* things, all objects. First philosophy is the study of being simply as being, and not being as magnitude (mathematics) or being as life (biology) or being as celestial objects (astronomy).[10]

In Book IV of the *Metaphysics*, Aristotle raises the question, Does the study of being simply as being also study "what are called in mathematics the axioms"? (1005a20). An axiom is one of several kinds of "starting points" (*archai*) that Aristotle discusses in his *Posterior Analytics*, which is the study of "demonstrative science" (71b20 ff). "Starting points" in general are those propositions needed for a demonstration to take place, for it to begin. They themselves cannot be demonstrated, for they are what make demonstration possible. They must be accepted, therefore, by some other form of knowledge (be it intuition, induction, or dialectic) without proof.[11] The starting points are either subject specific or general and applicable to many subjects. The most general are like what Euclid called the "common notions," a frequently cited example of which is "If equals are subtracted from equals the remainders are equal."[12] These can be called the axioms and are what "the man who is to learn anything whatever must have" (72a17–18).

It is because axioms pertain to all studies that they are fundamental. They constitute the ground upon which any given science arises. "They belong to all things that are and not to any given particular genus in separation from the rest. Everyone uses them" (*Meta.* 1005a23–25). It is for this reason that it is the task of the first philosopher, he who studies being as being and not just a cut-off portion of being, also to study the axioms.

The most "certain" or "secure" (*bebaiotates*; 1005b22) of all these principles is the Principle of Noncontradiction, which Aristotle formulates as follows: "It is impossible at the same time for the same thing both to belong and not belong to the same thing and in the same way" (1005b19–20). (A more strictly logical version of the Principle reads, "The most certain of all basic principles is that contradictory propositions are not true at the same time" [1011b13]. In a more psychological formulation Aristotle says, "No one can believe that the same thing can at the same time be and not be" [1005b23].) It is impossible for some S to be both P and not P at the same time and in the same way. This is the most fundamental of all axioms, for it is the rock-bottom Principle constituting the ground of all rational discourse—of logos itself. "All men who demonstrate refer back to this ultimate belief" (1005b32–33).[13]

The Principle of Noncontradiction, with the question of being as being, is the most fundamental issue for Aristotle. Can it be debated? Can someone deny the Principle's truth and then argue with one who affirms it? If so, and only if so, will a philosophical dialogue be possible.

The first point is that the Principle cannot be directly proven. Any attempt to do so would beg the question, for the Principle is (in Aristotle's logic) the basis of all proof procedures and therefore the attempt to prove it would require assuming (using) it. There is therefore no possibility of a dialogue that culminates in a direct proof of the item debated.[14]

Aristotle states that the Principle of Noncontradiction can only be defended "elenchically" (1006a12). What this means is that someone denying it can only be refuted in the midst of attempting to defend his denial; he will refute himself in the very act of attempting to defend his own thesis. The only requirement that Aristotle makes of his opponent is that he "say something significant" (*semainein*; 1006a21). That is, in defense of his position the denier of the principle must say something that is significant both to himself and to his opponent in the debate. Once this occurs, however, the dialogue terminates. For simply by stating something significant the denier has actually affirmed what he thinks he is denying. Why? The Principle, for Aristotle, is the foundation of all significant discourse. The denier has affirmed that some single attribute, in this case "false," applies to some subject, the Principle of Noncontradiction, and not its opposite. His defense of the position depends on his making this claim. But it is just this dependence that destroys his argument: he has obeyed the Principle in the name of rejecting it. He should have said, "The Principle of Noncontradiction is both true and false." That, however, would have been a meaningless statement, for he would no longer have had a discernible position to defend.

The elenchic refutation, then, presents the denier of the Principle with two options: Either say nothing significant in defense of his position (in which case, says Aristotle, he is indistinguishable from a vegetable [1006a15]); or immediately be refuted upon articulating a significant defense. In both cases there is no philosophical dialogue. What this means is that for Aristotle it is impossible to enter into a dialogue about the most fundamental of philosophical issues.

The remainder of Book IV is a series of arguments intended to defend the Princple of Noncontradiction. Most take the form of an indirect argument (or a *reductio ad absurdum*). They begin by assuming the denial of the principle and then draw out what Aristotle takes to be the unacceptable consequences that follow.

In the first such argument Aristotle begins by asserting, "It is clear that this very thing, at any rate is true, that the term 'to be' or 'not to be' means something definite" (1006a29). The term "man," for example, means one thing: Let this be "two-footed animal." If this is the case, then in the statement "S is a man," being two-footed is what being a man means about S. If S is a man, then S is two-footed and is not not two-footed. The predicate refers to, and therefore means, something definite. If this were not the case, then when I said, "S is a man," it could not be determined what I was talking about. That to which the predication referred would be indefinite and as a result there could be no discourse significant both to myself and to the person with whom I was speaking. To state Aristotle's general formula: "For not to speak significantly of some one thing is not to speak significantly at all" (1006b7).

Denial of the Principle of Noncontradiction implies that it is possible to have significant discourse without there being any restriction on the number of true predications attributed to a given subject. Therefore, denial implies that it is possible to speak significantly without speaking definitely of one thing. This, for Aristotle, is absurd.

Aristotle's reasoning here sounds circular, and in a way it is. He begins with a particular conception of significant discourse and then shows that rejection of the principle, which establishes the nature of that discourse, leads to the absurdity of there no longer being any significant discourse. The circularity here is not, however, vitiating. The point is that if the issue is what counts as legitimately significant discourse, the argument must be circular: That mode of discourse must itself be used in order to establish itself as significant. There can be no philosophical dialogue concerning the nature of significant discourse itself.

Logos now recognizes the reason for its discomfiture at the hands of Cleitophon and Hesiod. It began with the belief that it could refute such opponents. Then it learned it could not do so without begging the question, without violating a basic precept of rational argumentation. Logos next approached its enemies in the hope of at least having a dialogue with them. The revelation of this section, which is the most abstract of any that has yet transpired, is that it is impossible for two fundamentally opposed views of the world to debate what counts as significant discourse. And precisely this question has been at stake throughout the various encounters found in this book.

It is because of this impossibility that a gap exists between Socrates and Cleitophon. In the *Republic*, Cleitophon falls silent. In the *Cleitophon*, Socrates falls silent. The gap between the two men is one that logos cannot bridge. Instead of examining the differences in their positions, Cleitophon opts for Thrasymachus, for rhetoric, as his mode of significant discourse. He decides no longer to use his powers of reason and speech in the attempt to discover the Truth about beings in the world. He no longer attempts to attach single predicates (good, true, bad, false) to single subjects. Instead, he (like Rorty) suspends his loyalty to Socrates and the project of Truth, he terminates his flirtation with logos, and joins forces with Thrasymachus. Socrates' silence in the face of such a defection is his acknowledgment that logos cannot prevent it.[15]

A similar situation obtains with Hesiod. Since *chaos* is the residual principle of all the world, there is no stable reality to which one may univocally attribute true predicates. Mus-ical poetry is the poet's version of significant discourse. Hesiod's call to the Muses, and their response to him, is evidence that he (like Derrida) is self-conscious of the conception of significant discourse that he adopts. And such a conception the philosopher cannot refute, cannot even debate. To do so (as we have seen so often) would require begging the question and thus would violate a basic precept of reason.

To return to Aristotle: He argues that if the Principle of Noncontradiction is denied, then the doctrines of "substance" and "essence" must also be denied (1007a20–21). It would take a long time to explain what these terms mean. Suffice it to say that a substance is a stable being that exists in its own right and that these two doctrines comprise the basis of the natural view of the world discussed at some length in Chapter I above. Substances are what are "seen" by the discerning intellectual eye. They are the objects of Aristotle's confident assertiveness. If their existence were denied there would no longer be any possibility of an "essential predication." This is a statement that says that S is P and must be P in order to be S. As such, if S were to cease being P, then it would cease being S. For example, Aristotle says that a human being is essentially an animal with logos. Therefore, without logos a being is not human.

If the principle were to be denied, then essential predication would disappear. The reason for this is that the contrary to the essential predication could as equally well be predicated of the subject: S could just as well be not-P as P. If there is to be such a thing as "being essentially human," this must be different from "not being a human." If the two are not different, if the principle were denied, then there could be no essential predication. In sum, the Principle of Noncontradiction is, for Aristotle, the ultimate regulator of predication. In order for any predication to be significant it must refer to something definite and stable. We saw this in Chapter I; Aristotle's is a world of stable substances. Without the principle "anything goes," since essential predications would lose their privilege. To say anything goes means that without the principle there would be no articulable substance that can be identified as the recipient of essentially true predications.

Yet another way to put this point is that if the principle is denied there will be no univocally true propositions. For the denier, S is both P and not P; neither of the two statements, "S is P," "S is not P," is simply and solely true. Instead, in some sense both are true. In fact, denial of the principle leads to every possible statement being true (or being as equally true as any other statement). The result of all this is that anything that *seems* to be true can be counted as being true (1009a134–15). In short, if the principle is denied, then relativism is affirmed.

Aristotle identifies an old friend of ours, the Sophist Protagoras, as a proponent of both relativism and the denial of the Principle of Noncontradiction.

> Protagoras' position emerges from the same view . . . For if everything that seems true or appears true is true, everything must be true and false at the same time; for many people form judgments that are opposed to those held by others, and they believe that those who do not have the same views as they do are wrong. Therefore, the same thing must be and not. And if this is the case, all opinions must be true; for those who are wrong and those who are right hold views that are opposed to each other. So if things are really the way [Protagoras thinks], everybody will be right (1009a6–15).

Aristotle explains the conjunction of relativism and the denial of the Principle of Noncontradiction this way: If it seems to you that Sam is good, it is, according to Protagoras, true that Sam is good. (Remember Protagoras' famous dictum: "Man is the measure.") If in addition it seems to me that Sam is bad, "then it seems to me true that what seems true to you is false; so it is false. So it is both true and false that" Sam is good.[16] Denial of the principle goes hand in hand with Protagorean relativism to form a view in stark contrast to Aristotle's own.

To summarize: For Aristotle, the Principle of Noncontradiction is the most fundamental of all principles, for it is the foundation of all rational discourse. It itself, however, cannot be proven; it must be assumed. In fact, its truth cannot even be debated, for if it were debated in a manner that would please Aristotle, then that very dialogue would have to be conducted in accord with the principle. The denier, the proponent of Protagorean relativism; for example, would thus be well advised simply to ignore Aristotle's invitation to debate (and the abuse directed at him if he refuses).

If the Principle of Noncontradiction is paradigmatic of a fundamental issue, and if philosophical dialogue is to be about such issues, then it is clear that philosophical dialogue is impossible.

This thought should frighten—if the most basic beliefs, the very foundations of our conception of significant or rational discourse, cannot even be debated, then in what sense are they rational? Does rationality proceed upon irrational grounds? If so, then what differentiates the denial from the affirmation of the principle? One answer readily suggests itself: "the consequences that follow." Denying the principle, one might argue, gets us nowhere, while its affirmation makes possible the wholesome work of rational activity. But from where did these conflicting directions emerge? Is there any good reason to prefer one over the other? Upon what is each based? Such questions might of course be dismissed as pointless. But what if we, we who follow this story of logos, desire, indeed are driven, to pursue them? What happens then?

(3) The Misologists

By mentioning relativism in the previous section and identifying an old friend, the Sophist Protagoras, it should now be clear that the imaginary opponent in Aristotle's *Metaphysics*, the one denying the Principle of Noncontradiction, holds a position like that of logos's accusers (in both their ancient and contemporary guise). To use a term mentioned above, the accusers are "misologists," haters of logos. The expressions of Cleitophon and Hesiod each represent a form of discourse that differs fundamentally from Aristotle's. Implicit in their conceptions of significant discourse is the denial of the essential primacy of the principle and the (metaphysical) consequences that follow. This has already been noted. But that this is also true of the contemporary band of subversives, especially Derrida, is even more clear.

Derrida acknowledges in *Of Grammatology* that an enormous gulf separates him from the traditional version of logos or significant discourse, which he calls "phono-centrism" or "logocentrism." Logocentrism is based upon a "metaphysics of presence," a conception of the world that features Aristotelian substances, natures, stable realities. According to Derrida, logocentrism implies the primacy of the voice, which in turn implies that human beings can gain direct access to that which is present out there in the world simply and essentially as itself. An excellent example of logocentrism is Aristotle's statement in *De Interpretatione*, which I have already cited twice. There spoken words were said to be symbols of mental representations of things as they are. Commenting on, and I think illuminating, this passage Derrida says, "The feelings of the mind, expressing things naturally, constitute a sort of universal language which can then efface itself. It is the stage of transparence."[17]

Aristotle, if you recall, made writing a "symbol" or "sign" of spoken words. He thus placed writing a step further away from the reality of objects in the world. In other words, Aristotle conceived of a sequence: Things in the world, the mental experience of those things, spoken words giving voice to mental experiences, written symbols of spoken words. This sequence is phonocentric because it subordinates writing to speaking; it places spoken words closer to reality and thus grants them a better chance to articulate things as they are. It is just this subordination to which Derrida objects. His "nonphonetic" account of signification, his elevation of writing and rejection of Aristotle's sequence, "menaces the history and life of the spirit and self-presence in the breath . . . because it menaces substantiality, that other metaphysical name of presence and ousia."[18] ("*Ousia*" is the Greek word typically translated as "substance.")

With his nonphoneticism, with his grammatology, Derrida approaches just the view Aristotle describes as following upon rejection of the Principle of Noncontradiction. For Aristotle, if the principle is denied, a set of consequences follows that is unacceptable, but not quite refutable. It is not clear whether Aristotle thinks that an actual or serious philosophical position can include a denial of the principle. He implies, on the one hand, that the pre-Socratic philosopher Heraclitus, who seems to be such a denier, did not really believe what he was saying, that he was just talking. On the other hand, Aristotle spends a good deal of time explaining how it is that men come to adopt the view associated with the denial (see 1005b25 and 1009a22 ff.). Regardless, Aristotle knows that either acceptance or rejection of the principle is a fundamental decision in that it constitutes a whole conception of significant discourse.

So too does Derrida understand that his rejection of traditional logos, his rejection of the metaphysics of *ousia* and presence that regulated the classical version of predication, has enormous consequences. He knows that he is heading toward a version of "unregulated" (or "anarchic") predication. The single word that best captures what Derrida means is "playful." This is opposed to "serious," or traditional. The importance of play in subversive thought cannot be overemphasized. It is a notion Derrida inherits from Nietzsche, whom he rightly credits with making the first great move in the overthrow of traditional logos and metaphysics.

> Nietzsche, far from remaining simply within metaphysics (with Hegel and as Heidegger wished) contributed a great deal to the liberation of the signifier from its dependence or derivation with respect to logos and the related concept of truth or the primary signified, in whatever sense that is understood.[19]

By "liberation of the signifier" Derrida means rejection of the traditional conception of significant discourse wherein the signifier had to refer to something definite and stable. With logocentrism overthrown, language is free to roam, is not bound to the definite object, "the primary signified." The implications of this view are vast: an entirely different way of writing and thinking would have to emerge, one freed from the traditional task of simply stating things as they are. Derrida's experiments with different forms of writing, his playful use of language, his disdain for standard modes of argumentation, are evidence for this. Liberation means liberation from seriousness, the old way of saying things as they are, and an opening to a new way, to play. "One could call play the absence of the transcendental signified."[20]

In order to clarify the notion of misology further, and to understand a bit more about Nietzsche and Derrida, we need now to try to make sense of the notion of play. (I don't mention Rorty here because on the surface he is less playful than Derrida. Nevertheless, implicit within his sober critique of Philosophy is an attempt to overcome seriousness that is similar to that found in his French colleague. Consider, for example, the fact that Rorty diagnoses the cause of Heidegger's Nazism as a case of taking Philosophy too seriously.)[21]

As usual, my procedure will be to recall an ancient author. There was one Greek philosopher who greatly influenced Nietzsche (and therefore indirectly influenced Derrida): Heraclitus. And vital to Heraclitus' thought is the notion of play. To him, then, let us turn.

Who was Heraclitus? He lived in Ephesus, on the west coast of what is now Turkey, around 500 b.c.e. His writings have come down to us in the form of a group of unordered aphorisms, or short statements. These aphorisms are obscure and their language is peculiar. It is not at all clear how they fit together, and so they do not seem to express a coherent philosophical argument. As is true of much early philosophy, however, scholars are not certain what form Heraclitus' original writings actually took. It is possible that Heraclitus wrote a book and that the writings that have come down to us (which have been compiled from a wide variety of doxographical sources) were not in the form we have them today. For several reasons, some of which I'll explain, I think that Heraclitus' writings have come down to us exactly as they were intended to. As is true of Hesiod's poetry and Thales' prose, the aphorisms suit Heraclitus' intentions perfectly. The form of this writing is adequate to its content, to the thought its author wishes to express.[22]

It may seem odd to describe Heraclitus as a "misologist" since three of his aphorisms read as follows:

> Of this logos which always is human beings always come to be uncomprehending, both before they have heard it and after they have heard it for the first time. For even though all things come to be in accord with this logos, human beings are like those without experience, even when they experience

both words and actions of the sort that I describe as I divide each thing according to nature and say how it is. What they do when they are awake eludes the rest of human beings just as they forget what they do when they are asleep (1).

It is necessary to follow what is in common. Even though the logos is common, most men live as though their intelligence was private (2).

After having heard not me but the logos, it is wise to agree that all things are one (50).

These statements sound as if they belong to the tradition that Thales founded and Aristotle perfected. They seem to postulate a logos, an objective order existing out there and forming an intelligible world that human beings can (with their logos) apprehend. Indeed, Heraclitus is often credited with being one of the first of the Greeks to use the word "logos" in just this fashion.[23] But what is this logos to which Heraclitus asks us to listen? What is his world like? The following two aphorisms tell much:

Lifetime is a child playing (*pais paizon*) draughts; the kingship belongs to a child (52).

War of all things is father, of all things is king, and he reveals some as gods, others as human beings, he makes some slaves, others free (53).

Lifetime is a *pais paizon*: the Greek words for "child" and "playing" are closely related. (Draughts was probably a game like checkers.) The kingship is in the hands of a child. What does any of this mean? The world is not teleologically, reliably, predictably structured. There are no stable entities, no fixed purposes toward which living beings grow. Think of children playing a game; they make up the rules. They change the rules. They ignore or play without rules. They pick up a stick or a cup and their imaginations bring these objects to life; they shift their attention and these objects die. They play for no stated purpose. If an adult counsels a child, "It's a good time for you to go and play," chances of success are slim. If an adult suggests that a child play with a specific toy, the child may well reject this advice and pick up a kitchen utensil instead.

This is the play of a child: creative, imaginative, indifferent to command, spontaneous, fabulously alive, ever changing without definite purpose. And Heraclitus places the kingship (of what?) in the child's hands. What does this signify? The world to which he is trying to give expression is bereft of authoritative structure. The *pais paizon* tokens a world of constant, purposeless change.[24]

Nietzsche was fond of this aphorism and made the following comments about it:

> In this world only play, play as artists and children engage in it, exhibits coming-to-be and passing away, structuring and destroying, without any moral additive, in forever equal innocence.[25]

By "coming-to-be and passing away," Nietzsche refers to the ceaseless pace of change and the absence of any permanent, or "natural," structure in the world. All structure is fiction, a consequence of human creativity. For this reason Nietzsche associates the playing child with the artist. Both the child and the artist bring structures into being and then, when their attention shifts, let them pass away. This restless and creative energy is "innocent"; that is, it occurs without reason, without a preestablished goal. Children play, not because play is good, but because they just play. ("The child is innocence and forgetfulness, a new beginning, a play, a self-propelling wheel, a first motion, a sacred Yes.") Artists create, not because art is good, but because they are creative. The two thus exhibit coming-to-be and passing-away . . . the play of the world.[26]

To return to Heraclitus: What, then, should we make of his comments about war? How can the kingship be in the hands of a child and war be the father and king of all things? What could be further from child's play than adults making war? In an important sense, however, these two activities are similar. For example, the course or development of both a war and the play of a child are unpredictable. They are both spontaneous, incapable of being fully controlled, with outcomes undecided until the end. Two countries, A and B, go to war. Despite the carefully worked-out plans for defense, the army of A falters unexpectedly in the field; B defeats A, gains its territory, and expands its borders. The new borders, the new structure of B, are highly contingent. In other words, there is nothing natural, nothing fixed, about them; they are the consequence of the fortunes of war. Its newly expanded territory is more than B bargained for, and soon the citizens of A will revolt; the borders of B will change again. All is change, all structure is provisional. Nothing is fixed, there is no purpose to the ongoing conflict of A and B; nothing abides. War is the father of all, distributing its spoils to the occasional victor.

To reformulate this entire train of thought, consider what is perhaps Heraclitus' most famous aphorism: "It is not possible to step twice into the same river" (91). Why not? Because the river never ceases to flow; the water drifting by our feet is the continual change of the river. Because everything flows, nothing abides. This is Heraclitus' world.

Heraclitus is fond of statements such as these: "Donkeys prefer chaff to gold (9)"; "Pigs wash themselves in mud, birds in dust or ashes (37)." These can be read as straightforward descriptions of how various species of animals differ. Or, as I suggest, they can be read symbolically: Gold has no intrinsic value; ask the donkey. Mud is not intrinsically superior to ashes or water. It depends entirely on one's perspective. Nothing is good in and of itself. Why? Because if something were to be good in and of itself, it would require that something be fixed and stable, that it have a nature. And nothing does; everything changes, especially what is considered to be good. Consider the following two aphorisms:

> To god, everything is beautiful and good and just; but human beings suppose that some things are unjust and others are just (102).[27]

> The human abode contains no good sense; the divine does contain it (76).

The first aphorism states that the divine and the human understand things differently. Human beings make distinctions; they evaluate different people and things differently. They say, this is beautiful, that's ugly; he's evil and she's good. By contrast, to the divine everything is good. And as the second aphorism indicates, the divine is right.

What does it mean to say everything is good? To clarify, we might return to some comments Aristotle made in his discussion of the Principle of Noncontradiction. If the principle does not hold, he argued, then there would be no stable basis for predication, and the possibility of significant discourse (as Aristotle understands it) would be destroyed. It would no longer be possible, for example, to assert that a human being is essentially an animal with two feet, that H is T. Without the principle, H might also be not-T. If this were the case, then it would not be possible to identify securely an example of H. The name "human being" would no longer refer to or signify something definite and stable, an animal with two feet. In turn, this would lead to the breakdown of significant or rational discourse since, as Aristotle puts it, not to speak significantly of one thing is not to speak significantly at all.

Another way of putting this point is that if the principle is denied, then the doctrines of substance and essence, the stable components of reality, would also be denied. As a result, there would be nothing "behind" or in addition to "appearances" that could be invoked as a measure; all appearances would be counted as equally truthful (see 1007a20 ff. and 1009a10 ff). If it appears to me that Edna is good, then Edna is good. If to you she appears evil, then she is evil. Without a stable reality by which to measure them, all appearances are the same. In other terms, if the principle is denied, then all opinions would be counted as true (1009a10 ff).

Heraclitus is mentioned by Aristotle as one who denies the principle (1005b25, 1010a13, 1012a24). I do not think, however, that Heraclitus simply asserts that it is false. If he did, then he would obviously defeat himself (for he would be declaring that the principle was F and not not-F.) Instead of declaring it false, Heraclitus dismisses its relevance. What I mean is this: The principle contains a "time clause"—P cannot belong and not belong to S in the same way or *at the same time*. At different times S can obviously be P and then not-P. Socrates is bearded now but he can be not-bearded later. What Socrates cannot be is bearded and not-bearded *at the same time*. This last phrase presupposes that time has discrete moments that can be abstracted and separated from one another. The principle implies that S can receive the predicate P at some particular moment that is somehow outside of the flow of time. *At the same time*, S cannot be P and not-P.

Heraclitus denies that there are such isolated or frozen moments. Nothing is outside the continual flow of time, and so there is no moment at which S must be P or not-P. Of course, human beings can delude themselves; we can act as if time did have its discete moments. Finally, however, these are just fictions with which we comfort ourselves. There is no stable basis of predication, no basis for saying, "She is good and not evil." Since all things flow, she is just as evil as she is good. Human beings, fallen into error as they typically are, persist in making rigid value judgments (in presupposing that there are fixed moments of time). If they had good judgment they would realize that she is neither good nor evil; she is in fact nothing. Instead, she is becoming, changing constantly. Value judgments of the typical sort, therefore, stand at odds with the flow of things.

The goal of Heraclitus' aphorisms is to teach us to affirm, rather than to defy, the fact that everything is in flux and nothing abides. When he says, "To god everything is beautiful and good," we need not imagine some divinity nodding his head. Instead, we should recall what Aristotle describes as a consequence of denying the Principle of Noncontradiction, namely the truth of all appearances. All is the same, unified in its flux. All is good; that is, "It is wise to agree that all is one."

To elaborate, consider these aphorisms, which I translate quite literally: "The way up down one and the same (60);" Immortals mortals mortals immortals, living their death and dying their life" (62); "Want and fullness" (65). In each opposite words are placed directly next to each other. There are few connectives, no verbs, nothing except the bare juxtaposition of two words that "ought" not to be next to each other. Heraclitus writes this way because a consequence of his world-picture is rejection of the relevance of the principle of Noncontradiction. But if this is the case, what sense can we make of those aphorisms originally cited where Heraclitus asks us to listen, not to him, but to the logos? How can there be a logos without the basic principle of stability? How can there be an objective order in a world of constant change? If "the most beautiful cosmos a dust-heap piled up at random" (124), how can there be a logos or a person who uses well the human capacity for logos? If Heraclitus is the relativist he appears to be, how can he coherently say, "One man to me is worth thousands, if he is the best" (49)?

The key to answering these questions is, I think, this: Heraclitus' aphorisms are meant to *exhibit* the playful flux of the world. They are not intended to be a stable Aristotelian explanation of the way stable things stand. Instead, they themselves are meant to imitate the *pais paizon*. The aphorisms, with their apparent contradictions and obscurity have a coherence and expressiveness all their own. Precisely by being image-ridden aphorisms, rather than arguments or demonstrations, they exhibit the truth they mean to tell. They are an appropriate and adequate form to give voice to the world Heraclitus sees.

To illustrate what I mean consider these: "Nature loves to hide" (123); "The harmony invisible than the visible harmony better" (54). How is an invisible harmony, one that does not appear or manifest itself, better than a visible one? To answer, consider first what the visible harmony might be. This might be the appearance of regularity in change: "Cold things get hot, hot things get cold, wet things dry, the parched is moistened" (126). From opposite comes opposite. The cold night gives way to the hot day. To say "The day is cold and hot" is not a contradiction because the two predicates are attributed to the subject at different times. For many scholars, this is the way of explicating the Heraclitean aphorisms by explaining away their appearance of self-contradiction. Many scholars take him to be a member of the tradition founded by Thales, and his logos is interpreted as an obscure attempt to tell the truth about the rhythmic flow of nature.[28]

I think these scholars are wrong. The visible harmony is inferior to the invisible harmony. The appearance of the regular exchange of opposite for opposite, the apparent rhythm of nature, can be articulated: cold (night) gives way to hot (day) which gives way to cold (night). But this articulation, which to some seems to be a "law" of nature, conceals as much as it reveals. It reveals: it says something about the rhythm of natural change. But it conceals as well: precisely by being a stable articulation, it hides the fact that nature is not stable. To say something definite about nature is to employ a human fiction to conceal something about nature (which loves to hide.) Heraclitus is not like Aristotle. His aphorisms love to hide. This is why his language is so peculiar, why he offers bare juxtaposition of contradictories, why he so often leaves out inflections of the verb "to be." The meaning of these aphorisms cannot be "pinned down." They make no attempt to articulate firmly a natural realm. Instead, they reflect the play of the world.

The invisible harmony is better than the visible one. Heraclitus' aphorisms must make something visible; they must say something. But at the same time they allude to what is not said, to what is invisible, to what they themselves, just by being stated, conceal. "The lord whose oracle is at Delphi neither speaks (*legei*) nor hides, but gives signs (*semainei*)" (93). The lord at Delphi says nothing straightforwardly, gives no logos in Aristotle's sense. Nor does he hide; he does, after all, say something. Instead, he gives signs, indirect indications. The verb here, *semainei*, is the same one Aristotle uses when he states his general principle in *Metaphysics*, IV: "Not to speak significantly (*semainein*) about one thing is not to speak significantly at all." I change the English translation because Heraclitus and Aristotle attach such different meanings to the verb. Aristotle's logos is a direct pointing out of the shape of natural entities. For him, if language did not refer to one definite thing, to something stable, then it could not be meaningful. Heraclitus would disagree. His aphorisms are riddles that cannot be simply solved ("what we see and grasp we leave behind; what we neither see nor grasp, we carry with us" [56]); they indicate, allude to, a world of play that flows through our fingers as we attempt to grasp it.[29] "In the same rivers we both step and do not step, we are and are not" (49a).

The best of men, the one worth thousands to Heraclitus, is he who has the strength to affirm, and not to flee from, the potentially paralyzing thought that nothing abides. Nietzsche expresses his admiration for Heraclitus by imagining him saying the following:

> I see nothing other than becoming. Be not deceived. It is the fault of your myopia, not of the nature of things, if you believe you see land somewhere in the ocean of coming-to-be and passing away. You use names for things as though they rigidly, persistently endured; yet even the stream into which you step a second time is not the one you stepped into before.[30]

It takes great strength to admit that nothing abides. To believe, as Aristotle does, that there is something solid and dependable in the ocean of becoming is a consequence of weakness, of myopia. More specifically, to believe this is to be seduced by ordinary language (especially nouns). We think our names refer to beings, structures, islands. But, in fact, the name misleads for there is no being to correspond to that name. What is needed, therefore, is a different way of using language, one that will not mislead. And this is the Heraclitean aphorism. It plays. It changes. It contradicts itself. "One, which alone is said to be wise, is not willing and willing to be called by the name of Zeus" (32).

Heraclitus' aphorisms perfect the art that Derrida is now trying so hard to master: that of being playful, of creating a mode of assertion that retracts itself, that is both present and absent, that allows the signifier to roam in playful freedom from the signified.[31]

Heraclitus, Nietzsche, and Derrida, then, are misologists: They hate logos in its classical sense. For them there is no stable and unchanging principle of being; instead, there is becoming, world-play, unregulated flux. In such a view the Principle of Noncontradiction has no privileged status: there are no natural and enduring substances capable of admitting unequivocally true propositions. The goal of language and thought, therefore, is not to state the Truth about things as they are, but to go with the flow. The *pais paizon* rules, and logos is condemned as myopic weakness. This is anarchy, the view that fundamentally opposes itself to the principle and so to the conception of significant discourse held by Aristotle.

To digress briefly: One of the more interesting developments in the profession of American philosophy in recent years has been an eagerness to hold a dialogue with the misologists. I am referring to attempts to mend a split that has long characterized the profession, namely that between the "Continental" (European) and "analytical" (Anglo-American) philosophers. The recent Continentals are subversives, misologists, following the lead of Germans like Nietzsche and Heidegger and their French descendants like Derrida. As their title suggests, the analyticals are those following the Anglo-American tradition of sober-minded, rigorous, traditional analytical thinking. In one sense, these thinkers see themselves as following in Aristotle's footsteps; they adhere to the Principle of Noncontradiction; they are serious. These two camps have long battled each other for power and prestige in the academic world. Now, we are told, the time has come for reconciliation and dialogue.

A good example of this new spirit of harmony comes from a former president of the American Philosophical Association. He laments the fact that too often in the past much of discussion in the philosophical community "has been insular and has militated against the admittedly difficult but also essential exchange between basically different outlooks and approaches." He goes on to say that "the task before us now is to initiate a serious dialogue among the many different philosophical opinions represented in the Association."[32] A comparable statement is made by a spokesman for the Cambridge University Press, which recently commissioned a work titled *Modern French Philosophy*. This book aims "to increase mutual recognition and respect . . . on both sides of the same Channel." Even more recently, the author of this book was made an editor at Oxford University Press and has started a series devoted to Continental philosophy.[33]

The main purpose of this chapter has been to show that this hope is ill conceived. The two sides of the Channel, if they indeed represent, on the one side, the misologists and, on the other, the advocates of the Principle of Noncontradiction, cannot be bridged for they represent divergent views on fundamental issues. There can be conversion; Richard Rorty, for example, has transformed himself into a subversive. There can be mutual tolerance. But there cannot be philosophical dialogue. The recent developments in the profession of philosophy have recapitulated, yet again, the oldest of disputes: that between logos and its accusers.[34]

This, finally, is the insight logos attains: It cannot refute its opponents, its accusers, those who hate it. It cannot even enter into dialogue with them. This it now sees. And such seeing brings with it a recognition of a previous blindness. Logos screams: "Everything is now all too clear. I am not king, have never occupied a faithful throne. I, supposed lover of knowing, have never known who I am. Now I do, for now I know that I, the supposed knower, am ignorant. And this, my new knowledge, castigates me for my old blindness. Who was I to accuse my accuser . . . for I am guilty of the self-same crime. Even worse, I have compounded my crime with self-deception and arrogance. But I have learned; never again shall I see the world with these same eyes."

B Paradigms of Play

(1) The Athlete and the Child

Exhausted. Is logos finished? Must we (who for some time have admired logos) give up on all light, all possibility of using reason, the capacity to know, to make ourselves whole and well? Has the initial moment, the Aristotelian impetus, been exposed as nothing but deluded and oppressive fraud? Is there hope of any sort, or are we destined only for despair?

I am not sure. But if there is not hope in the sense of an expectation of resolution or rectification, there is yet another possibility: affirmation. Even after its reversals and hard-won recognitions, perhaps logos will yet be able to stand and say yes to who it is. It has confessed its blindness, but has not yet been fully crushed. Perhaps logos is newly understood.

Derridean play, the liberation of the signifier, the overthrow of logo-centrism, is the most contemporary and vigorous form of misology. It cannot be refuted nor can logos even engage it in a serious philosophical dialogue. This misology spreads like fire, deconstructing what was old and once thought good. As we have seen, Derridean play finds its ante-cedents in Nietzsche who, in turn, acknowledges his debt to Heraclitus' *pais paizon*. Child's play is the image of a world emptied of being, of structure and stability, a world in which reason has no true home, no ability to articulate with authority what is right or wrong, good or evil.

(It is worth recalling that this sort of misology is not restricted to those who are fashionably subversive; it is also the flip side of the view generated by those most apparently sober of men, Descartes and Spinoza. Descartes, for example, constructs a provisional morality in order to get on with the serious business of mathematical physics. He conceives of the world of purposes, values and meanings as a series of conventions produced by the human imagination and imposed by the will. There is no principle to guide the production of such conventions; their coming into being is a matter of creative energy. This is, I propose, akin to the view tokened by Heraclitus' *pais paizon*.)[35]

It is surprising, but true, that after all these pages play has become the issue. To the *pais paizon* logos must somehow respond, make its plea, perhaps capitulate. But does this imply that logos must totally renounce its serious purpose? Must it repress its erotic nature, that which energizes it as it strives to attain its goals? Must it bow to Nietzsche's character Zarathustra as he does battle against the "spirit of gravity," the impulse to deny the flow of time? The old king serious has indeed been de-throned; but do we yet understand what will take its place? Do we, in other words, yet understand what play is? Heraclitus' *pais paizon* is a specific image, or paradigm, of play and it is of course true that children wonderfully exemplify play. But adults play as well and do so quite differently than children. "There is, in other words, a crucial difference between mere playfulness and playing to win."[36] The question I will ask in this section is, Why should the child, rather than the adult, automati-cally be given pride of place when it comes to play?

Yes, the seriousness of Aristotle has been dethroned. After its three recognition and reversal scenes (the successive discomfitures at the hands of Cleitophon and Hesiod, the revelation that philosophical dialogue is impossible) logos can never again be so assertively serious. But this does not imply that logos must be supplanted by Heraclitean play. This would be necessary if there were only two options, Aristotelian seriousness and the *pais paizon*. What if, however, there is a third way, one that somehow falls in between the two just mentioned? I will explore this possibility by proposing an image to counter the Heraclitean *pais*, one that takes its bearings from an adult, not a child, playing to win. The subject of this section will be the athlete.

(And is this what logos has come to? Once so proud, it first offered an argument for itself, one that claimed nature as its warrant. Its second best way, the subjective or psychological argument, analyzed the structure of our erotic longings and language and concluded that they point upward to the Idea. Now, impoverished logos can only present an image. It can only hope what follows will exert some force of attraction on its reader, but it recognizes that if the reader feels no such force, sees no value in the image, then the game is over. The reader may well believe that this whole story has now degenerated into poetry, that the little semblance there ever was of argument in this book has now self-consciously given way to a battle of images. There is no argument to prove to such a reader that this image should compel and inform. At some point, all we can do is point and ask, "Do you see it or not?")

The most basic form of adult play is athletics, that type of organized and rule-bound competition in which the participants compete for a prize (in Greek "*athlon*," the root of "athlete," means "prize"). What I will suggest is that the athlete provides an alternative paradigm of play, one that shows a middle ground between child's play, the image used to represent the instability, the purposeless flux, of the world of human significance, and the old-fashioned quest for Truth and Goodness. The athlete, as a paradigm of play and an image of a stance to be taken toward the world, shares with traditional Aristotelian seriousness the belief that human energy directed toward agreed-upon goals is meaningfully well spent. At the same time, it shares with Heraclitus' child the belief that such goals do not abide, are insubstantial and in this sense meaningless. This sounds like a contradiction or a paradox, and in some sense it is. But it is a paradox that can be affirmed and lived and it is this possibility that will allow logos to go on.

As usual, a discussion of a select portion of a Greek text will provide the occasion to explain what I am talking about. This time it is the penultimate chapter (Book XXIII) of Homer's *Iliad*. Here the poet sings of the athletic contests held during the funeral of Patroklos, the Greek hero slain by the Trojan warrior Hektor. Briefly, the background to the story is this: The Greeks, led by Agamemnon, have gone to war against the Trojans to regain Helen. In the course of the protracted battle Agamemnon insults Achilles, the greatest of all Greek heroes, by taking away his prize, the woman Briseis. In response to this affront, Achilles refuses to fight with his comrades. As a result, the Trojans gain much ground. Achilles is intractable. Even though the Greeks suffer defeats and many of his comrades fall to the enemy, he refuses to reenter the battle. Only when the Trojans actually approach the Greek ships does Achilles relent: he allows Patroklos, his beloved friend, to wear his own armor and go to the aid of the beleagured Greeks. For a while Patroklos succeeds in shoring up the Greek defense, but soon he is killed by Hektor. At this point Achilles rejoins the fight. From Book XVII to XXII Homer sings of Achilles' murderous rage. He kills a great many Trojans. Finally he avenges Patroklos' death by slaughtering Hektor, a killing he culminates by mutilating the Trojan's corpse.

With the death of Hektor in Book XXII Achilles' rage at last is spent. Book XXIII recounts the games held in honor of Patroklos, and Book XXIV tells the story of what is perhaps the greatest reconciliation of enemies ever depicted: that between Priam, king of the Trojans and father of Hektor, and Achilles, hero of the Greeks.

The *Iliad* is framed by Achilles' rage (*menis*). It is his anger at Agamemnon that starts the action of the poem, and it is not until this rage is redirected, and then fully expressed, at the Trojans that the poem ends. What is quite extraordinary about Achilles is that despite his famous *menis*, he is not simply, one-dimensionally, a violent man. Indeed, he is as capable of love (*philotes*) and loyalty as he is of rage. As one scholar puts it, "The *Iliad* is as much about the *philotes* of Achilles as it is about his *menis*. The love he feels for Patroklos, his conversations with his mother, and his tender relationships with his surrogate fathers Phoinix and Priam are as exceptionally human and as unparalleled among the Greeks as is his divine wrath."[37]

In keeping with this human and social side of his character, Homer makes it clear that before the events depicted in the *Iliad* Achilles had behaved quite decently toward his enemies.[38] But with the death of Patroklos he is transformed into a totally antisocial, maddened killer. The following scene exhibits this well. Here Achilles slaughters Lykaon, a pathetic man who only a few days earlier had been captured by Achilles. In what had then been his typically decent and social manner, Achilles had allowed him to live. Lykaon has no such luck the second time.

> Poor fool, no longer speak to me of ransom, nor argue it. In the time before Patroklos came to the day of his destiny then it was the way of my heart's choice to be sparing of the Trojans, and many I took alive and disposed of them. Now there is not one who can escape death, if the gods send him against my hands in front of Ilion, not one of all the Trojans and beyond others the children of Priam. So, friend, you die also. Why all this clamour

about it? Patroklos also is dead, who was better by far than you are. Do you
not see what a man I am, how huge, how splendid and born of a great
father, and the mother who bore me immortal?
  Yet even I have also my death and strong destiny. (XXI, 99–110)

Hapless Lykaon spreads his bare arms wide in a final, lifeless gesture,
and Achilles slaughters him. He grabs the corpse and flings it into the
river shouting madly that "a fish will break a ripple shuddering dark on
the water as he rises to feed upon the shining fat of Lykaon" (XXI, 126–
127). "Die on," Achilles cries, addressing, it seems, the whole world.

There are scenes of comparable violence in these later chapters of
the *Iliad*. Achilles slays twelve innocent Trojan boys, mutilates Hektor's
corpse, and goes so far as to do battle with a river. Even within the warrior
world of the Homeric hero these are unacceptably violent actions for they
break the code that regulates this archaic warfare. In his rage Achilles is
no longer human; he becomes death incarnate and his mere scream
terrifies a whole army.[39]

Book XXIII, however, tokens a transformation. Here, when the funeral celebration begins, Achilles returns to the friendly ways of his past.
A series of games, of athletic contests, is held and for these Achilles acts
as referee, peacekeeper, and distributor of prizes. There are moments
when he even smiles (see line 556). A good example occurs during the
chariot race. A young man, Antilochos, becomes angry at the king's
brother, Menelaus. He voices a grievance not too different from the one
Achilles himself had leveled at Agamemnon in Book I, namely that he is
not getting the prize he deserves (lines 543-555). Achilles manages to
deflect Antilochos' anger and so prevents a second internal quarrel from
erupting among the Greeks. He acts toward Antilochos as Agamemnon
should have acted toward him.

The notion of celebrating a funeral with athletic games may seem
strange to us. In the *Iliad*, however, there is clearly something deeply
appropriate about these contests. What is it? Why does Homer have his
Greeks honor the life and death of the warrior Patroklos with games? In
one sense, the answer is easy: This was a traditional way of honoring the
deaths of distinguished men, and the *Iliad* is a poem that reflects traditional ways of life.[40] But as a poet, Homer does more than report accurately the ways of the society he depicts, and so the easy answer tells little.
Why games? Attempting to answer this question will help clarify how the
athlete functions as a paradigm of play, as an image of a stance to be
taken toward the world, one that is in-between traditional seriousness
and the *pais paizon*.

The athletic contests of the funeral and the war that comprises most
of the action of the *Iliad* are analogous. They are both competitive and

directed to a goal or prize, namely victory. In war, at least as Homer describes it, there is a need for strength, skill, daring and endurance, qualities required as well by the successful athlete. It is thus hardly surprising that in the *Iliad* the victors in the games (Diomedes, Ajax, Odysseus, Meriones) are among the best fighters.

Athletic contests, however, also differ fundamentally from war. Instead of destroying a society, they enhance it. They are socially productive and bring laughter rather than tears. (See lines 556, 625, 647, 789, 797, 840.) War is deadly serious, but games are not. Here we find the basic reason why athletics are an appropriate manner of celebrating the funeral of Patroklos. In honoring the death of a warrior the games rehearse many of the aspects of war without war's horrifying and all-too-serious blood. They celebrate physical vitality and, at least in part, the value system for which the warrior died. They reaffirm life and so integrate the warrior's death back within a socially viable context: they encourage the community to go on.

But there is more. In their graceful brevity games offer us miniature lives. For the athlete, the game, while it is being played, is totally consuming. The athlete is so thoroughly immersed in the game that he forgets the world outside. Those of us who have played know this experience well. The web of everyday concerns that generally occupy us are forgotten as we play. This is why games are capable of inspiring such enthusiasm. They generate a small world of their own, one whose rules, goals, and boundaries, unlike those of the everyday world, are clearly defined, agreed upon, and within reach. This is why the game is so immersing, why it is a small island in the flow of everyday time to which so many of us return again and again. Within the game there is no doubt about what is expected of the athlete, and when the game ends there is no doubt who won and who lost.

Unlike everyday life, games can be completed and then begun again. Unlike everyday time, whose indefinite future ever looms ahead (promising, threatening, causing a fracture between now and then), games are played with a fluid and concentrated motion that frees us from doubt. We simply play, always moving forward, always trying hard, unencumbered by all the qualifications the ordinary world with its hidden future and troubling past suggests.

If the game is a miniature life, then it is not surprising that in the heat of competition it can be experienced as something like a life-or-death matter. This is the source of what is frequently so objectionable about athletics. Athletes risk serious injury to themselves or to their opponents, they cheat, they explode into violence. Enormous sums of money are spent to achieve success, and games can become all too consuming. Athletes become *too serious* and forget the tired phrase, *"it's only a game."*

Indeed, such sensible counsel is regularly forgotten. Athletic play is precarious; it is tensely balanced between the two extemes that flank it. It can, on the one hand, easily become too serious and thus more closely resemble war than play. It can also lapse into the other extreme. If the athletes are not serious enough, if they cease to care who wins and hold victory in contempt, then the game is no longer a true contest. In order to be played well, the game must be played in order to win. If victory is not taken seriously as a goal, then the activity is more like child's play than athletics.

It is with the phrase "It's only a game" that the true nature of athletic play is illuminated. Games are *only* games. The goals athletes strive for are not really of life-or-death significance; athletes only act *as if* they are. Games are not really that serious because their goals are the products of artificial conventions. Winning a game of basketball, for example, might require putting a ball through a hoop fifteen times. How one is allowed to do this is circumscribed by the rules: one is not allowed to kick the ball, hit the defender, step on the boundary line, and so forth. In order for the game to occur these rules must be adhered to strictly, for the rules make it possible for the game to become the small, self-contained world that it is. Imagine if the prohibition against kicking the ball were not strictly enforced: there would be arguments, chaos; there would be no distinction between a well-played and a poorly played game, and it never would be clear what constituted victory. It would not be a good game. For the athlete, the rules make the game satisfying. This is why, even without an official referee (in "pickup" games), there is surprisingly little dispute over rules; athletes implicitly realize that their play requires acknowledgement of the conventions that constitute their game.

These rules, however, are arbitrary. The hoop placed on the backboard is not "by nature" ten feet above the ground. There is no reason why three steps should not be taken between bounces of the ball. These are conventions; they could easily be changed.[41] This implies that the goal of the game, victory, making fifteen baskets, is also arbitrary. As a result, in an important sense victory is quite meaningless; it has no enduring worth imbedded in the nature of things. Depositing a round ball in a hoop fifteen times has no meaning outside of the temporary, highly conventionalized, world of the game. This is why games frequently look so peculiar or childish from the outside.

What has just been said, however, does not imply that the experience of athletics, playing the game, is meaningless. The ordinary experience of athletes, our return again and again to the court in order to find a small segment of time meaningfully well spent, testifies to the deep attraction of the game. Despite the fact that the goal is constituted by something artificial, we feel our playing to emerge from our natures; we are compelled by the experience of competitive play and relish the small but engrossing life-world of the game. What the above implies is that the simple achievement of victory cannot account for the experience of playing. Winning does not exhaust the meaning of the game. We must, it seems, play for the sake of playing and not for the sake of winning.

This may sound "idealistic" and so someone will object: For the serious, the real, athlete winning is the only thing that counts. But this is not so. If victory as an isolated fact were the only thing that really mattered in a game, then a list of an athlete's victories would be equivalent to an account of what was meaningful in the athlete's experience. It simply is not the case that the phrase "200 victories, 150 defeats," adequately explains the experience of years on a basketball court.

The cliché is quite right: It isn't who wins or loses, but how one plays the game. The cliché of course gets forgotten at the highest reaches of televised athletics where the prizes for victory include enormous sums of money. But the overwhelming number of athletes are not professionals. It is street-play, pickup games played over the lunch hour, the games where the name of the victor is soon forgotten, that are the animating force behind all athletics. They are what initially sparked, and usually maintain, even the professional athlete. It is the pickup game, and not the Super-Bowl, that tells us what athletics mean.

Victory, the prize, is the goal of athletic play, but it is not equivalent to the meaning of play. It's not who wins or loses, but how one plays the game. But we must not become so intoxicated with the cliché that we forget a crucial fact about athletics: If it is true that good play, not just victory, is what really matters, it is equally true that play can only be good when it aims for victory. This is peculiar. How can the athlete play so hard, so seriously, on a rectangular court whose dimensions are arbitrary? Why should the athlete direct her intense energies toward achievement of an all-but-meaningless goal?

Athletics are a most peculiar, even paradoxical, phenomenon. In them we find a nonserious, forgettable, or meaningless goal, victory as arbitrarily defined, making possible a serious, an erotic, activity which itself is experienced as meaningful. There is thus a dimension of absurdity in athletics. We compete for a goal soon to be forgotten. Athletes act as if life itself were at stake when what is really at issue is nothing but fifteen baskets. *It's only a game.* But in the midst of competition athletes play, indeed must play, as if the goal of the game, victory, really did matter. We play for that which, upon distanced reflection, dissolves into absurdity. This is why those who are outside of a game are often incredulous, or even contemptuous of, those of us who play. This is why some athletes, when the game ceases, feel almost ashamed at having taken it all so seriously. Why should a rational adult risk bodily harm playing a game when the game is, from the outsider's perspective, a silly bundle of conventions?

To note this dimension of absurdity in athletics is not to condemn them. Quite to the contrary, it is precisely this paradoxical nature of athletics that is their enduring charm and why, compared to the petty pace of everyday life, they stand out as islands of such brilliance. In order to play well, the athlete must play to win. Not to do so is virtually to cheat, for the game is defined by its rules, which in turn mandate victory as the goal. But victory, in and of itself, is bereft of meaning and so not a serious goal. After the pickup game has ended, who won is of little or no consequence. And yet the athlete returns to play, to attempt to win, again and again, for the game is experienced as deeply compelling. We play for a goal which, upon reflection, is empty. But our play is not empty.

Athletic competitions so appropriately close the *Iliad* because they represent and affirm in succinct, graceful, and nondestructive form the paradox of human striving. They are analogous to the actual war from which they are a reprieve. In the Homeric world war is the most serious of activities, for it is the only arena in which a meaningful life (or in Homeric terms, glory) can be achieved.[42] The Trojan War, however, is fought for the most absurd reason: the abduction of a Spartan woman, Helen, who was stolen by a Trojan prince, Paris, son of Priam. As Homer makes us realize time and again, the cause and goal of the war are desperately out of proportion with the destruction they bring. Troy, a living city of women, men, and children, is annihilated by the rampaging Greeks only for the sake of Helen and men's pride.

One scene in particular makes this pain sharp and clear. Here Hektor pauses briefly from the battle to return to the walls of Troy. He visits his wife Andromache and infant son. When he reaches to pick his boy up, the child is frightened by his father's crested helmet. To comfort him, Hektor kisses his boy and prays that he "may be as I am, preeminent among the Trojans, great in strength, as I am, and rule strongly over Ilion" (VI, 477–478). The reader, and to some extent even Hektor, knows that both Hektor and Ilion are doomed for destruction, and so this prayer, emanating from the love of a father, is really a prayer for the death of a son. Homer tells us that Andromache, witnessing this peaceful and affectionate moment, "laughed through her tears" (VI, 484). Human laughter, generated by the warmth of the family, is forever laced with the tears of pointless battle. Unlike the gods, we are mortal and cannot keep for long the prizes we hold dear. Our losses are continually impending and cannot be reclaimed.

Even the sadness of this scene, sparked by the richness of domestic life and the intuition of its demise, does not imply that Homer condemns the war Hektor fights. Homer is not a pacifist, for in an important sense he affirms war. As stated, given the very limited world of the Homeric hero, war is the only arena in which glory, the most meaningful and serious of goals, can be achieved. But glory is bought at a disproportionately high, or even paradoxical, price: the death of fundamentally similar men seeking the very same goal. Even this fact, however, does not provide grounds for pacifism. War typifies the tragedy of human striving. All striving is, finally, for goals, like Helen, whose substance vanishes. This does not imply, however, that striving for such goals is itself meaningless; tragedy does not imply despair or paralysis. Instead, the situation can be clarified by athletics. In order to play well the athlete strives for a victory soon to be forgotten. In order to fight well, the warrior does the same. The difference between war and athletic play in Homer's poem is that only the latter, because it ends and then begins again, allows us to see sharply and to affirm appreciatively what our striving is.[43]

We strive for goals: glory, money, publication, wisdom, power, large families, pleasure. The achievement of such goals is but a moment. Our goals fade: There is not some nature of things to certify them with enduring value. They vanish. And so what to do? Join forces with Nietzsche and Heraclitus and proclaim that all is a flux whose king is a playing child? Are we to renounce all our erotic strivings because goals are not imbedded in an eternal structure? Are we to abandon our attempts to understand the world if it cannot be shown that the world is definitively, naturally, structured? No, not if we take our bearings from the athlete. As an image of a stance to be taken toward the human world, the athlete allows us to say yes to our striving, whether it is on the battlefield, in the political arena, or in our conversations. Even though our goals are no more than hoops nailed back to a board, our striving is to be prized.

The athlete gives us a middleground. The ephemerality of our goals, the fact that they are not imbedded in the nature of things, should inhibit us from taking them too seriously. But without serious and goal-directed activity, we lose ourselves and cannot play well. Heraclitus' *pais paizon* is a distortion. As an image of human experience it fails, for people do play games, try to win, and take their goals seriously. They do play well or play poorly. This must be taken into account and as an image the athlete, not the child, is able to express this.

Unfortunately, there is no argument, no appeal to human nature, to certify claims such as the ones just made. Indeed, objections could be offered. (One could argue, for example, that athletes just delude themselves by taking their their games so seriously.) For the moment, however, let us agree only on this: logos has been forced to acknowledge the primacy of play. But what is play? Is it necessarily the *pais paizon*, or is there an alternative? As a paradigm of play, athletics provide an option in between Heraclitean (Derridean) child's play and the Aristotelian seriousness fundamentally opposing it. This paradigm has only been asserted and not defended. No reason has been provided as to why the athlete is any more acceptable than the *pais paizon*. The two paradigms have simply been juxtaposed.

At this point habit will force (some of) us to ask: Which of these two paradigms is "better"? What would happen if the two paradigms were brought into competition, if they were to "debate" and rationally contest each other's merits? The answer is all too obvious: The athlete would "win," for the athlete is essentially a competitor, while the child is not. The obviousness of the answer shows the problem with the question: As we have seen all too often, entrance into a competition such as this one between the two paradigms of play is hardly a neutral act. Even to ask for such a competition is to predetermine its outcome. Simply to begin the game is already to declare allegiance to one of the two paradigms, namely the athlete, for it is the athlete who plays such games. Therefore, if given a choice the proponent of the *pais* (the misologist) should, in order to remain true to herself, refuse to enter such a game. Instead of attempting to defend herself against a competitor, she should speak in the voice of a Heraclitean aphorism or ask for assistance from one of Hesiod's Muses. The game of rational defense is one in which she should express no interest and take no part.

The proposed competition between the two paradigms of play thus recapitulates the various confrontations we have seen throughout this book. The proponent of the *pais paizon* is like the Sophist. Therefore, if faced with an invitation to debate against a representative of logos, like Socrates, she should follow the lead of Cleitophon and reject the model of Thrasymachus; that is, she should refuse to debate Socrates. Debating Socrates requires entrance into a game. But once the Socratic game begins, it is over, for like every game it has rules (or presuppositions). To say yes to Socrates' invitation to debate is to agree that competition is good, that the prize of victory should be sought. This is, however, a fundamental decision, one that gives shape to an entire view of the world (one in which knowledge is made good). The Sophist (the poeticist, Heraclitus, the misologist) disagrees with Socrates on the most fundamental of levels. Therefore, she cannot win against Socrates when the game is played according to the philosopher's rules.

The introduction of the paradigm of the athlete does not obviate the dilemma, the tragedy, of logos. The juxtaposition of the two images leaves us still at an impasse, for it provides no avenue of rational adjudication. Nevertheless, from this chapter emerges a modest form of self-affirmation. Logos, whose fortunes have been terribly reversed throughout the course of this book, will exit the stage dressed like a beggar and not a king. But it will exit standing and not crawling—for logos, as we will now see, is *conditionally*, and not unconditionally, good. It is good contingent upon acceptance of one condition: that there be some other person (out there) who is willing to talk with logos, to approach it even as an opponent. If there is an opponent who attempts (or is persuaded to attempt) to defend himself in a rational contest, then he is willing to play Socrates' game. If the opponent is not so willing (and in its own way this is a coherent, perhaps even reasonable, option) then logos has no legitimate authority to compel him to do so: the gulf that separates Socrates from someone like Cleitophon, or Hesiod from Thales, cannot be rationally or unconditionally bridged. Still, there is something to be gained from this chapter: *If* the opponent wishes to debate, to enter the competition, *then* the victory of logos can be secured.

And there is something else: We can observe that human beings, for whatever reason, frequently—perhaps typically—do want to enter such contests. (If "typically" is objectionable in the previous sentence, then substitute "people we know" for "human beings.") They do want to defend their positions (even when their positions denounce logos) in public display. Once they attempt to do this, they enter Socrates' game, they capitulate to the paradigm of the athlete even while attempting to defend the paradigm of the child. They thus recapitulate the incoherence Aristotle exposes in those denying the Principle of Noncontradiction: In the midst of denying logos they affirm it. And this spells their defeat.

Old habits die hard: Some of us are tempted to say, it is natural for human beings to want to play Socrates' game, to enter into rational contest. But saying this would only restate the Aristotelian maxim that human beings are the animals with logos. Therefore, the affirmation of logos made here is far less grand than that made during its first scene (Chapter I.A.1.) Here it is strictly conditional. If someone enters the Socratic game, he commits himself to its rules. And these rules stipulate that victory in debate is possible, that rationally certifiable knowledge is the goal, that the Truth should be sought. Such rules, however, represent just the position that the opponents of logos would like to argue against.

While the *pais paizon* is viable, and in an important sense irrefutable, it is thus faced with one enormous restriction: It cannot claim for itself a position that it is prepared to defend. Claim-making is a temptation that the followers of Heraclitus should, for their own good, resist.

In the next section we will briefly discuss another of Plato's dialogues, the *Ion*. In it we will find an excellent example of someone, the rhapsode Ion, facing, and then succumbing to, the temptation of claim-making. We will see how carefully Plato analyzes Ion's dilemma and how he even offers Ion the potentially fruitful option of resisting the temptation and avoiding Socratic refutation.

There are three reasons to engage in yet another dialogue such as this. First, doing so will allow for a quite explicit statement of why Plato is the hero of this book. Second, discussing the *Ion* will culminate the treatment of the all-important quarrel between the philosopher and the poet. Finally, the issue of techne, which has been discussed piecemeal throughout this book, will be raised and concluded. In the introduction it was said that "techne," along with "tragedy" and "logos," was one of three words that would function as guiding paths for the argument of this book. The meaning of this statement should finally be clarified in what follows. The three paths will meet and (I hope) this story will draw to a reasonable close.

(2) The Philosopher and the Poet (Continued)

In a short dialogue titled the *Ion*, Socrates confronts a man named Ion who is a rhapsode, someone who makes his living reciting poetry, particularly that of Homer. Ion is a skilled performer. He can make tears appear in the eyes of his audience when he sings of woeful Andromache; his recitation of the battle between Hektor and Achilles is so thrilling that his hair stands on end (535b–c).[44] This gift of rhapsody is one that Socrates professes to admire, and he approaches Ion with the intention of having him explain what knowledge it is that allows him to accomplish these extraordinary feats.

> And indeed, Ion, I often envied you rhapsodes for your techne. For at the same time that it is always appropriate for your techne to adorn your body and make it seem as beautiful as possible, it is necessary for you to spend time with many good poets, and especially with Homer, the best and most divine of the poets. Furthermore, the fact that you must come to understand Homer's thought, and not only his words, is enviable. For one would not be a good rhapsode if one did not comprehend that which is said by the poet. For the rhapsode should be an interpreter (*hermeneus*) of the poet's thought to his listeners. And if he does not know what the poet means he cannot do this well. (530b5–c6)

As this paragraph makes clear, Socrates conceives of Ion as more than a mere performer. Socrates suggests, and Ion agrees, that the rhapsode is an "interpreter" as well as a singer, who should understand the thought of and comprehend that which is said and meant by the poet. (*"Hermeneus"* is the root of our word "hermeneutics.") Even further, Ion claims (or is persuaded to claim) to possess a techne (530b6, b7, c8), a determinate knowledge or expertise about his subject.

After these initial remarks, the dialogue falls into three distinct parts. The first contains a typical Socratic refutation. Socrates demonstrates that Ion cannot substantiate his claim to having a techne. Obviously, then, the tone of this section is negative: Socrates reveals the inadequacy of his opponent's boast. The second section, however, is quite different. In it Socrates discusses what gift the rhapsode does possess. While it is true, he says, that Ion does not have a techne, he does have a very real and positive talent. This Socrates goes on to describe. At the end of this second section Socrates presents Ion with a choice: He can rest content with the positive, but nontechnical, characterization of poetry, or he can reassert his claim to a techne. Ion chooses the latter option, and in the third section of the dialogue he is again refuted by Socrates.

The transition between the second and third sections is highlighted by the choice Socrates presents to Ion and is the crucial juncture of the dialogue. As we will see, this choice, whether to claim a techne or rest content with the nontechnical characterization Socrates offers to Ion, is equivalent to a choice between entering or refusing to enter Socrates' game. If Ion relinquishes his claim to a techne, he could refuse to play Socrates' game. He could not be refuted for he would have no rational claim to defend. He, like Cleitophon or Hesiod, could thus carve for himself an inviolable space, one immune to Socratic refutation. On the other hand, if Ion continues to profess a techne, which in fact he does, he commits himself to certain presuppositions and is then quite easily refuted. Like other Socratic opponents, Ion cannot resist the temptation of claim-making. Once he succumbs, he is doomed to refutation.

What happens to Ion illustrates the point made in the previous section: *If* someone chooses to argue against Socrates, he commits himself to the rules of Socrates' game. These rules, however, are not neutral—for they presuppose the outlines of a philosophical position. (They imply that knowledge is good, authoritative, capable of being rationally defended and explicated, and should be sought.) Simply entering the game thus implies affirmation of Socrates' position. Therefore, when an opponent such as Ion, who thinks he holds an anti-Socratic position (that poetry, not logos, is the higher good), enters the game, he loses it.

In the first part of the dialogue Ion professes to have a techne. Socrates refutes him by getting him to agree to the following assertions (which occur on lines 531a–533b and which I paraphrase): If Mike professes to have a techne about subject S, then Mike professes to be a master, an expert about S. As a result, Mike ought to know S thoroughly. Therefore, if Jan and Dean talk about S, with Jan doing so well (knowledgeably) and Dean doing so poorly (with ignorance), then Mike should be able to evaluate, comment upon, speak intelligently about, both Jan and Dean. For example, if Mike is an expert in arithmetic, and Jan and Dean both venture to comment on a problem in addition, with Jan getting the problem right and Dean wrong, then Mike should be able to criticize and evaluate both their efforts.

Ion claims to have a techne whose subject is poetry. Therefore, he should be able to comment on all who enter this field. Hesiod and Archilochus (a poet of the 6th century b.c.e.) are both poets, but Ion is unable to comment on their work. He is interested in and knowledgeable only about Homer and thus fails to meet an essential criterion of a real expert (in Greek, a *technites*, one with a techne). Therefore, Ion's claim is illegitimate.

Ion responds to the loss of his techne with a certain innocent charm. He says: "I cannot argue against you on this point, Socrates. But I am conscious of this ability in myself, that of all men I speak most finely about Homer and have plenty to say. And everybody else says that I speak well [about Homer], but not about the other poets. Can you tell me what this means?" (533c4–8).

This plea leads Socrates into the second part of the dialogue where he tries to explain to Ion what gives him the power to rhapsodize so beautifully about his beloved Homer.

> I do see, Ion, and I am going to make clear to you what this talent of yours seems to me to be. For, as I was just now saying, it is not a techne which allows you to speak about Homer so well, but a divine power which moves you, just like the power that is in the stone which Euripides called "the magnet," but which most people call "Heracles' stone." For this stone not only attracts the iron rings themselves, but injects a power into these rings so that they too can do the very thing which the stone can do, namely attract other rings. The result is often a long chain of iron rings attached to one another. And it is the power from that stone which joins together all these pieces.
>
> In a similar fashion the Muse herself makes men enthused and through these enthused men, who make other men enthused, a chain is fastened. For all the good epic poets compose all their fine poems, not by virtue of a techne, but by being enthused and possessed. The same is true of the lyric poets. Just like corybantes who dance when they are not in their right minds, so too are the lyric poets not in their right minds when they compose their fine lyrics.[45] Instead, when they embark upon their harmony and rhythms, they act like bacchants and are possessed, just like the bacchants are possessed when they draw honey and milk from the rivers. And the souls of

the lyric poets, not being in their right minds, do this very thing and they themselves admit it. For the poets tell us, I think, that from the gardens and glens of the muses they bring us their songs, plucking them from the honey-flowing fountains like the winged bees. For they are thus winged. *And the poets speak the truth.* For the poet is a light thing and winged and holy and he is not able to compose before he becomes enthused and out of his senses and his mind is no longer within himself (533c9–534b6).

Socrates explains that Ion speaks well about Homer, not by virtue of a techne, but because he enjoys a "divine dispensation" that moves him. Socrates likens this divine power to a magnet, one that not only moves iron rings, but magnetizes them as well. The rings, in turn, move other iron pieces and the result is a well-linked chain. Analogously, the Muse causes the poet to become enthused or inspired. In turn, the poet inspires the rhapsode, who finally communicates this electrifying power to his audience. The spectator is the last of the rings, the poet the first.[46] Both the rhapsode and the poet, then, are able to speak as well as they do because of the very "mus-ical" inspiration we discussed above when examining Hesiod. The poet has no techne. Instead, he is possessed (533e7), not in his mind (534a1). The poet is like the bacchant, out of his mind (534b5).

Was I right to describe this passage as positive? Does Socrates add to "the greater glory of poetry" by apotheosizing its origin? Or is Socrates "making a nasty joke on poetry" by exaggerating its passive and inspired nature?[47] The passage, I propose, is ambiguous; it is both positive and negative. It is negative, but only from the vantage point of techne. Techne requires rational explanation of a determinate subject matter. This the poet cannot supply: he is inspired, his subject matter (to be discussed below) is not determinate and so cannot be rationally explained. But the passage is also positive, for Socrates credits the poet with an ability to speak about wonderful things wonderfully. What is perhaps the crucial line from above occurs after Socrates cites the poets describing themselves as "winged bees." He then says about these poets: "And they speak the truth."

The poets, in likening themselves to bees, use a simile; they describe themselves, explain themselves, poetically. Surprisingly, Socrates says they speak the truth. How can this be? Surely poetry is not the language of truth; surely, the "bare" words of philosophical prose, following the tradition invented by father Thales, are the appropriate voice for those seeking the truth. Why then would Socrates praise the poets who use a simile, instead of a straightforward rational explanation? Of course when he says "And the poets speak the truth," he may be ironic. But I suggest otherwise: Socrates here credits the poets with an appropriately self-referential, and in this sense truthful, account of themselves. By describing themselves poetically as winged bees they relinquish all pretense to a rational justification for themselves: They know they are inspired, somehow out of their minds.

This phrase, "out of their minds," sounds terribly damning. However, Socrates does not here condemn the poets for being psychotic. Instead, he credits them with a capacity to speak about that which is beyond the grasp of typical rational or technical thought. And what is this, the "subject matter," about which the poets sing? Socrates tells us in the following lines:

> Does Homer speak about any subject other than that which all the poets speak about? Does he not narrate, for the most part, about war and about associations of all kinds: those between good and bad men, and private and public men; and about the gods, how they associate with each other and with men. And does he not narrate about heavenly matters and about the things under the earth, and about the genesis of the gods and heroes? Are not these the subjects about which Homer has composed his poems? (531c2–d2).

The subject of the poets ranges from the subterranean to the heavenly, from the human to the divine. As such, what is described here might be called "everything." The poets do not restrict themselves; they are not experts in any particular field. Instead, they sing without limitation about all aspects of human being and the world. We have already seen an example of this in Hesiod. His *Theogony* is an account of the genesis of the cosmos, of the physical, human, and divine worlds. In this sense, Hesiod's subject matter is everything.

This may sound quite peculiar: How can anyone, even a poet, sing or speak of everything? Later in the dialogue, when Socrates professes his skepticism about the possibility of anyone doing this, Ion reformulates this claim. He says that he knows "what is appropriate for a man to say and what sorts of things are appropriate for a woman, and what sorts for a slave and what sorts for a free man, and what sorts for one who is ruled, and what sorts for one who is ruling" (540b3–5). In other words, here Ion claims as his "field" of expertise the whole range of human discourse. This is not as ludicrous as it may sound.[48] Homer, whose epics contain characters of all sorts, is somehow able to speak for all of them. The poet, the storyteller, is somehow able to depict the great variety of human experience; he can talk or sing, he can imitate, what everybody else says when they talk about the values, meanings and hopes that animate them. In other words, his "subject" is the world of human significance.

If either of these two characterizations of the subject matter of poetry, literally everything (or "the whole"), or the entire range of human discourse, is accurate, one consequence follows: Poetry cannot be a techne. Techne has a determinate, or strictly limited, subject matter and neither of the two characterizations suggested is determinate. There is no techne that can master the whole range of human significance, that can know with certainty what is good for human beings. (This is why, of course, Descartes despairs of the possibility of any "moral" knowledge.) The achievement of the poets that Socrates highlights is their implicit acknowledgment of this "limitation" in their poetry. They understand themselves and the nature of their subject: By claiming inspiration, rather than techne, by employing a simile rather than an analysis to describe themselves, they admit that in order to speak about their subject they must be "out of their minds." In other words, since their subject is indeterminate, access to it cannot be typical, cannot be technical. A Muse is required.

What is being described here is similar to what was said earlier about Hesiod. His *Theogony* tells us that *chaos* is the origin (*arche*) and at the heart of the world. This means that the world is perpetually stricken by indeterminacy, for *chaos* is no-thing. Because of this, there is a radical discontinuity between the world about which Hesiod sings and Hesiod who somehow "knows" how to sing. Unaided reason, logos on its own, cannot bridge this gap: Hesiod cannot clearly explain how he knows how to sing. Thus, he *must* invoke the Muses. The poet requires, but never can totally rely upon, his Muses—for they "know how to speak many false things as though they were true." There is no independent power of reason to assess the inspirational communications of the Muses. Instead, the poet is in their grip, and so the poem can never claim for itself certainty or solidity. Its source is beyond the poet. As a result, he must be out of his mind, inspired, to begin his poetry, to engage that source. He must be a "light thing" in order to let himself be transported.

Invoking the Muse, being self-consciously poetical, relying upon inspiration—these are ways of acknowledging that the world is inaccessible to the probings of reason. If the world is such, then poetry is the most adequate way of saying so. Thus when the poet describes himself poetically as a winged bee, he evinces a type of self-referentiality: His poetry refers to itself coherently. Poetry reflects and expresses a vision of the world as fractured, as having no unbroken avenue of access between the human mind and the origin of things. If the world is such, then a muse is required to say so. Far from being "merely poetry," the mus-ic of poetry is a perfect match of form and content.

What we see in Socrates' poetical description of the poet is the same type of self-referentiality we have seen not only in Hesiod, but in Cleitophon as

well. As a radical relativist disenchanted with Socratic promises, Cleitophon believes there is ultimately no structure to the world and so no
reason to follow the siren call of Socratic protreptic. For him, there is no
meaningful difference between silence and speech (for there is no reason
to speak rather than to remain silent) and so no reason to play Socrates'
game. It is precisely by not playing the game, by resisting that temptation,
that Cleitophon carves an inviolable space for himself, one Socrates cannot invade. The poet, who describes himself poetically and thus acknowledges the limitations of his claim, occupies a similar space. Socrates
realizes this and even goes so far as to offer it to the rhapsode Ion.

Far from being the simpleminded hater of poetry and the single-
minded advocate of classical reason that the subversives typically take
him to be, Plato appreciates the profound alternative poetry offers.[49]
Well-crafted and self-conscious poetry, that which invokes a muse, gives
voice to a vision of a world not fully accessible to the rational workings
of logos. There is no way of proving this poetical or sophistic worldview
false, since attempting to do so begs the question, presupposes the very
position in question. Socrates is incapable of refuting an opponent who
understands himself. A dialogue such as the *Ion* is meant to teach its
reader this lesson, to teach, in other words, the limits of logos.

Socrates presents Ion with a choice. In essence he says to him, "You
can, if you wish, represent the poet and claim for yourself the electrifying
power of inspiration. If you do, there is nothing more I can say. You will
be out of your mind, in the grip of the Muse, and I will remain a devotee
of logos. But if you choose to represent the poet, beware—for with this
choice you must steel yourself against a temptation: that of claiming for
your rhapsodic ability the status of a techne. A techne requires that you
be able to explicate rationally the connection between yourself and your
subject matter. Therefore, you must choose between them."
Unfortunately, Ion makes the wrong choice. He claims a techne for
his rhapsodic abilities. (It should be remembered that Ion is not a real
poet, but a representative, or *hermeneus*, of the poet. [As such, he corre-
sponds rather nicely to what today we call a literary critic.]) At the crucial
juncture of the dialogue, immediately following its second part, he says
to Socrates, "You speak well, Socrates. However, I would be astounded
if you should speak so well that you would persuade me that I am
possessed and mad when I praise Homer" (536d4–6). Ion refuses Socrates' offer of a poetic self-description. As a consequence, he becomes fair
game for refutation.[50]

(A clarification: In the above, poetry and techne seem to be placed in
opposition to each other—Ion is asked to choose between them. This

may appear to contradict an earlier point, namely that technicism and poeticism are two flip sides of a single coin. Cartesian technicism, for example, led to the provisional morality, which in turn corresponded to a poeticist interpretation of the world of human significance. There is an important difference between Descartes and Ion, however. Descartes admitted, as Ion does not, that there is no techne concerning the world of human significance. He was willing to relegate that world to the irrational and restrict his techne to mathematical physics. He tried to keep the two flip sides quite separate. By contrast, Ion wants to bring them together; he wants to have some sort of poetic techne. Since poetry includes within its subject matter the world of human significance, which is indeterminate, it cannot be a techne. When the rhapsode states that it can he exposes himself to Socrates' refutation.)

In the third part of the dialogue, Ion is defeated by the following argument (536e–542a): Technai are "field specific." For example, a doctor, and only a doctor, knows about medicine, and only about medicine. Only the doctor can comment knowledgeably about the specific field in which she is an expert and only in that field is she an expert. Therefore, when Homer speaks about medicine, only the doctor is able to determine whether he does so *well*. That is, only the doctor is able to judge whether Homer speaks about medicine *correctly*. The only techne Ion professes is that of being a rhapsode. Therefore, he should limit his commentary to those few passages in which Homer speaks about rhapsodes. But Ion professes much more than this, namely to be able to comment upon all of Homeric poetry (which, in turn, comments upon or imitates all sorts of people). Given the initial assumptions about the nature of techne, this claim is rendered ridiculous.

This second refutation is obviously flawed. Ion claims to speak *well* or *finely* about Homer (see 538b2). Socrates takes this to mean that he speaks *correctly*, with technical expertise (538c4). Furthermore, Socrates assumes Homeric poetry is nothing more than an encyclopedia of technai. If this were the case, then it would be true that to judge Homer would mean to determine how much he knows about medicine, carpentry, and so forth. But obviously there is more in Homeric poetry than technical information. Socrates clearly exaggerates and overly intellectualizes (or "epistemologizes") poetry. He reduces the beauty of the epics to correctness and thus distorts them.

Why does he do this? I suggest that it is in order to highlight the relationship that holds between techne and poetry. Ion is not clever. He is easily persuaded by Socrates that to speak well is to speak correctly. But the reader of the dialogue shouldn't be as easily duped. We should instead imagine the response that a better representative of the poet would make. He might say, "You're wrong, Socrates. Of course Homer does more than provide technical information. Speaking well is not equivalent to speaking correctly, with technical accuracy. Speaking well is speaking beautifully, musically, wonderfully about wonderful things. The muse breathes her voice into me and I sing electrically. Only listen to me and you will hear."

By assimilating poetry to techne, Socrates "defeats" Ion. This defeat, however, is predicated upon the foolishness of the poet's representative and not the inherent vulnerability of the poet. Ion should have accepted Socrates' poetical description of poetry. He didn't. Instead, he entered into Socrates' game. To return to an idea mentioned long ago, he abided by the "techne-analogy." In other words, he let Socrates treat his professed knowledge as analogous to the ordinary knowledge found in a typical techne. A techne requires no muse; it should be able to explain itself. The possessor of the techne, the expert, should be able to identify the specific field of his expertise. But Ion has no such field. His voice, inspired by the poetry of Homer, bespeaks the entire and indeterminate range of human discourse. And so in the third part of the dialogue, the one framed by the techne-analogy, Ion is made to look extremely foolish.

The careful reader should realize that despite Ion's defeat, the ancient dispute between philosophy and poetry is hardly resolved by Plato's dialogue. Quite to the contrary, Plato *preserves* the dispute and weaves it into the very fabric of his dialogue. Ion's choice, his giving in to temptation, at the crucial juncture shows us what happens *if* Socrates' opponent ventures to play the game of refutation. The fact that it is a choice should remind us that the outcome of the game is strictly contingent. The further fact that Socrates himself offers to Ion a coherent, that is poetical, self-description shows how the alternative of poetry is incorporated within the Platonic conception of logos—a conception that is revealed not just in Socrates' arguments, but in the dialogue as a whole—as an option, an opponent, that cannot be defeated.[51] The dialogue shows how this option can be rendered invulnerable. It also shows how strong the temptation is for the opponent to claim a techne.

Techne is the paradigmatically teachable form of knowledge; it is that which is most easily recognized and rewarded as knowledge. With a techne one who professes to know something can readily secure himself in the eyes of others as one who actually does know. Ion is not quite ready to admit that he is "out of his mind" or inspired. Techne tempts him to give up his purely poetical account of himself. The dialogue shows this lure at work. It does not prove that one ought to aspire to a techne or that it is good. Indeed, there is no reason that Socrates can provide to compel Ion to desire a techne for himself. Instead, Ion's claim is induced only by his own desire for a certain public status.

(It is precisely this desire, by the way, that characterizes many of today's deconstructionist/literary-critical professors. With typical scholarly sobriety they profess their poeticist and relativistic "doctrines." Finally, this leads them into incoherence . . . not because they are poeticists, but because they have doctrines. What they should do instead is call upon a Muse. Of course they don't do this: if they did, how could they rise through the ranks of the fashionably academic?)[52]

The game Socrates plays against the poet (or the poet's representative) is contingent upon his opponent's having a desire for a public recognition of himself as one who knows and can teach a techne. If that desire is present, if that first step is taken, a common ground shared by Socrates and his opponent will be staked out. Ion takes that first step; as a consequence Socrates refutes him upon the common ground they share. The dialogue in its totality should, however, force its reader to reexamine the maneuvers that induce Ion to take that step. Are they themselves rationally defensible, or are they rhetorical ploys? Does Socrates use logos to defeat Ion, or does he just manipulate him? Is Socratic refutation predicated only upon something as precarious as Ion's desire? Is it predicated only upon a foolish opponent who is ignorant of his own self-interest? (Recall, if you will, what happened when Socrates encountered someone who wasn't foolish, namely Protagoras.) If so, then perhaps we should conclude that Cleitophon was quite right—*Socrates is good only at protreptic*, that mode of discourse that encourages people to play a game that the philosopher knows in advance he will win. Far from having any real knowledge about human nature or the Good, perhaps logos can do no more than exhort people to adopt the particular paradigm of play advocated by Socrates.

(3) The Protreptic Logos (Continued)

Cleitophon was right. Socrates speaks most beautifully, but only about speeches yet to come. He exhorts men to care about, to speak about, the Good, but he does not tell them what the Good is. As he does with Ion, he frequently makes use of the techne-analogy in his conversations; but he has no techne of the Good to teach. With Socrates there are no answers, no proofs. He cannot, for example, prove that the radical relativism tempting Cleitophon is false. Socrates offers the protreptic logos, but this is finally unsatisfying to someone like Cleitophon, a man who like so many of us wants answers, wants a techne. When Cleitophon realizes these are not forthcoming from Socrates, he abandons him for Thrasy-machus and rhetoric.

Cleitophon was right that the Socratic protreptic is most beautiful. But he did not understand the full implications of, and so was unable to evaluate properly the status of, Socrates' logos. Protreptic is the effort to persuade others to accept the essential condition, to take the first step in a game, whose very rules imply that logos is good. We just saw an example of this game: If Ion makes a certain claim, if he agrees that the techne-analogy is an appropriate way for him to formulate his own claim to knowledge, then he has agreed to the essential condition that will, eventu-ally, secure the supremacy of the Socratic position. Ion does agree and so he commits himself to providing a rational defense of his rhapsodic abilities. Ultimately, this implies an affirmation of the goodness of logos. The only problem is that the position Ion believes he can defend, namely his poeticism, is a denial of the goodness of logos. Therefore, he contra-dicts himself and is easily defeated by Socrates.

Socrates cannot demonstrate that logos is unconditionally or necessar-ily better than the poetry Ion represents. He cannot prove with certainty that philosophy is superior to poetry. Instead, the lesson the reader learns from this dialogue is that once Ion makes the choice to defend poetry in accord with the standard rules of rational disputation he must fail. It is vital to make this clear: Plato does not declare that philosophy is simply, demonstrably, or unconditionally superior to poetry. Instead, he depicts what happens if the representative of the poet makes certain claims. If he invades the territory of logos (by affirming the techne-analogy, by acquiescing in the rules of the Socratic game), the poet will be defeated by the representative of logos. But this defeat is conditional upon the poet himself taking that first step.[53]

Protreptic is the effort to encourage others to play the Socratic game, to enter the conversation, to accept the techne-analogy, to embrace logos. If Ion exemplifies someone persuaded to do this, then Cleitophon is a prime example of someone who is sufficiently confident and self-con-scious to resist Socratic protreptic. The silence that follows his brief speech in the *Republic* and Socrates' parallel silence in the *Cleitophon* represent Plato's acknowledgment of the gap that separates these two men. Logos cannot mend this gap; it cannot argue, without begging the question, that one ought to argue on Socrates' terms, accept the analogy, or deem logos good.

The protreptic logos employed by Socrates is not itself a a techne.[54] That is, it is not a knowledge of a determinate subject matter. Instead, it is a knowing how to exhort, urge, encourage an indeterminate variety of human beings to care about and pursue wisdom. But Socrates frequently uses the term and the concept of techne within his exhortations. It is necessary next to consider the relationship between these two pivotal words, "techne" and "protreptic." As promised in the introduction, techne will help illuminate the Platonic conception of logos, in which, as we are now seeing, protreptic plays an extremely important role.

A good example of how Socrates incorporates techne into his protreptic logos was already noted in our discussion of the *Protagoras*. There Socrates used the techne-analogy to encourage Hippocrates to think critically about Protagoras. If you recall, this young man was terribly eager to gain the famous Sophist's wisdom. By asking him a series of questions Socrates forced Hippocrates to consider closely what Protagoras actually had to offer. If Hippocrates were to study with a doctor, he would receive tutelage in medicine. If he were to study with a sculptor, he would learn sculpture. In both of these cases it was relatively easy to determine the subject matter and the credentials of the professor. But what about studying with a Sophist: What is the analogous subject that Hippocrates would learn? Socrates used the analogy to exhort Hippocrates to think through this question and thus to protect himself from the Sophist's great charms.

Another example of Socrates' protreptic use of the analogy comes from a dialogue titled the *Laches*. Here Socrates faces two older men, Lysimachus and Melesias, who wish to have their sons educated. The education they seek to obtain is not the typical sort found in a specific subject. Instead, they want their sons to be made excellent; they wish to obtain for them an education in excellence, in virtue, in *arete*. They wonder whether they should have their sons trained by a master in the techniques of fighting in armor. Would this, they ask, be a reasonable way of educating their sons in virtue? They solicit the opinions of two respected military men, Laches and Nicias (178a–180b). Nicias says yes, Laches no. Lysimachus asks Socrates to cast the deciding vote (184d).

The fact that Lysimachus makes such a request shows that he is not eager to think through the issue of education on his own; he wants someone else to settle it for him. It is clear that Lysimachus is a thoughtless man willing to rely on the opinions of the majority to mold his own. Socrates does not cooperate with Lysimachus' democratic proposal. Instead, he uses the analogy to exhort him to settle this debate by means other than a vote. He asks him (and I reformulate), "Suppose you were about to have your son trained in gymnastics. Would you take a vote how most effectively to accomplish this, or would you enlist the services of an expert trainer?" Melesias answers that he would of course employ a trainer. The issue would be resolved not by the majority, but by someone with knowledge. Similarly, if the issue were how to treat a problem with the eye, one would consult a trained doctor instead of taking a vote (184d–e).

The analogy that Socrates urges Lysimachus to accept is this: As the trainer is to the exercise of the body, and as the eye doctor is to the treating of the eye, so X is to the education of the young in virtue. Socrates does not supply the X here. (And this, of course, was what frustrated Cleitophon.) Instead, he uses the analogy to encourage Lysimachus to abandon his reliance on the principle of majority rule and instead seek some sort of knowledge in order to decide on a teacher for his son. The analogy is used by Socrates, not to explain or deliver his own version of the X, but as a protreptic device designed to exhort Lysimachus to care about knowledge of *arete*.

In addition to exhortation, the techne-analogy is useful in refutations. In the *Protagoras* Socrates uses the same analogy with which he exhorted Hippocrates to refute Protagoras himself. If Protagoras is a true teacher who deserves to be well paid for his teaching, Socrates argues, then he should be able to disclose fully the subject matter that he professes to have mastered. After all, if Hippocrates were to study with an expert painter or flutist, it would be clear what he would learn and how success in his lessons could be measured. Socrates demands that Protagoras provide an analogous disclosure and unambiguous criteria against which his claim can be measured. As shown in chapter I, Protagoras is far too clever to be taken in by Socrates. He therefore hedges on the question, Does he have a techne? He does so beautifully and to his good advantage: He knows that if he straightforwardly claims to have a techne he will be refuted by Socrates. (On the other hand, if he straightforwardly denies having a techne, then he will have nothing to teach.) By hedging so artfully he avoids refutation by avoiding a clear claim to a techne. Other interlocutors, among them Thrasymachus, Gorgias, and Ion, are not so perspicacious. They profess to have a techne, and then are refuted for they cannot successfully disclose and then defend their expertise of their professed subject matter.

It is very tempting to infer from Socrates' use of the analogy in exhortations and refutations that he himself has a techne. Indeed, many scholars have made this inference the basis of their interpretation of Plato's dialogues. I believe they are mistaken. By contrast, I believe that Cleitophon, who questions whether Socrates possesses any real knowledge at all, is far more perceptive in his appraisal of Socrates.[55]

There is no question that Socrates believes that in some sense techne is good; this we saw above. There is also no question that he often uses the analogy to encourage men like Hippocrates and Lysimachus to think about what they hope to learn and to refute men like Protagoras and Ion who claim to know much. But neither of these two facts necessarily implies that he has a techne.

Socrates believes that what is good about techne is that it is knowledge. Someone, like Thrasymachus, who affirms the goodness of a techne, has made an important value judgment, namely that knowledge is good. Socrates proceeds to use this judgment against him. Thrasymachus had proposed a version of relativism, which, if true (and taken to its most extreme conclusion), would render all values relative. But by declaring techne to be good, as Thrasymachus implicitly does, he elevates techne to the status of nonrelatively good. This judgment about techne thus contradicts his own relativism. Socrates forces Thrasymachus to acknowledge this contradiction and eventually defeats him.

It should be noted that to say that techne is good does not imply that it is the best or the exclusive mode of knowledge. In fact (as we saw in Chapter 1.C.2), it implies something quite different. Since (as was argued in the introduction) it is value-neutral, techne is incapable of evaluating itself. If techne is judged good, then the knowledge that is responsible for making this judgment cannot itself be a techne. Techne is thus located in an in-between position. It is superior to ignorance, but some other, higher, mode of knowledge, namely knowledge of what is good, is needed to evaluate it. Therefore, the fact that Socrates believes that techne is good does not necessarily imply he has a techne. He may have a "nontechnical" form of knowledge that is capable of judging the goodness of techne.[56]

The same type of argument can be made about his use of the techne-analogy in his refutations. Techne is ordinary knowledge. ("Ordinary" means knowledge that is generally recognized, admired, or easily identified.) Since its subject matter is determinate, someone who professes to have a techne can easily be checked: His claim can be measured against the subject matter. If someone professes to be able to play the flute, he can be tested by putting a flute into his hands. Because of this, techne is a very useful device in refuting those who profess to know something. It forces them to disclose their professed expertise. It is especially useful in refuting those who, like Protagoras or Ion, claim knowledge about an unusual or atypical field, one that is not obviously determinate. (In Protagoras' case, this is political *arete*; in Ion's, the whole range of human discourse.) The techne-analogy reveals the inappropriateness of their claims. Again, however, the fact that Socrates uses the analogy in this manner does not necessarily imply that he himself has a techne. He may simply be using an effective device to refute those who make inappropriate claims.

Finally, the same point can be made regarding Socrates' use of the analogy in exhortations. Techne is knowledge we can trust and identify. It is particularly useful in pointing out to those, like Lysimachus, who would abandon the possibility of knowledge altogether, that their ordinary practice implies an affirmation of knowledge. Lysimachus seems to believe something like this: "Attaining knowledge that can resolve questions about value is hopeless. I might as well abandon the search and rely on the opinion of the majority." In response, Socrates points out to him that when he is sick he goes to the doctor, and does not take a vote on what medicine he should receive. Ordinary practice includes an affirmation of knowledge, and Socrates continually reminds his interlocutors of this. He uses this ordinary awareness of knowledge to exhort his listeners to seek knowledge about the extraordinary question of value. Yet again, the fact that he employs the analogy to do so need not imply that he himself has a techne.

Many scholars, however, would agrue that Socrates does have (or wishes to or thinks that he does have) a techne. This is quite plausible; after all, he so frequently makes use of the techne-analogy in his arguments that it is hard to imagine that he himself doesn't have one. These scholars would argue that techne need not be value-neutral, that there is some "higher-order" techne whose object is precisely the good.[57] Again, I disagree with this interpretation. The real question at issue here (and it is one that is hardly restricted to Plato scholars) is this: Is there a techne that can take up the world of human significance (of *arete*, of the Good) and treat it as a determinate object to be mastered and then taught? If the answer is yes, then the next and obvious question is, what is it and who has it? Precisely as Cleitophon demands, one would wish to see it if Socrates professes to have it. Cleitophon never gets to see such a techne, and so quits Socrates for Thrasymachus.

If the answer is no, then the next question is, if there is no techne of value, must the realm of human significance be relegated to the junk pile of the irrational? Descartes, for example, thought that questions of value could not be treated with technical precision, and so the junk pile (in the form of his provisional morality) was precisely where he placed such questions.

It is possible to agree with Descartes that no techne can satisfactorily and with certainty handle the world of human significance, but disagree that techne is the sole model of knowledge. The fact that there is no such techne does not preclude the possibility of knowledge of the human world. Instead, there may be a nontechnical, nonordinary, form of knowledge—or conception of logos—that in fact can know about this world. This, I suggest, is the teaching that can be extracted from Plato's dialogues.

The reason that there is no techne to treat the world of human significance is this: The human world cannot be made into a determinate, stable object capable of being mastered. Human beings are simply not such objects. In a sense, much of what has been written throughout this book (and the way it has been written) has been an attempt to show this. Human beings, as the *Symposium* teaches, are erotic: We desire, strive, run madly after objects not our own. But eros itself is not a fixed object; it is not-a-thing; instead, it is a force that directs itself to, and so is shaped by, things other than itself. Because of its indeterminacy, it cannot become the object of a techne.

To approach this point from a different angle: The human world (the one depicted in the Platonic dialogues and in a far inferior manner in this book) is populated not only by the admirable and sober Socrates and the other friends of logos, but also by Cleitophon, Hesiod, Callicles, Protagoras, Descartes, and Spinoza. The desires that propel human life only take shape upon being directed toward objects other than themselves. And these objects, these desires, vary widely, even madly. The characters mentioned are intensely hungry, terribly in search of satisfaction. They do not capitulate to those who would oppose them. And all are residents of the one world we are trying to understand. Because they each have a justifiable claim to citizenship, this is a world unstable and rife with oppositions, for these are powerful characters eager to dispute. As a result, the world they populate cannot become a determinate and clean subject like medicine or arithmetic. Unlike the realm of number, or of the body, the human world is not fixed; it is electrified by competing desires. The subject matter is we who are self-consciously alive, ever fluid, competing, and hence indeterminate. We cannot be held down to be observed and counted.

To reformulate again: Throughout this book we have repeatedly seen what occurs when there is a debate or conflict between two fundamentally opposed positions. When Socrates confronts the radical relativist, when the philosopher Thales confronts the poet Hesiod, when Aristotle argues against Heraclitus, when the contemporary subversive squares off against the traditional conception of logos, we witness human beings, whose ideas differ at the most fundamental of levels, attempting to communicate with one another. In each case rational communication at some point breaks down. This is not due to some accidental, and therefore remediable, deficiency in the opponents. In situations such as these, failure is necessary. This is because fundamentally different positions are based on different "starting points," on divergent presuppositions. Communication between them must break down, for it requires agreement on just such starting points. Therefore, no such position can be defended against the most pressing of objections without assuming itself.

It is just these starting points that we would like to understand fully and see debated. Is the world "out there" accessible to the probings of human reason, or is it not? Are the goals and values that constitute the world of human significance manufactured by us, or do they exist in natural independence? Are they stable or fictitious? Is human being the measure, or are there purposes that abide in the nature of things? Does an athlete or a child at play best image the human relationship to the world? Should we invoke a Muse before we sing or speak straightforwardly about the nature of things in words bare of embellishment? Is silence no worse than speech? Is there a good reason to argue with those with whom we disagree? Answers to questions such as these represent fundamental assumptions; and these must collide. The human world is the sum total of such collisions.

Human beings, madly different, forever assume fundamentally divergent positions. That most ancient and basic dispute between the poet and the philosopher has gone on for centuries. It rages yet today as the deconstructionists do battle against the "Platonists." Because human beings adopt such different positions, the world we occupy is always one of internal opposition. Conflicts daily emerge in any polis, for men such as Thrasymachus or Callicles always demand more than their fair share. Their desires, their view of the world, are not amenable to reason's gentle suasions. Indeed, the audience that proves to be receptive to any given speech, to any logos, is always limited to those who already agree on its fundamental, its originative, assumptions. There never will be widely spread agreement or a beneficent silencing of the cacophany of competing voices. Here all is turmoil.

These sorts of remarks would seem to place their author in the camp of the subversives, for don't they express an all too Nietzschean or Heraclitean message? Doesn't the above deny rational structure and ask that rhetoric and the politics of power substitute for philosophical dialogue? Doesn't it echo Rorty's complaint that Philosophy never gets anywhere and should therefore be abandoned? No. For only two related admissions emerge from the above: First, it is true that there is no techne of, no solution to the problems of the human world. This does not mean, however, that the human world is utterly irrational. It would mean this only if techne were the sole form of human logos (only if finding solutions were the sole task of logos) and this, as will be discussed below, is not the case.

The second admission is that the scope of logos is indeed destined to remain "insular." In other words, logos cannot convince everyone, all its opponents, of its goodness. In the context of the Platonic dialogues, this means that Socrates occasionally (but pointedly) fails in his attempt to refute his opponents. There are always some, like Cleitophon and Callicles, who remain unmoved by his arguments. Logos, as Plato teaches, has limits. Against such limits it is driven (by its erotic nature) to collide. Logos began its drama by wanting more than it could legitimately claim for itself. On the basis of its progressive understanding of itself, it now has come to recognize its insularity. Logos cannot persuade everyone and thus should make no further pretense to a universal throne. Instead, it is destined to wander only in the company of kin. This does not imply, however, that logos, that Philosophy, should be abandoned. The fact that we admit that logos will never fully succeed and will always collide against its limits, the fact that we now recognize that the drama of logos is tragic, need not cause us despair. Tragedy somehow affirms.

The preceding paragraph remains obscure. The concluding sections of this chapter will attempt to clarify it. For now, consider only this: The author of this book takes his bearings from Plato and not Heraclitus or Nietzsche. Within these pages is a desire for knowledge of the world of human significance. It is true that this cannot be technical knowledge. Therefore, the goal animating this book should be described as "nontechnical" knowledge. By definition, such knowledge, if it exists, must be difficult to articulate and display. Techne is paradigmatically clear, reliable, and noncontroversial. Nontechnical knowledge of the world of human significance would share none of these features. Its object would not permit it to do so. Therefore, such knowledge is terribly difficult to exhibit or see. Cleitophon, for one, simply doesn't see it. He's not just being petulant; he has a reasonable complaint. What, then, is this nontechnical conception of knowledge? Again, let me postpone this question until the concluding section and return to the issue more immediately at hand: The relationship between techne and protreptic.

The fact that Socrates uses the techne-analogy in exhortations and refutations, the fact that he thinks techne is good, does not imply that he has one. What his use of the analogy does imply is that he believes that knowledge of the world of human significance is desirable. The analogy itself does not bind Socrates to a conception of what this knowledge is like. It only implies that it is good and should be sought.[58] It is, in other words, *essentially protreptic*. The analogy encourages Socrates' listeners to affirm the goodness of logos. Protreptic, singing the praises of logos and the evils of relativism, turns its audience forward, upward, toward the project of being rational. But is it itself rational? Protreptic is the attempt to redirect the desires and cares of others toward logos. But on the basis of what? Again, old habits die hard: One is tempted to say, on the basis of what it means to be a human being, or on the basis of the structure of eros. Such temptations manifest a vestigial trace of Aristotelianism. But if Aristotelianism has been discarded, then the notion of a human nature cannot be appealed to in order to provide a basis for the protreptic logos.

Is the step toward logos, then, arbitrary and irrational? No, not quite. There is no basis for such a step if by basis one means a certain, verifiable ground upon which an indestructible edifice can be constructed. If one means a Cartesian foundation, then there is no basis for being rational and thus no real difference between being rational and irrational. The architectural metaphor fails when applied to logos. There are no conclusive arguments to demonstrate the goodness of logos. We are not, however, faced with utter irrationality or baselessness, sheer emptiness, as a consequence of this failure. There are yet reasons to play Socrates' game.

What reasons? First of all, whatever the explanation might finally be, we can observe that people (the ones we know, the ones reading this book) are drawn into this game. They wish to claim that their position is demonstrably superior to their opponents' (even if their position is one—like Rorty's—that denies that "superiority" can be demonstrated). Maybe this is just a bad habit, a remnant of a bygone authoritarian age that would best be left behind. I do not know. But one simply needs to observe human beings at work to conclude that so often we make claims, describe our positions as good, and then prepare to do rational battle for them. Such claim-making is the essence of Socrates' game and the lifeblood of logos. Even the misologists, when they think themselves able to defend their misology, participate in this game. As we have seen, the ability to resist the temptation of claim-making is rare. The misologists, so many of whom work in universities, make claims constantly and then write books in their defense. As a result, the Socratic affirmation of logos, the philosophical position that views logos as essential to living a good life, can account for a good deal of human behavior.

To reformulate the above, ordinary life gives testimony to the goodness of logos. We walk around walls and not into them. In other words, the ordinary practice of walking around a wall implies a judgment: Bumping into a wall is bad, not good, and not good and bad at the same time. Ordinary life seems to offer evidence for the Principle of Noncontradiction and, eventually, for the goodness of logos. When sick, we go to the doctor. When building, we rely on the expert carpenter. The subversives' denial of knowledge, their relativism, if translated into the ordinary world, becomes absurd. Therefore, their denial of knowledge of values and purposes should be disregarded as mere academic talk.

But the opponent of logos can quickly reply: Why should we take our bearings from and give privilege to ordinary life? (Contemporary science doesn't do this, and it's flourishing.) Doesn't ordinary life vary from culture to culture so greatly that appeal to it is futile? Another, less compelling, reason can then be offered: The game is traditional. Giving reasons and defending judgments in public argument has been the standard procedure by which the intellectual tradition of the West has been regulated. Of course, and unfortunately, such a view is but a version of conventionalism. Why should any of us adhere to the traditions of the West?

A final reason, then, and one related to the first: The Socratic game is able to absorb its opponent within itself. Within the game, fundamental disagreement cannot be tolerated. As we have said so often, there are no misologists who can argue successfully against Socrates, since their participation in the argument belies their own misology. One cannot argue against logos without acceding to it. It is this feature of logos, however, that leads Derrida to make the following complaint. (He is talking specifically here about those who are mad. His remarks, however, could be generalized to refer to logos's many accusers.)

> The misfortune of the mad, the interminable misfortune of their silence, is that their best spokesmen are those who betray them best; which is to say that when one attempts to convey their silence *itself*, one has already passed over to the side of the enemy, the side of order, even if one fights against order from within it, putting its origin into question. There is no Trojan horse unconquerable by Reason (in general). The unsurpassable, unique and imperial grandeur of the order of reason, that which makes it not just another actual order or structure (a determined historical structure, one structure among other possible ones), is that one cannot speak out against it except by being for it, that one can protest it only from within it.[59]

For Derrida, reason is imperial; it is a tyrant who cannot be overthrown from within: When one speaks out against it, one is really for it. The capacity of logos to absorb its opponents is, for the deconstructionist, a grand strategy,—a forceful, and not a rational, imposition of power. What Socrates sees as a virtue, Derrida sees as an authoritarian vice. For him, then, the step toward logos, acceding to Socratic protreptic, is willful and arbitrary rather than rational and natural.

Perhaps Derrida is right. Logos, lover of knowledge, is a tyrant and uses more than just "reasons" (which really are no more than signs or suggestions) to certify its goodness. It knows, too well, that reasons such as the ones given above can be deconstructed, exposed as presuppositions rather than as rational conclusions rooted in solid ground. Logos must, therefore, confess its ignorance here. It must admit that it cannot give a complete account of itself and its goodness. It must rest content with its conditional, and not unconditional, goodness.

Logos: "Oh darkness and memory . . . what, then, is left for me to affirm? Without certain knowledge, how can I go forward? Without a techne, how can I teach? Having been stripped of my authority to command, with what voice shall I speak? Are my words destined only to fly aimlessly wherever the wind would take them?"

C QUESTIONS

(1) Eros and Logos (continued)

Logos retains a voice. As it exits the stage it is dressed like a beggar and not a king. It is destined to wander, homeless, shoeless, sleeping on doorsteps. But to wander such is not the same as collapsing in a heap of despair. Logos is alive and in its own, newly discovered way, well. It will make no further attempts at the throne. It knows its ignorance, understands its limits, and is prepared to say that they are somehow good. It will wander, but with a happiness all its own.

With what voice can logos still speak? In what tone? No longer can logos assert with regal and untroubled confidence. Instead, its paradigmatic form of expression is now the question. The assertion was Aristotle's. The question is Plato's, and he is the hero of this story.

To explain, let us return briefly to the ascent passage of the *Symposium*. There we saw the intimate bond between logos and eros. At each stage of the ascent the initiate is impelled to speak, and each speaking forces him to realize the discrepancy between his speech and the object that he loves and speaks about. Dissatisfaction is experienced and so the initiate has to move on, upward, from the love of one particular body to the love of souls, institutions, particular sciences, and finally to the love of "beauty itself," the "Idea of Beauty." In pursuit of this final, universal object the initiate engages in philosophical logos.

Logos uses the ascent passage as a justification for itself. By presenting a structure of human desire, with logos at its pinnacle, Diotima seems to argue that the goodness of logos is unconditional. Such a claim seems similar to Aristotle's assertion that human being is by nature the animal with logos. As such, it can no longer be accepted as definitive. The ascent passage does not, however, have to be totally rejected because there is another way of reading it that will lessen its Aristotelian assertiveness and make it better able to account for all the hard recognitions and painful reversals that logos has suffered.

Diotima presents a picture or history of an emerging philosophical psyche and the type of logos affiliated with it. Philosophical logos is erotic in origin. It is perverse; that is, the philosopher turns away from all that is usually desired by most human beings, namely the particularized world of bodies, cities, and sciences. His desire is somehow for everything; the object of philosophical logos is the "Idea of Beauty." The philosopher desires to speak about that perfect object whose beauty is *not* in the eye of the beholder, that universal object that brings order and unity to the particulars of experience. It is not clear, however, whether such an object can be "theoretically" articulated. The Idea is not presented as a clean, determinate entity that simply exists "out there" to be seen and then articulated without distortion by a windowlike mind. Instead, the passage describes all objects, even the most universal, as appearing only as objects of desire. The ascent passage speaks only from the side of the subject. The "Ideas," those glorious objects, ultimate structures, and supposedly reliable barriers against relativism, are invoked, but only as objects of a certain psyche that desires them.

As a result, the passage does not clearly construct a line to separate the philosopher, with his belief in the objectivity of knowledge, from the subjectivism of the poet or the Sophist. The ascent passage does not make clear how the philosopher, or representative of logos, is fundamentally different from his enemies. This is because the passage does not prove that the Ideas are independent or natural beings that have not been fabricated by the human imagination. Since they are invoked only as objects of desire, it is possible to conclude that this is all they are, that they are dependent for their existence on human desire. If this proves to be the case, then the Ideas would become open to all the vagaries, the shifts and flows, of life. They would be no more than debris floating in Heraclitus' river.

The question that thus surfaces, for the final time, is how, if at all, does Plato differentiate philosophy from poetry or sophistry?

Three conceptions of human discourse, of speaking, can be elicited from Diotima's ascent passage. Two are extreme and can be explicated rather straightforwardly. The first, and the most optimistic, is based on an Aristotelian reading of the passage. As we have discussed, Aristotle thinks it is possible for human logos to see and then say what is really "out there." His version of logos is capable of becoming a window through which the world of natural entities shows itself. As such, the truth is within human grasp. The ascent passage can be interpreted as containing this sort of teaching. One can read it to imply that the Idea of Beauty can ultimately be explicated by the philosopher at the pinnacle of his ascent. Philosophy, on this reading, can articulate "everything"; it can supply a techne whose object is that which brings unity to experience.

Of course, various objections have been raised against this interpretation of the passage. The possibility of a clear-eyed gazing at objects is not obviously offered by Diotima: the lens through which the initiate sees the Ideas is more "kaleidoscopic" than windowlike. It allows the initiate to see what he wants to see, namely beautiful forms. The fact that such forms are what the initiate wants to see does not imply that they actually exist. People may well delude themselves and fabricate beautiful purposes and order. Such fabrications would be impositions, fictions, of the human imagination. Therefore, on this, the second reading of the passage, a sophistical or poetical conception of discourse is elicited.

These, then, are the two extremes: On the one hand, the Aristotelian views reality simply as reality. On the other, the Sophist or the poet views reality only as an object of desire. To broach the third conception, the one in between, let me state a theme for a final time: The Sophist's relativism, his poeticism or belief that reality is ultimately shaped by desire, cannot be refuted. Socrates can use all his self-referential arguments, can appeal to the goodness of techne, can try his protreptic best, but he cannot provide conclusive reasons to demonstrate that the position held by the radical relativist or Sophist should be rejected. Or, to add a necessary qualification, he cannot refute the Sophist who resists the temptation to make the claim that he has a techne or a defensible position. The Sophist, if he is careful, is an irremediable and looming presence who challenges (by conditioning) all the claims of the philosopher. To the extent that the ascent passage does not clearly stipulate the objectivity of the Ideas and prove that they are not fabricated by the human imagination, the Sophist lurks as a threat even within Diotima's speech.

If, however, the Sophist does make a claim that his position is deserving of rational validation, if he desires (for whatever reason) to defeat the philosopher in public debate, then he can be refuted by Socrates. Once the debate commences certain conditions implicitly become operative. Most important of these is that the opponents agree that in principle the debate can be won. To enter into this game implies doing so armed with a defense of one's position and a resolve to settle the dispute. Therefore, a standard must be evoked by which the two competing positions can be measured. Such a standard is what makes the game between Socrates and his opponents intelligible, for it makes victory—the necessary goal of such a game—possible. As a result, once the sophist or the poeticist enters the debate, he implicitly becomes a Platonist, one who affirms the existence of just such standards and thereby rejects relativism. To put this into stronger terms, everyone who enters into such a debate automatically becomes a Platonist. Since such debates are the essence of philosophy, every philosopher is a Platonist.

Yet again: None of this implies that Platonism is absolutely true or that philosophy is unconditionally superior to poetry or sophistry. It only means that if someone tries to argue against Socrates, to refute Platonism on its own terms, he will fail; in attempting to show that logos should be rejected, he will in fact affirm it.

According to Diotima, the Ideas are the objects of desire operative in philosophical discourse. In their existence the philosopher invests his belief, not because he is sure or can prove that they exist, but because he cannot make sense of what he is doing as a philosopher without them. This, I propose, is the teaching of the ascent passage. It is very close to what is sometimes called a "transcendental argument," an argument that tries to explain what conditions must obtain for a given experience to be possible. The ascent passage, however, is not really a transcendental argument. Its "conclusion," that the Ideas are there to be secured by logos, only emerges when a particular psyche, engaged in a specific form of logos, pursues the farthest reaches of its desire. When this occurs, that psyche must invest its belief in the Ideas. When this does not occur, there is no reason for the Ideas to exist. There is no necessity that the search be undertaken. The Ideas cannot, then, be proven to exist necessarily or independently of those searching for them.

The ascent passage is an analysis of that erotic agent who is compelled by some pressing need to philosophize. Such a compulsion implies a certain set of beliefs. In this sense, the ascent passage is strictly psychological, a logos of the psyche. It concludes that a certain type of psyche, that belonging to both the philosopher, as well as anyone wishing to argue against the philosopher, must affirm the existence of the Ideas. This is not the same, however, as a demonstration of the truth of Plato's "theory of Ideas," for it does not prove that the Ideas are not fictions of the human imagination.

The point is this: The Platonist believes that there are ultimate structures or standards which he then describes as being self-sufficient, altogether nonchanging, and even eternal. The intensity of these descriptions reveals the desire to resist all forms of relativism. The Platonist also understands that these descriptions do not simply reflect the nature of things. What they do reflect are the beliefs or commitments at work when someone acts upon a desire for a certain kind of conversation; when we defend our views in public debate, argue against opponents, try with others to know, we play Socrates' game. The intelligibility of such activities requires the belief in nonrelative standards. But such activities are ephemeral; they are borne on the wings of desire and can give no sure evidence of what is built into the nature of things.

The third form of discourse, the way of talking, that the ascent passage invites us to consider is philosophical. This term is now used strictly in the Platonic, and not the Aristotelian, sense. The latter, as beautiful as it is, is simply a matter of going after the truth. The former is precarious, unstable, difficult to pin down. Philosophical logos has something to do with pursuing the universal structures of reality, but these are not simply out there to be seen through the window of the mind. Philosophical logos has more to do with dialogue, with talking to others, especially opponents, for in the midst of such conversation a certain set of conditions, mandated by the desire that animates the conversation, gets charged into operation. Philosophical logos wants knowledge, but it accepts the fact that in an important sense its goal is unattainable.

(2) Asking Questions

Philosophical discourse, logos in its Platonic variety, never reaches its desired terminus. It is forever the love, and not the possession, of wisdom. To reformulate this, and much of the above: *Philosophical discourse is fundamentally interrogative.* Its paradigmatic sentence is the question, and not the assertion. This is not to say that all philosophers do is ask questions; that would be ridiculous. They ask questions, entertain possible answers, review such answers, and then proceed forward once again. Nevertheless, the question is the animating force of philosophy, for it is the most erotic of sentences.[60]

To question is to seek an answer. Doing so implies that the answer is not possessed, not known, by the questioner. The fact that the question is posed, however, implies that the questioner does know a great deal. He knows, for example, that he does not know the answer; that is why he asks the question. Furthermore, posing a question implies that an answer is desirable and a belief that, in some sense, it is possible.

Consider this: I ask you, "Who won the game on Monday?" That I do so means that I know there was a game, that I know enough about games to understand that there was a single victor, that I realize that I do not myself possess the answer to the question, and that I acknowledge in myself the desire to attain it. I also know, or at least suspect, that you are a reasonable candidate to assist me, which is why I ask you and not someone else.

In short, a great deal of knowledge is packed into the asking of a question. As such, the question is located somewhere in between knowledge and ignorance. The questioner is not totally ignorant, for he knows enough (about himself and the object of his question) to pose the question. He is not totally knowledgeable, for he lacks an answer. The questioner seeks, strives for objective knowledge, for an answer.

The Platonic version of logos is not poetry. It seeks objective answers, it loves wisdom, it wants to speak about what is Good and Beautiful for all. For the very same reason, it is not Aristotelian. It is erotic, incomplete; it does not issue in an unambiguous, unclouded, theory. It is in between, interrogative, protreptic. It urges us to ask questions and it subjects this very urging to examination. It seeks out dialogue with those who object even to the asking of such questions. It believes in the goodness of the question and is sufficiently aware of its limitations as to condition all its expectations and conclusions. Precisely this awareness of limits makes questioning so vital, for the question affirms the precariousness of the entire project of logos. It proceeds with knowledge of itself: It knows that it does not know. This is knowledge, but of an altogether peculiar sort. The question discloses a desire to know and sparks entry into Socratic dialogue. With such entry comes the implicit commitment to those structures that would make answers possible. Yes, such standards exist; they exist insofar as we seek them. Yes, there is a basis for protreptic: One ought to seek knowledge of the Good, one ought to attempt to answer Socrates' questions. What is Beauty? What is Good? Socrates gives no answers, has no techne. But the very asking is capable of sustaining for a lifetime.

The question has a logic, a structure of its own. It is posed between knowledge and ignorance, aiming for the former and fleeing the latter. It is on the way, in motion. It somehow sees the goal toward which it strives. But it is not yet there.

Logos is fundamentally interrogative. An obvious objection can be directed at that statement: It is not self-referential. That is, although it purports to praise the question, it itself takes the form of an assertion. Throughout this book self-reference has been a standard used to criticize others. (The relativist, for example, was accused of failing to refer to himself coherently.) Therefore, the same standard should be used to measure any position this book would advocate.

While it is true that the first sentence of the previous paragraph is not literally a question, I would yet maintain that this book has exhibited an interrogative conception of logos throughout its many pages. There has been no systematic argument, no attempt made at a comprehensive interpretation of Plato or Aristotle or Descartes or Spinoza. Instead, a series of texts have been placed into opposition with one another in the hope of generating a story, one that sparks its readers and draws them into its reflections. From these chapters, all of which were inspired by the Ancient Greeks, it is hoped that readers have been persuaded to pursue certain questions and perhaps read, or reread, certain books. If nothing else, this book, if at all successful, has been an invitation.

EPILOGUE

I have attempted to defend a conception of logos characterized as Platonic. I began with an assumption that has been well defended by other scholars: The dialogue form is essential to a philosophical appreciation of Plato's thought. For this reason I have focused a great deal of attention not only on Socrates and his arguments, but also on his opponents and their challenges, confusions, and silences. Characters such as Protagoras, Ion, Callicles, Thrasymachus, and Cleitophon represent positions that are essential to a complete understanding of the dialogues. These are troubling figures with powerful views that cannot happily or straightforwardly be dismissed as false or evil. Other ancient authors, especially Heraclitus and Hesiod, were introduced to amplify this side of the "ancient dispute" and to demonstrate how basic it is—not only to the dialogues, but to Greek culture in general.

Because of the above, Martha Nussbaum's description of Plato as the author of an "anti-tragic theater" seems quite wrong. Far from being "pure" or "crystalline" the dialogues are kaleidoscopic. They are works of drama constituted by the complex lines of interaction between their polymorphous characters. Far from denying the human experience of contingency, as Nussbaum believes the dialogues do, they incorporate it within their very structure. Plato writes dialogues in which his Socrates can, for example, be awakened by Hippocrates, spurned by Cleitophon, or mocked by Callicles. As a result, I dispute the central thesis of *The Fragility of Goodness*: That Plato's views are fundamentally at odds with those preserved in Greek tragedy.

Nussbaum advocates much the same position as that proclaimed by Nietzsche: That by trying to achieve a "god's-eye perspective" Plato showed his hate of human life. Again, this seems wrong. Human experience, as the *Symposium* teaches, includes the desire to achieve a god's-eye perspective; we are erotic and seek immortality. This desire belongs not only to some mystical elite, but is reflective of ordinary human striving and talking. While it is therefore true that the desire for philosophy is urged by the dialogues, it does not follow that they are "crystalline" arguments to consummate that desire through the work of pure reason. Instead, they are dramas; philosophical desire is conditioned by the contingencies of the dramatic context Plato so carefully weaves. One of the most important elements constituting that context is rhetoric, which steadfastly keeps its gaze focused on that which is altogether human. Another is poetry, which denies that a logos unaided by the Muse can achieve reliable knowledge. The dialogues, populated as they are by representatives of both rhetoric and poetry—two options that the philosopher cannot dismiss as demonstrably false—thereby reflect the boundaries against which logos must collide and the conflicts by means of which it must be understood.

How to end? One question that arises is, Does this book, which argues that the philosopher can refute neither the poet nor the rhetorician, culminate in skepticism? If we simply hearken to the Greek root of "skepticism" (*skeptomai*: to look at carefully, to consider), then the answer is yes. The story ended with a call to question. But we are not left with skepticism as classically formulated by Pyrrho and preserved by Sextus Empiricus. The goal for the Pyrrhonian is tranquillity (*ataraxia*). By learning how to oppose any argument about the real nature of things with another argument of equal weight, this skeptic systematically learns how to suspend judgment on all such issues. He learns how to distance himself from and to cease to be disturbed by traditional philosophical questions. The result, so it is claimed, is peace of mind.[1]

Pyrrhonian skepticism seems to be flawed in its empirical observations about human psychology; in other words, it gets the appearances wrong. The discovery of the equal balance of opposed arguments hardly needs to lead to tranquillity. What if human beings are erotic? What if we push for answers, demand satisfaction even when it is not apparently forthcoming and continually disrupt the balance? If such desires are reflective of who we are (or appear to be), and if certain beliefs must attend them, then Burnyeat's verdict on skepticism seems just: "When one has seen how radically the sceptic must detach himself from himself, one will agree that the supposed life without belief is not, after all, a possible life for man."[2]

To reformulate: It is skepticism, and not Platonism, that is truly, even systematically, "antitragic." By denying an impulse to greatness, to knowledge, it forecloses the possibility of a tragic collision against the limits of human efficaciousness. If that impulse is, for whatever reason, strongly felt, then skeptical *ataraxia* will be neither compelling nor even plausible.

One further point: Even though this book ended in questions, I did lay a claim to some sort of knowledge that I hoped would reflect that described by Socrates as "human wisdom."[3] This knowledge consists in an understanding of the contours of those debates that ensue when various versions of the "ancient dispute" arise again and again. It consists, in other words, in knowing what happens when people disagree on very basic issues and then attempt to champion their ideas and discuss their disagreements. If successful, this book showed what happens when the philosopher meets the poet or the rhetorician (or the subversive) and attempts to engage her in an argument over her fundamental beliefs.

It is true that such arguments cannot be conclusively and rationally settled. This need not, however, lead to a skeptical abandonment of the dispute. Precisely because the issues are so basic and compelling, the representatives of the various positions rarely relinquish their desire to defend their claims. As a result, the battles, it seems, must be fought again and again. Articulating the patterns that such arguments regularly follow was the content of this book; if it succeeded, such an articulation constitutes its claim to knowledge. The skeptical notion that the battles could some day cease seems to be neither accurate, coherent, nor desirable.[4]

Only a small selection of passages from a few of the many dialogues was used to substantiate the thesis that the conception of logos this book proposed was in fact Platonic. As a result, and as any classical scholar will surely realize, not nearly enough textual material was analyzed to warrant a claim about Plato *simpliciter*. A vast number of scholars have commented on virtually every line of text that was cited. About most of these commentators the book was silent. This is not because their works are unimportant. It is because this book was animated mainly by a desire to confront directly and accessibly certain issues that the Platonic dialogues raise. Far from being merely of antiquarian interest, the dialogues provoke questions that occur continually to reflective people. They treat such questions coherently and with an unmatched fidelity to our experiences. As a result, even today they can play a significant role in shaping our lives. Using ancient books as a guide, I tried to enter into a debate that is alive and well: What role should logos play in our lives? Can it speak to our deepest longings, or must we abandon or deconstruct it in the name of our humanity?

From a variety of perspectives, logos has been damned as the culprit and made accountable for the barrenness that plagues the twentieth century. The subversives counsel us to say "farewell to Reason" and to welcome an age that comes "after Philosophy." Not surprisingly, I shall end this book by reiterating a protreptic response: To relinquish the desire for Truth, for answers, for a rational understanding of our experience and a certification of our values would be a disaster. The desire for

Truth is, for whatever reason, felt within and spoken about. This, our logos, sustains our openness to the deepest questions that we are sparked to ask and thereby nourishes us. A life without such logos does not seem worth living for a human being. I hope that you agree; if you do not, I ask only that you try to explain why.

NOTES

PROLOGUE

1. The relationship between Plato and Socrates is notoriously complex. In this book "Socrates" will refer *only* to the character appearing in Plato's dialogues. I do not mean to imply here that Nietzsche follows the same procedure. I only mean to indicate that I am not willing to broach the issue of Socrates versus Plato in itself or as it appears in Nietzsche's work. Doing so would lead into scholarly disputes of a magnitude so great that they would distract from the main purpose of the book.

2. Friedrich Nietzsche, *The Birth of Tragedy*, trans. Walter Kaufmann (New York: Vintage, 1967), 97.

3. Ibid., pg. 18.

4. Kenneth Baynes, ed., *After Philosophy* (Cambridge, MA: MIT Press, 1987), 7.

5. On this point see Rorty's "Pragmatism and Philosophy," in *After Philosophy*, 26–65.

6. Martha Nussbaum, *The Fragility of Goodness* (Cambridge: Cambridge University Press, 1986), 133. As will become apparent, Nussbaum's book treats many of the same issues as my own. I have commented on her work in some detail in "The Tragic Philosopher: A Critique of Martha Nussbaum," *Ancient Philosophy* 8 (1989): 285–99. Among its other virtues, Nussbaum's book has an extensive bibliography, and I shall refer the reader to it often.

7. Since she is an Aristotelian, this remark obviously does not apply to Nussbaum.

8. Of course, Plato's letters are an exception.

9. Charles Griswold's *Platonic Writings, Platonic Readings* (New York: Routledge, 1988) contains numerous essays that provide a good overview of the issue of how to read the dialogues. His bibliography is an excellent guide to the literature.

10. Charles Griswold's "Plato's Metaphilosophy: Why Plato Wrote Dialogues?" in *Platonic Writings, Platonic Readings*, 143–67, argues for a similar thesis.

11. This remark should begin to make clear where I diverge from Nussbaum's reading of Aristotle.

12. Paul Feyerabend, *Farewell To Reason* (London: Verso, 1989).

INTRODUCTION

1. "Techne" and "logos" and their plurals ("technai," "logoi") are Greek, but will be used so often that they will not be italicized.

2. A good introduction to the historical background of tragedy can be found in the articles "The Origins of Tragedy" and "Tragedy in Performance" in *The Cambridge History of Classical Literature*, vol. I (Cambridge: Cambridge University Press, 1985).

3. There is no "H" in Greek, only an aspirated iota.

4. This is a point made by John Herrington with regard to the fragments of the other plays by Aeschylus. See his *Aeschylus* (New Haven: Yale University Press, 1986), 45–60.

5. The Greek text is Hude's edition of the *Poetics* (Oxford: 1969). In general, I will use Oxford editions and supply page numbers of quoted material in the body of the book.

6. These two examples were selected almost at random (for their titles alone) and were written by Herbert Muller and Miguel de Unamuno.

7. The phrase is Stephen Halliwell's translation of 1452a22. See his *The Poetics of Aristotle* (Chapel Hill: University of North Carolina Press, 1987).

8. See T.C.W. Stinton, "*Hamartia* in Aristotle and Greek Tragedy," *Classical Quarterly*, 25 (1975): 221–54.

9. Examples of where Aristotle cites *Oedipus Tyrannus* in his *Poetics* are 1452a25, 1452a33, 1453a20, 1453b6, 1454b8, 1455a18. I would use these and other references to defend the familiar assertion that this play is for Aristotle the paradigmatic tragedy.

10. The Greek text is Pearson's edition (Oxford: 1975). The translation is mine, but R.D. Dawe's commentary, *Sophocles, Oedipus Rex* (Cambridge: Cambridge University Press, 1982) and David Grene's translation in the Chicago series (*The Complete Greek Tragedies*, ed. David Grene and Richmond Lattimore) have been consulted.

11. See Nussbaum, *The Fragility of Goodness*, 388–89.

12. The term "*tyrannus*" can be usefully opposed to "*basileus*." The latter refers to a king whose rule has been inherited; the former is someone from the outside who has gained the rule of a city. Oedipus thinks he is the former, when in fact he is the latter. Bernard Knox has made this point in "Why is Oedipus Called Tyrannos," in *Word and Action* (Baltimore: Johns Hopkins University Press, 1979), 87–95.

    In this book the movement is from logos thinking itself a *basileus* to realizing it is a *tyrannus*.

13. This is controversial. The question of what did Oedipus know and when has been debated frequently. I provide evidence for my own answer below.

14. Bill Scott reminded me of another question: Why exactly does Oedipus ask for a sword at 1255? He also first suggested that, since we are left with no stage directions, one of the most pressing questions faced by a would-be director of this play is how to situate Oedipus during the last scene. When exactly does he leave the stage? Is he fully erect or is he bowed?

15. Because of their grammar and meter these last lines are frequently declared spurious. Dawe claims that they are obviously so: see *Sophocles, Oedipus Rex*, p. 247. Perhaps they are. Nevertheless, they can be fruitfully employed to formulate what I take to be the essential question of the play.

16. Liddell and Scott's *Greek-English Lexicon*.

17. Fragment number 50, from Hermann Diels, *Die Fragmente der Vorsokratiker* (Berlin, 1952). See also fragments numbers 1 and 2. Heraclitus will be discussed at some length below.

18. A great exception to this statement, one far too complex to discuss here, is Hegel's *Phenomenology of Spirit*. I realize the short shrift given to Kant. An interesting modern

example of a theoretical argument designed to show the limits of reason is Nicholas Rescher's *The Strife of Systems* (Pittsburgh: University of Pittsburgh Press, 1985). Rescher even uses the phrase "the tragic fate of philosophy" (pg. 54) to describe his conclusions.

19. It is not necessary for the reader to agree that the physicist must perform exactly the task I have just outlined, only that something like it is required for the physicist, or the philosopher of physics, to justify her conception of logos.

20. I base this discussion on Richard Robinson's "Begging the Question," *Analysis* 31 (1970–71): 115–17.

21. Jorge Kube, *Techne und Arete* (Berlin: De Gruyter, 1969), 14. Pages 9–35 of this book present a good history of the word.

22. The Greek text is Murray's edition (Oxford: 1975). The translation is mine, but I have consulted Mark Griffith's commentary, *Aeschylus: Prometheus Bound* (Cambridge: Cambridge University Press, 1983) and David Grene's translation in the University of Chicago series.

23. Martha Nussbaum, *The Fragility of Goodness*, 95. I substitute "chance" for her "*tuche*." Terence Irwin, throughout *Plato's Moral Theory* (Oxford: 1977), wrongly equates techne with productive knowledge.

24. See Jacob Klein's *Greek Mathematical Thought and the Origin of Algebra* (Cambridge: MIT Press, 1968), especially pages 46–61, "The Concept of *arithmos*," for an informative discussion of these issues.

25. For a discussion of the question, Is techne (or technology) value-neutral? see Langdon Winner, *Autonomous Technology* (Cambridge: MIT Press, 1977).

CHAPTER 1

1. *Politics*, 1253a9–10. The line reads, "Human beings, alone of the animals, have logos." My Greek text is Ross's edition (Oxford: 1988).

2. "Soul" typically translates the Greek "*psuche*." The latter, however, has a quite different connotation than the former. Rather than use the familiar translation, I employ the cognate "psyche" and hope that its meaning will emerge. The best text to consult for what Aristotle means by the term is of course *De Anima*, "On the Psyche."

3. See the *Physics* 194b16 ff. for a discussion of the "four causes." A good introduction to the subject of Aristotelian teleology is Martha Nussbaum's essay, "Aristotle on Teleological Explanation" in her *Aristotle's De Motu Animalium* (Princeton: Princeton University Press, 1978), 57–106. Her bibliography is useful in getting a sense of the literature on this subject.

4. This sentence requires one qualification. A human being without a polis cannot live a good *human* life. Such a being is either a beast or a god (1253a29).

5. See W. Wieland, "The Problem of Teleology," in *Articles on Aristotle*, ed. J. Barnes (London: 1975).

6. To begin the long argument required here to establish that Aristotle's work is thoroughly "theoretical" and then to explain what this means I would examine his frequent use of the verb "*theoreo*" and then see if this meshes with his description of cognitive activity in the *De Anima*. One difficulty that plagues any attempt to decide upon the character of Aristotle's "prose" is that it is probable that what remains of his written work is lecture notes.

7. Martin Heidegger, *Being and Time*, trans. MacQuarrie and Robinson (New York: Harper and Row, l962), 56. Heidegger is talking here about the Greek conception of logos in general. I think he is wrong in applying it to Plato, but helpful in thinking about Aristotle.

8. The Greek text is W.D. Ross's critical edition of the *Metaphysics*, vol. I (Oxford: 1970). Note that hearing is required for learning at 980b23.

9. The second citation is from a chapter of the *Metaphysics* that may not have been written by Aristotle. (See Ross's commentary, p. 213.) Even so, it is, I believe, Aristotelian in spirit and therefore illuminating in the context in which I cite it.

   For a recent discussion of Aristotle's view of perception see Deborah Modrak, *Aristotle: The Power of Perception* (Chicago: The University of Chicago Press, 1987).

10. Aristotle uses this sort of "argument" at *Metaphysics* 1008b15–16, which I will discuss in a later section. This section of the *Metaphysics* exemplifies what it means to approach logos from the perspective of the true and false.

11. My Greek text of *De Interpretatione* is Minio-Paluello's edition (Oxford: 1966). J.L. Ackrill's translation and commentary (Oxford: 1968) has also been consulted.

12. As Nussbaum's "Aristotle on Teleological Explanation" shows, this modern project was prefigured in antiquity by Democritus.

13. See Derrida, *Of Grammatology* (Baltimore: Johns Hopkins, 1976), 11 and 30, where he specifically mentions this Aristotelian text. See Rorty, *Philosophy and the Mirror of Nature*, 40–41.

14. I borrow the phrase "dead dog" from Paul Feyerabend who writes that Aristotle isn't one in *Science in a Free Society* (London: NLB, 1978), 53 ff. See also his "In Defence of Aristotle," in *Progress and Rationality in Science*, ed. G. Radnitzky and G. Andersson (Dordrecht: D. Reidel, l978), 143–180.

15. Nussbaum, *The Fragility of Goodness*, 261. Her entire section on Aristotle should be consulted both to illuminate the reading I propose as well as to offer an alternative to it.

16. My Greek text is Bywater's edition (Oxford: 1962).

17. The material I place in square brackets are my own attempts to clarify the text.

18. This is a highly controversial argument. See Nussbaum, "The Function of Man," in *De Motu Animalium*, 100–106. Her notes provide a good introduction to the literature on this issue.

19. Friedrich Nietzsche, *Thus Spoke Zarathustra*, trans. Walter Kaufmann. (New York: Penguin, l968), 52.

20. In this section I imitate the protreptic arguments that are given by Socrates in Plato's *Euthydemus*. Aristotle himself wrote a protreptic work which probably was similar to those arguments. Today it can only be speculatively reconstructed. See for example *Aristotle's Protrepticus: An Attempt at Reconstruction* by Ingemar During (Göteborg: 1961).

21. See *Metaphysics* 1006a25.

22. My formulation of relativism is idiosyncratic. I do not believe, however, that acceptance of it in all its detail is required for the argument to progress.

    Relativism comes in several varieties—ethical, cognitive, ontological, vulgar, etc.— and there is a mountain of literature on each. Two recent anthologies are *Relativism: Interpretation and Confrontation* (Notre Dame: University of Notre Dame Press, 1989) and *Relativism: Cognitive and Moral* (Notre Dame: University of Notre Dame Press,

1982), both edited by Michael Krausz (the latter volume with Jack Meiland). Also see Paul Feyerabend, *Farewell to Reason*, 19–89.

I focus on ethical relativism because it is familiar and rather easy to think about. I later shift to epistemological relativism when talking about truth. Ultimately I think such a shift is justified. The pursuit of the truth is a human activity and as such requires a positive evaluation before its commencement. In this sense, ethical precedes epistemological relativism.

23. This view is accepted by J.L. Mackie in *Ethics: Inventing Right and Wrong* (New York: Penguin, 1977). What is interesting about Mackie's position is that although he accepts this point he maintains that on a "higher level" relativism is nevertheless true. He admits "that a belief in objective values is built into ordinary moral thought and language, but [holds] that this ingrained belief is false" (p. 49).

24. Much of my discussion of silence is inspired by what Stanley Rosen has to say in *Nihilism* (New Haven: Yale University Press, 1969).

25. Rorty does not explicitly follow Nietzsche. His heroes are Wittgenstein, Dewey, and Heidegger, whom he describes as "therapeutic" and "edifying," rather than "systematic," thinkers. See the introduction to *Philosophy and the Mirror of Nature*.

26. Doing this of course prejudices the argument in favor of Plato. No attempt will be made to do justice to the historical Protagoras except insofar as I quote his famous dictum (the text for which comes from Diels, *Die Fragmente der Vorsokratiker*). The types of arguments that will later be brought to bear against Protagoras will be similar to those employed in the *Theaetetus*.

Since Protagoras antedates Aristotle it is peculiar to say that he challenges him. As stated in the prologue, the strategy informing this book is to position various Greek texts not into a chronological sequence, but into a dramatic one. The ideas championed by Protagoras were surely available to Aristotle and so I do not think that this procedure is distorting.

27. Laszlo Versenyi, in his *Socratic Humanism* (New Haven: Yale University Press, 1963) 8–38, is sympathetic to Protagoras and has an interesting analysis of "things" in his famous saying.

28. I think in particular of how Plato treats Protagoras in his *Theaetetus*.

29. Despite what I have just said, the historical Protagoras apparently had a reasonably good reputation in Athens. For a defense of him see Nussbaum, *The Fragility of Goodness*, 100–106.

30. For a more detailed and sympathetic view of the Sophists see G.B. Kerferd, *The Sophistic Movement* (Cambridge: Cambridge University Press, 1981). For a polemical defense of sophistry see Brian Vickers, *In Defense of Rhetoric* (Oxford: Oxford University Press, 1989).

31. This definition comes from the *Republic* and will be discussed below.

32. Nietzsche. *The Will to Power*, no. 429 (New York: Random House, 1967). For the connection between Nietzsche and Callicles see the appendix to E.R. Dodds's commentary on the *Gorgias* (Oxford: Oxford University Press, 1959), titled "Socrates, Callicles, and Nietzsche."

33. Nietzsche, *Thus Spoke Zarathustra*, 59. This is from Kaufmann with some small modifications.

34. I have discussed this issue at length in "Socrates' Use of the Techne-Analogy," *Journal of the History of Philosophy* 24 (1986), 295–310.

35. *"Dunatotatos"* is somewhat ambiguous here. In this context it means "most capable." In others, it could well mean "most powerful."

36. In other dialogues Socrates also formulates, or reformulates, an opponent's claim to make it include profession of a techne. I think, for example, of *Gorgias* 449a, *Ion* 530b, *Charmides* 165c (*"episteme"* is used here, but in this context is synonymous with "techne"), and *Republic* 332c.

37. Nussbaum also finds him quite sympathetic: *The Fragility of Goodness*, 89–121. So does Rorty: *Philosophy and the Mirror of Nature*, 157. For an extended defense of Protagoras see D. Loenen, *Protagoras and the Greek Community* (Amsterdam: 1940).
    My translation should be compared with that found in the Loeb edition. I occasionally omit some lines in order to shorten the text.

38. The issue of myth will be discussed in the two sections titled "The Philosopher and the Poet."

39. See, for example, Loenen, *Protagoras and the Greek Community*, 22–23.

40. *"Dikaiosune"* and *"sophrosune"* replace *"aidos"* and *"dike."*

41. I refer to 329c where Socrates abruptly changes directions and begins the "unity of virtue" argument.

42. A view somewhat similar to my own is presented by A.W.H. Adkins in "Arete, Techne, Democracy and the Sophists," *Journal of Hellenic Studies*, 93 (1973): 3–12.

43. This is in stark contrast to Socratic myths where the soul figures so prominently. Consider, for example, the "palinode" of the *Phaedrus*.

44. C.C.W. Taylor, *Plato: Protagoras* (Oxford: Clarendon Plato Series, 1976), 101.

45. Protagoras' fragment on religion reads: "Concerning the gods I cannot know either that they exist or that they do not exist, or what form they might have, for there is much to prevent one's knowing: the obscurity of the subject and the shortness of man's life." (The text is *The Older Sophists*, edited by Rosamond Sprague [Columbia: University of South Carolina Press, 1972], 20.)
    My view diverges sharply from the more typical one, such as that held by Loenen, that Protagoras and Callicles are extremely different kinds of characters. My own, and I believe Plato's, view is that Protagoras is simply more artful in disguising his position.

46. Stanley Rosen has made a similar point in a series of complex and useful writings. I refer to his *Hermeneutics as Politics* (New York: Oxford University Press, 1987), especially "Transcendental Ambiguity: The Rhetoric of the Enlightenment." Also see his "A Central Ambiguity in Descartes," in *The Ancients and the Moderns* (New Haven: Yale University Press, 1989), 22–36.

47. The word "fable" appears on page 4 in the *Discourse*. For a discussion of what Descartes means by it, see Etienne Gilson's text and commentary on the *Discourse* (Paris: 1967). In citing page numbers I refer to the standard Adam and Tannery edition, *Oeuvres de Descartes* (Paris: 1897–1910). I use the English translation of Donald A. Cress (Indianapolis: Hackett, 1980). Cress includes the standard pagination in his edition.

48. Gilson's commentary, 109–19, has a detailed discussion of Descartes' curriculum.

49. Gilson, pp. 130–31, states that Descartes probably had Seneca and the Stoics in mind here. Even so, his remarks would seem to apply fairly to logos as well.

50. This section refers to *Phaedo* 89d–91c. It should be noted that Socrates explicitly says that logoi are not like human beings, most of whom are *metaxu* (90b4). Also, note that Socrates does use the phrase *techne peri tous logous* at 90b7. Finally, it's obvious that Descartes himself speaks of "morals . . . the highest and most perfect moral system,

which presupposes a complete knowledge of the other sciences and is the ultimate level of wisdom" (*Principles of Philosophy*, 14). I shall comment on this line shortly.

51. Le Corbusier here comes to mind.

52. The more complete presentation of the method is given in his *Rules for the Direction of the Mind.*

53. The point I make here, which could be described as a critique of the Enlightenement, is surely not original. Rosen has made versions of it numerous times. From a different perspective, so have Horkheimer and Adorno in a work like *Dialectic of Enlightenment*, trans. John Cumming (New York: Herder and Herder, 1972). The literature criticizing the "Cartesian" scientific world is voluminous.

To return to the last point made in note 50: It is obvious that in my discussion of Descartes I have said nothing about his "theology" or his other works. These, one could argue, are precisely his attempt to comment upon the world of human significance. I believe that finally a reading of these works would confirm what I have said so far, but in this book I do not document that assertion. Attempting to do so would force me into a scholarly argument that would go beyond the limits of this short section.

54. Hiram Caton, *The Origin of Subjectivity* (New Haven: Yale University Press, 1973), 56. Caton here is voicing agreement with the position of Gilson and Alquie. The metaphor of the tree of knowledge comes from the *Principles of Philosophy*, 14.

The key to Cartesian "morality" is "generosity": "I believe that true generosity, which causes a person's self-esteem to be as great as it may legitimately be, has only two components. The first consists in his knowing that nothing truly belongs to him but this freedom to dispose his volitions . . . The second consists in his feeling within himself a firm and constant resolution to use [his freedom] well—that is, never to lack the will to undertake and carry out whatever he judges to be best" (*Principles*, 446).

55. By contrast, consider the following assertion by Rorty: "Unlike Nietzsche and Heidegger, however, the pragmatists did not make the mistake of turning against the community which takes the natural scientist as its moral hero—the community of the secular intellectual which came to self-consciousness in the Enlightenment. James and Dewey rejected neither the Enlightenment's choice of the scientist as moral example, nor the technological civilization which science had created. They wrote, as Nietzsche and Heidegger did not, in a spirit of social hope" (*Consequences of Pragmatism*, 161).

Given Rorty's assumptions, I do not understand what he means when he accuses Nietzsche of making a "mistake." I think what he means by "spirit" in the last clause is actually just a mood.

56. Nietzsche, *Thus Spoke Zarathustra*, 75. I have modified Kaufmann somewhat here.

57. I should note that this is a quite traditional reading of Descartes, which would be challenged by someone like Hiram Caton in his *The Origin of Subjectivity*.

58. My text for Spinoza is *The Complete Works of Spinoza*, trans. E. Curley (Princeton: Princeton University Press, 1986). I only cite Curley's pagination.

59. Again, see Nussbaum, "Aristotle on Teleological Explanation," in *De Motu Animalium*, 59–106, for an extended discussion of this issue.

60. See, for example, the Introduction to *Philosophy and the Mirror of Nature*, 3–13.

61. See *Theaetetus*, 179e ff. The issue of self-reference as applied to Protagoras is frequently discussed in the literature. See, for example, M.F. Burnyeat, "Protagoras and Self-Refutation in Plato's *Theaetetus*," *The Philosophical Forum*, 85 (1976): 172–95. My own discussion of this issue occurs in "Can the Relativist Avoid Refuting Herself?" *Philosophy and Literature*, 14 (1990): 92–98, where I criticize Barbara Smith's *Contingencies of Value*.

62. In fairness to Protagoras, he never quite does this in the *Protagoras*. Instead, he presents a myth, a story, and not an argument designed to verify his position. The significance of myth will be discussed below in the sections titled "The Philosopher and the Poet."

63. See note 23.

64. See *Philosophy and the Mirror of Nature*, 315–322.

65. Ibid., 394.

66. Rorty doesn't think he is a relativist. See "Pragmatism, Relativism, and Irrationalism," in *Consequences of Pragmatism* (Minneapolis: University of Minnesota Press, 1982), 160–75.

67. There is a great deal of literature on Thrasymachus. For recent examples, see B. O'Neill's "The Struggle for the Soul of Thrasymachus," *Ancient Philosophy*, 8 (1988): 167–86; F. Sparshott, "An Argument for Thrasymachus," *Apeiron*, 21(1988), 55–67; and P.P. Nicholson's "Unravelling Thrasymachus's Arguments in the *Republic*," *Phronesis*, 19 (1974): 210–32.

68. Again, it is Socrates who first uses the term "techne" in the dialogue (332c). He thus establishes, at the outset, the terms of this discussion.

69. In typical fashion, Socrates is quick to generalize after only a few examples.

70. Perhaps it is going too far to call him a technicist; the word "techne" is so common and its meaning usually so broad, that to adopt it as a description of one's abilities may simply reflect ordinary usage.

71. This is a highly truncated version of Spinoza on teleology. After all, he did have an elaborate political philosophy. The issue of whether it is possible, for example, to have a nonrelative theory of rights without teleology needs to be explored.

72. Baynes, *After Philosophy*, 7.

CHAPTER 2

1. I translate this, the shortest of all Plato's dialogues, almost in entirety because it is so rarely read. To make it slightly shorter I left out 407d–e.

   I coin an English word, "to protrepticize," in order to keep the Greek visible to the reader. For an alternative translation see that by Clifford Orwin in *The Roots of Political Philosophy* (Ithaca: Cornell University Press, 1987), 111–116. Orwin's interpretive essay should also be consulted.

2. *Ergon* can mean "product," "result," or "activity."

3. I have commented at length on this dialogue in an earlier version of this section, "The Riddle of the *Cleitophon*," *Ancient Philosophy* 4 (1984): 132–145. I think I succeed in showing that the dialogue is genuine.

4. This is the key point made by Jan Blits in his article, "Socratic Teaching and Justice: Plato's *Cleitophon*," *Interpretation*, 13 (1985): 321–334.

5. I can think of no other character in the dialogues who is treated this way.

6. This sense of silence is articulated by Stanley Rosen in his chapter on Wittgenstein in *Nihilism*.

7. Also consider Philebus' silence in the *Philebus* and Callicles' in the *Gorgias*.

8. An earlier version of parts of this section appeared as "The Erotics of Philosophical Discourse," in the *History of Philosophy Quarterly* 4 (1987): 117–130.

9. A famous opposition is between eros, the "pagan" or "epithumotic" conception of love, and *agape*, the Christian conception. On this subject see Anders Nygren, *Eros and Agape* (Philadelphia: Westminister Press, 1953).

10. Of course, a more accurate way to put this is to say that human beings love nothing other than what they think is good.

11. All material in brackets is my commentary. The various "stages" I label could be debated: I use them only for convenience. I use the term "initiate" because the language here is that of religious initiation. For a more idiomatic translation see Nehamas and Woodruff's (Indianapolis: Hackett, 1989).

12. "To have more" translates "*pleonechein*," a word used by Callicles and Socrates in the *Gorgias*.

13. Such a view is, I believe, compatible with the political teaching of the *Republic*. Saying this puts me in the camp of the notorious Leo Strauss and Allan Bloom. Bloom's interpretive essay in the *The Republic of Plato* (New York: Basic Books, 1968), 307–436 is a good introduction to this line of interpretation. I do not intend to try to defend it myself. Let me only say that, in response to Strauss's many critics, I think that a sober, clearly argued interpretation can validate the apparently strange idea that the principal teaching of the *Republic* is that political justice is impossible.

14. Among contemporary scholars Plato's theory of Ideas is perhaps his most talked about legacy. The amount of literature on it is vast. A. Wedberg's "The Theory of Ideas," in *Plato: I*, ed. G. Vlastos (Notre Dame: University of Notre Dame Press, 1978), is a clear introduction to the issue.

15. I refer to Phaedrus and Pausanias, who if not Sophists themselves are surely friends of the Sophists, Eryximachus the doctor, and Aristophanes and Agathon the poets.

16. "Realize" translates "*katanoesai*" at 210a8. Verbs related to seeing abound: *theasasthai* at 210c2, *idein* at 210c4, *blepon* at 210c7, *theoron* at 210d4 are only some examples.

17. Parts of an earlier version of this section appeared as "The First Philosopher (and the Poet)" in *Classical and Modern Literature*, 6 (1985): 39–54.
     The first quote in this paragraph comes from R.E. Allen *Greek Philosophy*: *Thales to Aristotle* (New York: Free Press, 1966), 1. The second and third come from G. S. Kirk and J.E. Raven, *The Presocratic Philosophers* (Cambridge: Cambridge University Press, 1957), 98, 73.

18. D. R. Dickes, "Thales," *Classical Quarterly*, 9 (1959): 298. See also Diogenes Laertius, I.23. This little piece of information could be put to good use by a deconstructionist.

19. For a sense of the literature see Leo Sweeney, *Infinity in the Presocratics*: *A Bibliographical and Philosophical Study* (The Hague: Nijhoff, 1972).

20. It is true that the philosphers Empedocles and Parmenides also wrote poetically. I would argue, however, that in their case the form of their writing is not an essential component of their thought; in other words, their thought could be translated into prose without being damaged. As we will see, this is not the case with a genuine poet like Hesiod.

21. The translation I use is that of H.G. Evelyn-White in the Loeb Classical Library.

22. Pietro Pucci, *Hesiod and the Language of Poetry* (Baltimore: Johns Hopkins University Press, 1977), 12. Pucci's reading of Hesiod is somewhat similar to my own; this is especially true of his comparison between Hesiod and Derrida.

23. For this point see Norman O. Brown, *Hesiod's Theogony* (Indianapolis: Bobbs Merrill, 1981), 10.

24. "Void" is Brown's. M.L. West, in *Hesiod: Theogony—Works and Days* (Oxford: Oxford University Press, 1988) uses "chasm" and says in a note, "This is the literal meaning of the Greek name Chaos; it does not contain the idea of confusion or disorder" (p. 64).

25. On this point see Norman O. Brown, *Hesiod's Theogony*, 11–13. He refers to this as the human cosmos.

26. See Aristotle's *Metaphysics* 984b23–31 and 989a10.

27. I call this simple but the problem of no-thing or non-being is hardly that. From its initial articulation in Parmenides to Plato's *Sophist* to Hegel's treatment of it, it is of decisive importance in the history of philosophy. Stanley Rosen has an interesting essay on nothing: "The Limits of Analysis: Linguistic Purification and the Nihil Absolutum," in *Ancients and Moderns*.

28. Jacques Derrida, *Positions*, trans. Alan Bass (Chicago: University of Chicago Press, 1981), 22

29. Many of these comments about writing are prefigured in Plato's *Phaedrus*. Derrida has commented on this text in "Plato's Pharmacy," in *Dissemination*, trans. Barbara Johnson (Chicago: University of Chicago Press, 1981.) A good analysis of Derrida's commentary on the *Phaedrus* is found in Charles Griswold's *Self-Knowledge in Plato's Phaedrus* (New Haven: Yale University Press, 1987), 230–242.

30. Jacques Derrida, *Margins of Philosophy*, trans. Alan Bass. (Chicago: University of Chicago Press, 1982), 318.

31. See Pucci, *Hesiod and the Language of Poetry*, 13.

32. Jean Baudrillard, *Simulations* (New York: Semiotext(e), 1983), 127. This sentence was brought to my attention by my colleague Tony Smith. For an entertaining critique of Baudrillard, see Robert Hughes, "The Patron Saint of Neo-Pop," *New York Review of Books*, 36 (June 1, 1989): 29–32.

33. Derrida, *Margins of Philosophy*, 7. The affinity between "postmodern" and "preclassical" thought is easily documented by noting the esteem in which the pre-Socratic philosophers are held by both Nietzsche and Heidegger. See, for example, Heidegger's *Early Greek Thinking*, trans. David P. Krell (New York: Harper and Row, 1984). I will discuss one such pre-Socratic, namely Heraclitus, shortly.

34. It should be recalled that Protagoras employed a myth in order to respond to Socrates. His doing so should be seen as testimony to his self-knowledge.

35. See Diogenes Laertius, I.401.

36. Charles Kahn, *Anaximander and the Origin of Greek Cosmology* (New York: Columbia University Press, 1960), 6.

37. These three fragments come from Aristotle's *Metaphysics* 983b6–21, his *De Anima* 411a7, and Diogenes Laertius, I.9.

38. Aristotle, *Metaphysics*, 983b22–29.

39. Drew A. Hyland, *The Origins of Philosophy* (New York: Putnam, 1973), 100. Hyland's entire essay on Thales should be consulted.

40. The order might be reversed: perhaps one begins with a certain form that demands an attendant content.

41. To ask, Who is right? presupposes that one position can actually be "right," a notion unacceptable to the deconstructionist.

I should address an issue that perhaps has occurred to some readers. What is the relationship between the type of argumentation I present here, and will continue to present in later sections, and classical skepticism? Many of my arguments will indeed resemble the skeptical method of balancing equal options. I differ as follows: The goal for the Pyrrhonist skeptic is a life without belief, which in turn is said to constitute a life of tranquillity or *ataraxia*. This seems to me to be based upon a thesis about human nature that is both wrong in itself and incoherent on its own terms. I will return to this issue in the epilogue.

CHAPTER 3

1. Parts of this section appeared in an earlier form as "The Impossibility of Philosophical Dialogue," in *Philosophy and Rhetoric*, 19 (1986): 147–65.

2. A former president of the American Philosophical Association, John Smith, said this. (*Proceedings of the American Philosophical Association*, 56 [1982]: 6.) My reason for citing this speech will be made apparent soon.

3. The argument I present has been formulated in various contexts. There is, for example, the issue of the incommensurability of scientific theories (and the translatability of their terminology) generated by Kuhn's work.

4. Rorty, *Philosophy and the Mirror of Nature*, 316.

5. My colleague Tony Smith put this to me as a version of a Habermasian objection. I should state that it was a disagreement with Smith that started me on the train of thought represented in this book.

6. Rorty, *Consequences of Pragmatism*, xiv. He is quoting Sellars.

7. Ibid., xl.

8. My remark is meant to call into question the coherence of Rorty's attempt to argue philosophically for his position. His real business should be that of getting into conversations with strangers and not arguing with philosophers in learned books. With his discussions of Proust and Nabokov in *Contigency, Irony, and Solidarity* (Cambridge: Cambridge University Press, 1989), perhaps he has done this.

9. The strategy of the *ad hominem* mode of argumentation should be considered as an alternative. When practiced by someone like Socrates, this can be taken as a form of irony. Socrates frequently will adopt his interlocutor's position as his own in order to expose its flaws. I do not think, however, that such a strategy succeeds when dealing with fundamental disagreement: the position is so foreign that, if adopted, there could be no dialogue.

10. I oversimply here in that I ignore the question of theology. The notorious question plaguing the *Metaphysics* is whether first philosophy studies "being qua being" or "god" or both.

11. See *Posterior Analytics* 71b27–28 and *Nicomachean Ethics* 1140b31 ff. The text of the former is the Loeb Edition, ed. Tredennick (Cambridge, MA: Harvard University Press, 1976).

12. For a good discussion of this see H. Lee "Geometrical Method and Aristotle's Account of First Principles," *Classical Quarterly* 29 (1935): 113–124.

13. This may not be true. See, for example, Jan Lukasiewicz, "On the Principle of Contradiction in Aristotle," *Review of Metaphysics*, 24 (1971): 485–509. Also, note the striking phrase *eschaten doxan*, at 1005b33: in what sense is affirmation of the Principle a *doxa*?

14. R.M. Dancy in *Sense and Contradiction* (Dordrecht: Reidel, 1975), disagrees with this. See pp. 29–34. This is a valuable work and should be consulted.

15. I suppose Rorty would deny any affinity with Thrasymachus. He is a tolerant man who has dedicated his most recent book to the "memory of six liberals" (*Contingency, Irony, and Solidarity*); presumably he is not interested in power politics. He says he is not a relativist. Nevertheless, I remain unconvinced. As is true of many contemporary theorists, Rorty's position is a complex attempt to embrace some version of relativism without becoming vulgar. The reader should investigate whether I am being fair to him or not.

16. These are Dancy's words: they come from *Sense and Contradiction*, p. 61. The translation of *Meta*. 1009a6–15 I cited was based on his translation as well as that found in the Loeb edition.

17. Jacques Derrida, *Of Grammatology*, 11.

18. Ibid., 26.

19. Ibid., 19.

20. Ibid., 50.

21. Richard Rorty, "Taking Philosophy Seriously," *The New Republic*, April 1988: 31–34.

22. For a discussion of Heraclitus' possible book see G.S. Kirk and J.E. Raven, *The Presocratic Philosophers*, 183–85. When I cite Heraclitus I follow Diels and simply place the aphorism number in parentheses.

23. See Kirk and Raven, *The Presocratic Philosophers*, 187–88.

24. Two immediate objections can be raised against this statement. First, one could argue that child's play *is* teleological. For example, even apparently purposeless play can be interpreted as being for the sake of learning. This may well be the case. Still, on the surface child's play *seems* to be purposeless. The second objection is that Heraclitus speaks so often of the regularity of change. This will be discussed shortly.

25. Friedrich Nietzsche, *Philosophy in the Tragic Age of the Greeks*, trans. Marianne Cowan (Chicago: 1962), 55.

26. See the section in Nietzsche's *Thus Spoke Zarathustra*, titled "The Three Metamorphoses." To see how seriously play is taken, see Eugen Fink, "The Ontology of Play," in *Sport and the Body*, ed. Ellen Gerber (Philadelphia: Lea & Febiger, 1972), 76–86 and Hans-Georg Gadamer, "Play as the Clue to Ontological Explanation," in *Truth and Method* (New York: Crossroad, 1982), 91–118.

27. Charles Kahn, in *The Art of Heraclitus* (Cambridge: Cambridge University Press, 1979), argues that this aphorism is not genuine (183–85).

28. Kirk and Raven's book is a good example of this rather standard view of reading Heraclitus.

29. For an interesting commentary on this aphorism see Robert Rethy, "Heraclitus, Fragment 56: The Deceptiveness of the Apparent," *Ancient Philosophy* 7 (1987): 1–7.

30. Nietzsche, *Philosophy in the Tragic Age of the Greeks*, 54.

31. Examples of Derridean playfulness are his use of an "X" to "cross out" the word "is" (see *Margins*, 5–6), his playing with his signature in *Margins*, 330, and the typography of *Spurs*.

32. See note 2 to this chapter.

33. See Vincent Descombes, *Modern French Philosophy*, trans. L. Scott-Fox and J. Harding (Cambridge: Cambridge University Press, 1981). Descombes is the editor of the Odeon series at Oxford. Its first release was Stanley Rosen's *Hermeneutics as Politics*.

34. Of course, I oversimplify the continental/analytical split. These are two camps which have many diverse members. It is surely possible for an analytical philosopher to discuss points of interest in Heidegger's *Being and Time* or the works of Husserl or Marx.

35. Again, I would attempt to substantiate this assertion about Descartes with an analysis of his key virtue, "generosity."

36. Stanley Rosen, *The Ancients and the Moderns* (New Haven: Yale University Press, 1989), ix.

37. Seth Schein, *The Mortal Hero* (Berkeley: University of California Press, 1984), 98. Schein's book is a good introduction to both the *Iliad* itself and to the enormous amount of scholarship that has been devoted to it.

38. See, for example, VI, 416–20. The translation I cite is that of Richmond Lattimore (Chicago: University of Chicago Press, 1961). When no book number is cited, the lines are from XXIII. Parts of this section appeared in earlier form as "Iliad XXIII: The Tragicomedy of Athletics," *Arete*, 3 (1986): 159–68.

39. See XXII, 345–49; XXI, 175 ff.; XVII 229–30.

40. Homer's treatment of traditional material is a major concern of Schein's. For a discussion of the role of athletic games in funerals see L.E. Roller, "Funerary Games for Historical Persons," *Stadion*, 7 (1981): 1–18.

41. There are, of course, "natural" limitations to such conventions. The hoop could not, for example, be placed fifty feet high. No one could reach it.

42. Again, Schein's book is a good place to start to understand the Homeric notion of glory.

43. An eloquent defense of the position that Homer is opposed to war itself comes from Simone Weil, "The *Iliad* or the Poem of Force," trans. M. McCarthy. (Wallingford, Pennsylvania: Pendle Hill Pamphlets, 1957).

44. This section appeared in preliminary form as "Plato's Critique of Postmodernism," in *Philosophy and Literature* 11 (1987): 282–91.

45. "The Corybantes were priests of Cybele, the Phrygian mother-goddess:" *Plato's Ion*, a commentary by Andrew M. Miller (Bryn Mawr: Bryn Mawr College, 1985), 10.

46. For an elaboration see N. Tigerstedt, *Plato's Idea of Poetical Inspiration* (Helsinki: 1969), 13–18.

47. These two possibilities are mentioned by Paul Woodruff in his English edition of Plato's *Ion* and *Hippias Minor* (Indianapolis: Hackett, 1985), 9.

48. This is rather typical of the sort of claim a Sophist might make. Consider, for example, that Gorgias says he can answer *all* questions (*Gorgias* 447d) or the claims made by the Sophists in the *Euthydemus*.

49. My view is in stark contrast to the more orthodox way of reading Plato's relationship to the poets. There is a mountain of literature on this subject. Again, consult Nussbaum's Plato interpretation in *The Fragility of Goodness* to get a sense of the position I oppose as well as the literature.

50. There are, I believe, several such crucial junctures throughout the dialogues. One is Gorgias finally specifying a specific object of his techne at *Gorgias* 454b. Another is when Thrasymachus rejects Cleitophon's advice, a mistake Protagoras avoids.

51. Far too many Plato commentators ignore the dramatic context in which Socrates' various arguments are imbedded. The question of how properly to read the dialogues

is itself an old dispute. A good place to begin its study is Charles Griswold's introduction to *Platonic Readings; Platonic Writings* (New York: Routledge, 1988).

52. The best example of this tendency that I know is found in Barbara Smith's *The Contingencies of Value*.

53. Consider what Socrates says about the poets in the *Apology*: they have "many fine things to say, but they don't know what they're talking about" (22c). In other words, what they say is in itself fine; the poets cannot, however, give a logos defending what's fine about it. When they try to, they get into trouble.

54. A question should be asked: Is techne as strict as Socrates makes it out to be? Is it possible that a more flexible notion of techne, such as that found in Isocrates and which later came to be known as "stochastic," is a viable option? I shall explore this issue in depth in a future work.

55. A few of the many commentators who argue that Socrates has, or thinks he has, a techne, include Jorge Kube, *Techne und Arete*, Terence Irwin, *Plato's Moral Theory*, Rosamond Kent Sprague, *Plato's Philosopher King* (Columbia: University of South Carolina Press, 1974), and Morimichi Kato, *Techne und Philosophie bei Platon* (Frankfurt: Peter Lang, 1986). There is a great deal of literature on this issue. This, too, I plan to discuss in a later work.

56. Paul Woodruff discusses what he calls "non-expert knowledge" in "Plato's Early Theory of Knowledge," in *Epistemology* ed. Stephen Everson (Cambridge: Cambridge University Press, 1989).

57. The notion of a second-order techne is Sprague's. See note 55.

58. This seems to violate the usual Socratic procedure of specifying what something is before discussing what it is like.

59. Jacques Derrida, *Writing and Difference*, trans. Alan Bass. (Chicago: University of Chicago Press, 1978), 36. (There is a quite peculiar feature of my copy of this book. After page 20 comes page 36 which is followed by page 35, 34, etc. This happens until page 21 which is followed by 37. I've assumed this was just a printing error. Maybe it's not.)

60. As anyone familiar with his work will realize, this section and the previous one on play were inspired by my teacher Drew Hyland. (All errors and confusions are, however, my responsibility.) His *The Question of Play* (University Press of America, 1984) and *The Virtue of Philosophy* (Athens, OH: Ohio University Press, 1986) represent his own elaboration of the themes of eros, play, and questioning.

Epilogue

1. A good introduction to skepticism is *Sextus Empiricus,* ed. and intro. Philip Hallie (Indianapolis: Hackett, 1985). For a discussion of the modes, see Julia Annas, *The Modes of Scepticism* (Cambridge: Cambridge University Press, 1985).

2. Myles Burnyeat, "Can the Sceptic Live his Scepticism," in *Doubt and Dogmatism*, ed. M. Schofield (Oxford: Clarendon Press, 1980), 53.

3. "Human wisdom" translates *anthropina sophia* at *Apology* 20d8.

4. A final formulation of my divergence with skepticism: It is ultimately "Buddhistic." I mean this metaphorically, but there is a possibility that Pyrrho was in fact influenced by the Buddhists: see Everard Flintoff, "Pyrrho and India," *Phronesis* 25 (1980): 88–108. Robyn Smith kindly showed me this article.

INDEX

Achilles, 166–9
Aeschylus, 1, 2, 21; *Prometheus Bound,*
  18–20
Anaximander, 137
Arche ("first principle," "origin"),
  130–32, 135–9, 144, 181
Arete ("excellence," "virtue"), 59–62,
  64, 93, 99–103, 187, 188, 190
Arithmetic, 19, 21
Aristotle, xii, xiii, 16, 17, 29, 30, 44,
  49, 53, 54, 56, 57, 62–9, 77, 79, 95,
  96, 108, 121–2, 129, 130, 137, 159,
  175, 191, 196–8; *De Anima,* 27; *De
  Interpretatione,* 28, 29, 124, 154,
  155; *Metaphysics,* 26, 27, 148–153,
  163; *Nicomachean Ethics,* 30–3, 68,
  109; *Poetics,* 2–3, 8; *Politics,* 12, 23–
  6, 31, 32, 70; *Posterior Analytics,* 149
Athens, 1, 3, 45, 46, 47, 118
Athletics, 166, 168–174, 192
Axioms, 106, 149

Beauty, Idea of, 122–4, 196–8
Beauty, itself, 120
Beautiful, the, 111, 115, 120
Begging the question, 16, 17, 106
Burnyeat, Miles, 204

Callicles, 48–50, 63, 76, 77, 82, 84,
  86, 104, 106, 118, 191–3
Certainty, 71, 72, 74, 76, 82, 87
chaos ("chasm," "gap"), 128–131,
  134–6, 144, 152, 181
Cleitophon, 89–91, 97–109, 121, 141,

143, 151, 154, 174, 175, 177, 181,
  185, 186, 188, 190, 191, 193, 203
Conversation, 86, 87, 95, 141, 142,
  145, 146
Creativity, 44

Daimon ("spirit"), 111
Deconstruction, xii, 88, 134, 135,
  192, 195, 196
DeLillo, Don, xv
Democracy, 47, 141
Derrida, Jacques, ix, x, xii, xiii, 29,
  34, 44, 45, 50, 76, 95, 132–5, 163,
  165, 195; *Of Grammatology,* 154–6
Descartes, ix, xii, 15, 21, 44, 64–77,
  80, 82, 84, 87, 93, 94, 103, 107,
  165, 181, 190; *Discourse on Method,*
  65–75
Desire, 33, 34, 108, 110, 112–4, 116
Determinateness, 19, 20
Dialogue, xii, xiii, 98, 106, 107, 140–
  151, 153, 164, 192, 200, 203, 204
Diotima, 111–125, 196–99
Drama, 14

Epithumia ("desire"), 110
Eros, 109–22, 191, 196–9, 200, 201
Eudaimonia ("happiness"), 32–4, 36,
  37, 42, 111
Euripides, 1, 2

Fate, 3, 4
Forms, the, 95
Freud, 120

221